WILDFOWLING IN DAKOTA
1873 - 1903

Old-Time Duck and Goose Shooting on the Dakota Prairies

Best wishes!
Harold F. Duebbert
2004

Harold F. Duebbert

Windfeather Press

Bismarck, ND
2003

WILDFOWLING IN DAKOTA
1873 - 1903

Harold F. Duebbert
(Editor)

Library of Congress Control Number: 2003102370

International Standard Book Number: 0-9620122-2-X

Published by
Windfeather Press
Bismarck, ND
2003
Woodcut reproductions are from
A. M. Weinhardt
Engraving Co.
Wood Engravers and Designers
Chicago, IL

To order this book contact:

Harold F. Duebbert
P.O. Box 300
Fergus Falls, MN 56538
or
629 East Adolphus Ave.
Fergus Falls, MN 56537
218-736-4312
$29.95 (includes shipping & handling)

Material taken from the authorship of William B. Mershon is used with permission of the Bentley Historical Library, University of Michigan, custodians of the Mershon papers. Aside from the editor's annotations, all other material for this book is from the public domain and as such no right of ownership is claimed. Those wishing to quote or copy from it for educational or informational purposes are entitled that privilege. In so doing, the editor would appreciate credit.

HISTORICAL PERSPECTIVES

"The Cherokee believe the past is to be respected for its rich store of experience."

> Joyce Sequiche Hifler
> *A Cherokee Feast of Days* 1992

"Experience has taught me how necessary it is to probe deeply into the life and background of a region if the feeling of what has really transpired there is to be important."

"Knowledge of the past always adds spice to present observations."

> Robert Gard
> *Prairie Visions* 1987

ACKNOWLEDGMENTS

I am most appreciative of the encouragement and help of my longtime friend and hunting companion, Ted Upgren, in preparation of this book. Kaye Upgren performed the word processing and computer work for which I am grateful. My deepest gratitude goes to my wife, June, for her love and support. I express my sincere thanks to librarians in the Technology Department of the Minneapolis (Minnesota) Public Library for providing me with old sporting publications upon which this book is based. Articles reproduced in this book are in the public domain. To Galen and Lucille Bowerman go my heartfelt thanks for friendship and use of a house as a hunting camp for the past several years. It has also served as a fine place to write, as many of the hunts presented in this book took place within a few miles. Of course, the most important acknowledgment must go to those hunters on Dakota prairies a long time ago who cared enough about their experiences to put them into print.

FOREWORD

We owe hunters of bygone days a great deal of gratitude for our knowledge about the rich heritage of wildfowling. Our link to this recent past is documented in what they wrote and the images they conjure in our minds of venerable hunts on expansive prairies amidst wildfowl seemingly inexhaustible. The old hunter's affection for the hunt and for their hunting partners is alive in us today. Writings about gunning in an age when game was plentiful and the landscape less manipulated fascinate us as we compare the then and now of hunting. And from these accounts of hunting in bygone days our heritage lives on as does our foundation of sporting life.

An awareness of wildfowling literature was alive in my youth. However, not until I met Harold Duebbert did I know someone with a shooting library. As colleague wildlife biologists with the U. S. Fish and Wildlife Service our paths crossed while conducting field studies of waterfowl in the Dakotas and Canada. During those years we discovered a mutual passion for waterfowl hunting and an appreciation for the rich traditions of wildfowling. We shared many experiences while hunting ducks and geese.

I recall pleasurable nights visiting with Harold following a hunt together or during winter sitting in the warmth of his wood-burning stove. Late into the night we talked of early wildfowl shooting when intrepid men rode steam trains and creaked along in horse-drawn wagons on their way to hunt Dakota Territory of the 1880s. Nearby, an old oak bookcase always attracted my attention. On its shelves rested books such as William Bruce Leffingwell's *Wildfowl Shooting*, George Bird Grinnell's *American Duck Shooting,* Van Campen Heilner's *Duck Shooting,* Martin Bovey's *Whistling Wings,* Eugene Connett's *Wildfowling in the Mississippi Flyway*, and many others. More often than not one of Harold's books went home with me, a trusted friend, for which I am forever grateful.

Each of Harold's books came with a story about how and when it was acquired. For example, his copy of Leffingwell's *Wildfowl Shooting* (1888) had belonged to a great uncle, the same person who gave him the oak bookcase. Harold knew these books well and could talk at length about their contents. He especially appreciated those that mentioned early-day waterfowl hunting in the Dakotas. Many referenced top-quality marshes in North Dakota that he knew well and had hunted himself. In addition to the accounts of hunting the articles provided insights into the abundance of waterfowl and hunting conditions in those early times.

I shared many hunts with Harold over the years and carry fine memories of shooting canvasbacks over his own handmade decoys, mallards and bluebills in the wind and snow, wigeon in saline wetlands, or shooting geese in stubble fields, reminiscent of the ways the old timers wrote about. And that is important to Harold Duebbert. To him there is more to each hunt than the here and now. Tradition plays an important role in his hunting and he is particular about where he hunts, who he hunts with, where he blinds the duck boat he made 40 years ago, how he sets decoys, and how he selects individual ducks to shoot. These things are connected in a kind of timelessness and oneness with the past.

The early days of wildfowling in the Dakotas were not without some difficulties. Horse and buggy or wagon travel was the norm. At the end of each day the birds had to be cared for and equipment readied for the next day. None of that dampened the allure of gunning fall migrants that winged their way southward out of the Arctic and prairie Canada into the staging marshes in Coteau and Drift Prairie regions of Dakota. Those adventurous men and women who sought wing-shooting on the open plains apparently had the time and the means to pursue their passion for wildfowling. The fact that they wrote articles about their hunts and kept diaries and journals tells us not only of their hunts but also about themselves as sportsmen and the value they placed on those pursuits.

It is these links with the past that Harold has retrieved to share with us in this book. Times have changed since those halcyon days and so have the ways we hunt waterfowl. Today, by comparison, our access to waterfowl hunting is relatively easy. Modern bag limits mean we shoot fewer birds than those hunters whose hunts are described in these articles. Our hunting experiences are less pristine. Yet the thrill of seeing flights of wild ducks and geese and the challenges of wing-shooting still inspire in us an annual enthusiasm for the hunt. For those of us who go into marshes in the pre-dawn with memories of wildfowling's past there is always promise of a great day and anticipation of many more tomorrows.

I want to thank Harold Duebbert for helping to keep our hunting heritage alive, not only for what he so determinedly compiled in these pages from the past, but also for the example he sets in practicing the celebrated traditions of a wildfowler.

Jerry Serie
Bowie, Maryland

TABLE OF CONTENTS

ACKNOWLEDGEMENTS iv
FOREWORD v
PREFACE x

PART 1 - *THE AMERICAN FIELD* - Articles by William B.Leffingwell

Wanderings in Dakota - No. 1, December 17, 1892 1
Wanderings in Dakota - No. 2, December 24, 1892 11
Wanderings in Dakota - No. 3, December 31, 1892. 21
Wanderings in Dakota - No. 4, January 7, 1893 33
Wanderings in Dakota - No. 5, January 14, 1893 44
Goose Shooting at Minnewaukan - March 2, 1901. 55
An October Day at Dead Buffalo Lake - April 6, 1901 61
The Echos of Lac Qui Parle - June 1, 1901 70
Among the Barley Shocks (Minnewaukan) - July 20, 1901 79
The Land of the Dakotas (Dawson) - February 14, 1903 89
The Plateau du Coteau du Missouri (Chicago Lake) -
    December 19, 1903 96
Long Lake - January 16, 1904 104

PART 2 - *THE AMERICAN FIELD* - Articles by Various Authors

Duck Shooting in Northern Dakota (Pembina) - 1884 113
North Dakota Notes (Mandan) - 1885 120
Shooting Wildfowl in Dakota (Barnes County) - 1885 123
Jamestown, Dakota—A Sportsman's Mecca - 1886 126
Dakota Game Notes (Menoken) - 1886 132
Where To Go To Get Good Goose Shooting
    (Devils Lake, etc.,) - 1893 135
Game In Dakota In Olden Times (Red River Valley) - 1894. 144
An Outing at Devils Lake - 1896 151
Goose Shooting in Dakota (Kimball) - 1884 159

Goose Shooting in North Dakota (Island Lake) - 1892. 165
Sportsmen vs. Cinch Seekers - 1895 172
The Sportsman and the Farmer - 1904 176
Sport in Dakota (Devils Lake) - 1887 180
Duck and Goose Shooting at Lake Thompson (SD) - 1898 233
Among the Ducks in South Dakota (Day County) - 1902. 250
Ducking in Dakota (Sisseton, SD) - 1904. 265
Ducking in Dakota (Sisseton, SD) (Conclusion) - 1904 279

FOREST AND STREAM - **Articles by Various Authors**

A Trip on a Hunting Car (Valley City) - 1883 287
A Goose Hunt in North Dakota (Devils Lake) - 1891. 290
Dakota Game Birds (Towner County) - 1891. 293
The Saginaw Crowd (Dawson) - 1891. 297
The Saginaw Crowd (Dawson, No. 2) - 1891. 301
With Gokey (Dawson) - 1897 303
The Saginaw Crowd (Dawson) - 1902 319

PART 3 - OTHER SOURCES

Duck and Goose Shooting in Kidder County - 1889-1902 325
    (An account of the hunting records of William A. Bond and
    Albert R. Barnes of Chicago who shot during the 14-year
    period in Kidder County, North Dakota.)
Among the Geese and Sand Hill Cranes
    in North Dakota (Fred Kimble) 333
Hunting Records of William B. Mershon in Dawson Area. 335
The Old Hunting Car - (William B. Mershon) 346

CONCLUDING THOUGHTS. 349
REFERENCES CITED 351
BOOKS ABOUT OLDEN TIMES WILDFOWLING 352

PREFACE

A trait deeply ingrained in the human spirit is a curiosity about what life was like in years gone by. As a duck hunter I have always enjoyed reading about the experiences of others. From an early age up to the present time stories about hunts that took place a long time ago have held special appeal to me.

This book is the product of a lifetime duck hunter. I have been enamored with duck and goose hunting since my teen years hunting on Missouri River sandbars near my hometown of Wellington, Missouri. During the 1940s I enjoyed some outstanding mallard shooting often in the company of older hunters who were experienced river men. At the age of 15 I made a 16-foot rowboat and with it learned to navigate the river and hunt alone. That was the beginning of a lifelong association with water and waterfowl that remains strong to this day.

In 1958 I moved to North Dakota and in the intervening 40-some years I have hunted ducks and geese in some of the premier marshes and fields of the state. One of the best was Kraft Slough near Oakes in the 1950s where many limits of mallards came to our decoys after feeding in nearby corn fields. Later on, after spending two years in Oregon, and having great hunting on the famed Malheur Lake, I moved to Jamestown in 1966 where I lived and worked for 21 years. From that base it was possible to find excellent hunting within a radius of 50 or 60 miles. It is from my hunting camp in a favorite hunting area that I have chosen to work on this book. Looking out the window to the south I see the site of a skirmish between Sioux Indians and General H. H. Sibley's troops on July 24, 1863 known as the Battle of the Big Mound.

Within the distance of four miles from where I sit are five of the marshes which were favorite hunting places for over 20 years. I say "were" because since 1993 a series of high water years have converted them into open water lakes with depths of 15-20 feet. In their glory years they were much shallower and contained beds of sago pondweed, prime food for canvasbacks and tundra swans, and clumps and points of hardstem bulrush for blinding sites. One of my favorite sloughs, which is one mile from my camp, in 1989 held around 8,000 ducks when it was with low water level and had abundant beds of submerged aquatic vegetation. By 1995 it was an open water lake and attracted less than 200 ducks, mostly buffleheads, and some grebes.

In addition to actually hunting I have had a lifetime passion for reading about duck and goose hunts of other hunters. Of special appeal to me are the stories of hunting as it was in "the good old days."

In my library are most of the classic old wildfowling books. Authors such as Heilner, Mershon, Leffingwell, Long, Grinnell, Bruette, Forester, and one of the oldest—*The American Sportsman* by Elisha Lewis (1855).

During the 1990s I had an opportunity to review some of the most popular sporting publications of the late 1800s. One was *Forest and Stream*, a weekly publication, that began in 1873. I reviewed 1600 issues from the years 1873 to 1905 and while doing so discovered many fine articles by hunters who enjoyed wildfowling on the Dakota prairies. I found those articles to be very interesting and informative about hunting in the early days of Dakota history. Most of the articles were written a short time after returning home from the hunt. That resulted in the hunters recording their experiences accurately and with the expression of emotions and feelings they had while in the field.

Another publication in which I found many fine articles was *The American Field*. I reviewed the years 1884-1904 and since it was published weekly that amounted to about 1600 issues. It seemed to me that searching for the old articles, turning the pages one at a time, had some of the same fascination as hunting. There was the element of anticipation about what would be on each page and the excitement of finding articles of special interest. And finally "bagging the game" which was quite a process in itself. The weekly issues were bound into volumes 12 inches by 18 inches and four to five inches thick. *The American Field* was divided into sections and the one that appealed to me the most was entitled "Game and Shooting." To obtain the articles I wanted, it was necessary to make two 11 x 14 inch photocopy pages of each page in the publication. Then when I got home I cut and pasted back together the articles on 8 ½ x 11 inch paper for ease of storage and duplication. I often stayed in the library from 9:00 a.m. to 9:00 p.m. because the search was so interesting to me. Due to the age of the publications, as old as 130 years or more, the paper was very brittle and had to be carefully handled.

As the articles began to accumulate I shared them with some of my friends who are hunters. They all appreciated them like I did. The original publications are scarce and hard to find. Even where they exist in library collections their fragile condition may soon prevent them from being available for viewing. For those reasons I thought the articles too important to just leave in my files. So I decided to put together a book that would give interested readers an insight into what duck and goose hunting was like on the Dakota prairies around 100 years ago. I selected the years 1873-1903 as, in my opinion, those were some of the glory years of wildfowling on the prairies. My focus was on North Dakota and South Dakota which before 1889 was Dakota Territory. The Northern Pacific Railroad was laid across Kidder County, North Dakota in 1872 and reached Bismarck on June 3, 1873. That form of transportation gave hunters from the eastern United States easy access to virgin hunting grounds. In the next 20 years hundreds of hunters did just that and many left the written records contained in this book.

One hunter who came to North Dakota to hunt soon after the railroad was completed was William Bruce Leffingwell. He was a prominent citizen of Clinton, Iowa where he practiced law after

being admitted to the bar in 1872. He authored three excellent books (*Wild Fowl Shooting*, 1888; *Shooting on Upland, Marsh, and Stream*, 1890, and *The Art of Wing Shooting,* 1894). Of all the writings about wildfowl shooting that I have read those of Leffingwell have the greatest appeal to me. As a teenager I obtained *Wild Fowl Shooting* and *The Art of Wing Shooting* from a favorite great-uncle. Reading those books at an early age made a powerful influence on my lifetime as a wildfowler. I continue to enjoy them today.

The following statement found in the chapter, "The Wild Goose" written by C. R. Tinan, whose pen name was "Nanit," expressed what many of us feel about hunting on the Dakota prairies. It is in the book *Shooting on Upland, Marsh, and Stream* that was edited by Leffingwell. Tinan (Nanit), wrote, "...the pure air and bright sun of the Dakota prairies on an autumn day gives to the hunter a certain animation and buoyancy of spirits, and a peculiar sense of enjoyment, found in but few places."

For over 30 years I searched for another publication that I noted was authored by Leffingwell titled, "Wanderings in Dakota." I made inquiries to the Library of Congress, dealers in antique books, and looked in dozens of bookstores but could find no information about such a title. One day while going through *The American Field* page by page I spied the following statement in the issue for November 5, 1892.

"WANDERINGS IN DAKOTA. It affords us pleasure to announce that we shall commence in an early issue a short series of articles entitled "Wanderings in Dakota," descriptive of the feathered game in Dakota and how to pursue it. The articles will be written by the well-known writer on field sports, William Bruce

Leffingwell, author of *Wild Fowl Shooting, Shooting on Upland, Marsh, and Stream,* and *Manulito.* Mr. Leffingwell's reputation as a writer is so well known and his writings are appreciated so highly, our readers will feel confident that their expectations will be realized fully."

So at last I found *"Wanderings in Dakota"* and it turned out to be not a book but a series of five articles published in 1892 and 1893 in *The American Field.* I was elated to find these articles and learn that they contained the same colorful and emotion-charged writing style that I had enjoyed for so many years in reading and rereading Leffingwell's books. My interest was further enhanced by learning that in those articles Leffingwell described hunting over 100 years ago in areas I have also hunted. Examples such as that are reasons why to me a knowledge of history enriches present-day hunts.

In addition to "Wanderings in Dakota," I found seven other articles in *The American Field* that described Leffingwell's early Dakota wildfowling experiences. Those articles are under the authorship of Douglas Leffingwell but in my opinion they were by the same William B. Leffingwell. The writing is the same style and reference is made to having hunted in the same areas 10 years before. My investigation of the Leffingwell family history through the Iowa Genealogical Society has not revealed the name Douglas.

The five-part series "Wanderings in Dakota" and a collection of seven other articles by William B. Leffingwell make up Part 1 of this book. In Part 2 will be found articles by various hunters that I thought had special interest. I hope that you, the reader, will find articles of interest and read something in them to relate to your own days among the ducks and geese on the Dakota prairies. Part 3 is a series of articles by well-known hunters who hunted in Dakota in the early days.

Harold F. Duebbert

PART 1

Articles by William Bruce Leffingwell including a five-number series "WANDERINGS IN DAKOTA" (1892-1893) and seven articles under authorship of Douglas Leffingwell (1901-1904) that describe hunts at various places in North Dakota.

WANDERINGS IN DAKOTA - No. 1

Editor's Note: In this article Leffingwell describes his trip to North Dakota from Chicago. He was accompanied by two of his brothers, Frank and George, and a friend. The group traveled from Minneapolis to Grand Forks on the Great Northern Railroad. There they were met by their farmer-friend who was to be their host. It was mentioned that the farmer's home was three hours away. Since the travel was by a team of horses and wagon I do not know how far they could have traveled in that time. From statements made in later articles I believe their locations were the Stump Lake and Devils Lake regions.

> "Sir, you are very welcome to our house,
> It must appear in other ways than words,
> Therefore, I scant this breathing courtesy."

"Perhaps you do not remember me, but I have not forgotten you; besides your brother George is an old chum of mine, and my father and mother and my wife join me in writing you and your brother to visit us this fall, when I can promise you the grandest shooting you ever had. Here is the home of the wildfowl; their breeding places, and if you come, I promise you shall shoot to your heart's content."

When I received that invitation I was deeply engaged in office work. I held that welcome letter, that generous invitation, in my hand, and like a warhorse which scented the battle from afar, my soul went forth with sweet longing; in anticipation of the trip which proved the most delightful of my life. Experience had shown me in years gone by, that almost without exception, anticipation far exceeds the realization of an event. We look forward to an outing with keen desire; our hearts are in the trip we propose making, and the hours and days are passed with fervent discussions and active preparations, getting everything arranged for the contemplated trip. No storms, or lack of game; no disappointments darken with somber clouds the sunshine of our happiness, and we laugh and are merry with eyes ever on our beacon light—the day we take our departure. And yet, I find that years have slightly toned down the fervent desires and the thrillings which used to fill my thoughts with such long expectations.

Accustomed to scenes of beauty on prairies and in the woodland, I drink in those beauties as an expected draught which I have quaffed for so many years, and which by reason of long usage I have the right to expect. How delicious the thought stole into my mind that Summer's day when I read and reread that unexpected invitation! What, to go once more on the prairies I love so well! To breathe the pure fresh air of Heaven as it comes wafted to me o'er hill and through the valley! And then to stay concealed in the rushes of some great marsh where the wild ducks feed and play and roost. To wander in the stubble where the sharptail and the pinnated grouse were softly crouched, decided and yet undecided to take their flight. And to feel that in a few short weeks I was to see and enjoy those sights and to listen to the songs of the larks which I knew would frequent our drives; to hear again the mallard and the teal, the whistling widgeon and the gray duck, the laughing goose, the hoarse ah-unk of the Canada's! What delightful days the thought recalled to memory! And then when I read still farther into that welcome letter and learned that I was invited to the home of the royal canvasback and his congener the redhead, the two grandest birds that fly, I drew a long breath lest I might not hear the fierce rush of wings which had so often greeted my ears when at break of day I awaited the flight of those birds and it seemed as if a dark streak shot across the horizon and—a report, a splash, told the story.

My books have opened to me an avenue of delightful intercourse with fellow sportsmen, and I have been complimented with invitations to hunt from New York to San Francisco, from Memphis to British America, and I have learned from observation and correspondence, the fraternal feeling which animates the hearts of the gentlemen sportsmen of whom there breathes no loftier or more generous soul. Were my situations according to my desires, my days would be more often spent afield. The seed which bursted years ago and blossomed and ripened into fruits which flavor of the love of field sports, have taken deepest root with me, and the birds, the flowers, the fields and streams are ever beckoning me toward them.

I wrote my brother George, who lives at Chicago, enclosing him the letter I have received. I got a reply that he would go. And then my thoughts went out in sympathy to his patient wife, for I knew that for weeks to come she would be persecuted and haunted by hideous noises, as he attempted to call ducks and geese, swans and cranes, as if they were in every room from cellar to attic and would speedily come forth at his calling. But with me I had no time for aught but active preparation, and my boys took special pleasure in preparing me for the journey. The die was cast. The day was set and on September 27, 1892, I left home for a three weeks' trip, and resolved that business cares and monetary desires should be cast adrift, and that I would wander unconstrained by thought and lose myself so far as mental worry was concerned, until my hunt was over.

At Chicago, my brothers George and Frank and a mutual friend, Mr. Keener, joined me. They had purchased round trip tickets, and at 6 p.m. of the day mentioned, we squeezed into the crowd at the Chicago & North-Western Railroad depot and, with dogs and guns, grips and baggage, started for the great North. I was less familiar than they concerning the road we should take, but the service showed the wisdom of their selection. The train was the North-Western limited with compartment coaches, and was due in St. Paul the following morning at 7:25. The dining car was beautifully finished and furnished, being different in design from any I had seen. The seats were spacious, and withal there pervaded throughout the car a cleanliness that was most appetizing. But the buffet and compartment cars were a continued revelation to me. Divided into compartments royally furnished, each section a private stateroom with toilet accommodations, the tourist was placed completely at home and isolated from curious eyes. The furniture corresponded with the finish of the cars. In the buffet cars soft, leather covered chairs invited the tired traveler to easiest rest. The carpets were heavy brussels and the foot sank into their soft bodies with refreshing ease. The wood finish I could not determine; I thought it either cherry or bay wood. It was highly polished and frescoed and ornaments stood in bas relief representing the Corinthian period, while here and there tiny marble columns in various colors, added beauty and variety to these handsome cars. Tables were placed at the ends where pens and paper solicited their use, and a library of standard literature disclosed to the traveler works heavy, or of lightest reading. Incandescent lights, softened by opaque shades, threw a mellow light on these tables, at one of which I sat and mentally noted the magnificence of the car. The refreshment part of it was presided over by the slowest and blackest darky I ever saw. The appointments of the train were the subject of comment and many were the expressions of approval and admiration they caused, and compliments of their magnificence were frequently heard. I do not wonder at a remark I heard on the Great Northern later, when a man said: "There is but one road from St. Paul to Chicago, and that is the Chicago & North Western." Of course there are others, but this train was certainly perfection.

I retired early, and at break of day peeped into the uncertain gloom and learned the swift rate we had been traveling, for the hills and streams and the tall pines which stood as sentinels noted our approach and disappearance in a way that told me of our rapid running. The roadbed seemed smooth and I little imagined that while I was in the Land of Nod we had gone so speedily along. Shortly after I had arisen a car pin broke which caused a slight delay.

As we stood on the platform, a fine looking man seemed to eye us closely. As the darky said, "Ah, hedn't done nuffin," so I watched the gentleman. I liked his frank, manly appearance, for he carried in his face a confidence which was infectious. Approaching my brother Frank he said:

"Excuse me, but isn't your name Leffingwell?"

"Yes," replied Frank.

"Frank Leffingwell?"

"Yes."

"I thought so; I used to go to school with you at Notre Dame. My name is Johnson."

"What!" said Frank. " 'Sal' Johnson?"

"Yes, 'Sal' Johnson!:

"And how did you recognize me after twenty years?" said Frank.

"By your nose!"

At this George burst into a laugh and muttered sententiously:

"Here he thought he was not known,
But his nose has his identity shown."

We were introduced and our new-found friend said: "Yes, Frank, I'm still 'Sal' Johnson, and that name will probably be recalled every time I run across a fellow student."

"You see," said he, turning to me, "when I was at school I was very fond of playing ball. I threw overhand, like a girl. Some fellow noticed it and called me 'Sal.' That settled it, and I went by that name while I remained at school."

Our trip to St. Paul was made more pleasant because of his excellent company. We left him and his party at St. Paul and they went up the Northern Pacific to Jamestown and Dawson, among the best shooting grounds in North Dakota.

During the day we rested and saw but little of Minneapolis and St. Paul. The Chicago contingent made pointed comparisons as between these cities and their home. But I was not constituted champion for the Northwest, and I avoided discussions of the merits or demerits with them. We visited Barnhard & Son, also Kennedy Bros., at St. Paul, and made some slight purchases. They were all very busy and told us of marvelous bags sportsmen had been making in Minnesota and the Dakotas.

That night at 7 o'clock, we took the Great Northern and soon the twinkling lights of St. Paul and Minneapolis flittered and disappeared. The dark night was made still darker by the brilliant lights within, and we retired conscious of the fact that the following day would bring us into North Dakota and to the home of the game we had come a thousand miles to hunt.

The day had scarce begun to break, and while the dark pall was receding before the crimson light which preceded the sun, I drew my pillow near the window and the hundreds of wheatstacks assumed definite form, and I looked with wonder on the immense grainfields of the Red River Valley; for when I saw them, their multiplicity and the nearness of the fields told the story of the abundant harvest.

And what a magnificent country! From daylight till we reached Grand Forks, there was a pleasing sameness of fertile soil and evidences of agricultural prosperity. Handsome barns, pretty houses, acres and hundreds of acres dotted here and there with huge stacks of grain, which would have brought delight to any farmer's heart, and which convinced the most skeptical that divine promises had been fulfilled, for Dakotans had had both seedtime and harvest and their bins were filled to repletion. This was a busy time of the year, and teams primitive with oxen and teams modern with horses, hastened along conveying grain to elevators, or hauling it from steam thrashers, which seemed wonderfully plenty for so new a country.

All was activity and contentment. Prosperity breeds contentment, and Dakotans were happy, for the abundance of this and the previous year had brought Ceres to them with smiling face while she invited them to reach forth and garner the golden grain which she, as goddess of cultivation, had given them.

Grand Forks! Were you ever at Grand Forks! If not, and your friends ask you the name of one of the prettiest little cities of the great North, tell them Grand Forks. She is rich in the enterprise of her citizens, modest in her soft, creamy brick buildings, and in every particular presents the appearance of prosperity, and ought to be and doubtless is, the pride of her people. We bowled along, admiring the beautiful country, so different from what we expected, and weaned in part from the prairie land of Illinois and the rolling hills of my own native Iowa, to this great State which time served to increase our admiration for.

We were pleased tourists, and appreciated the uniform courtesies of the employees of the Great Northern Railway, who were unceasing in their efforts to make our trip a pleasant one. There was no unseemly intrusion on their part to advance the interests of the road, or of personal individuals, but our many questions met gentlemanly and prompt replies, and at the different stations we visited, the same uniform courtesy prevailed and although strangers to them, ourselves and our dogs received their prompt and unremitting attention. If the officials of the Great Northern have employed an instructor to instill into the minds of their employees gentlemanly traits, he has apt pupils, for they have learned their lessons well.

And now, although the train was late, we had reached our journey's end and found our host awaiting us. We saw the long train draw away from us without vain signs of regret, for we were now at the happy hunting grounds.

The afternoon was half gone, the home of our friend was still three hours away, and with two teams we started overland to that house beside the lake where

> "Nature paints not
> In oils, but frescoes the great dome of Heaven
> With sunsets, and the lovely forms of clouds
> And flying vapors."

The dogs freed from the restraint of chains and long confinement, bounded joyously forward venting their thanks with merry whisk of tail or noisy bark, ever and anon kissing the horses' noses as if soliciting sympathy because of their freedom.

We sped along through prairie grass, then along some little hill whose sloping sides led us gently to a tiny lake whose rushes concealed ducks and snipes by hundreds. We were getting the fever in a most contagious form and my companions could scarce restrain their ardor or await the coming of another day before intruding on wildfowl which, in places, had as yet not been fired at.

I believe that I was in a normal state. It seems now that I was, and yet, ducks arising before us and then alighting again, had a most demoralizing effect on me, which was allayed by the remark: "That's nothing to what you will see!" And it wasn't. The horses jogged along, the scenery beautiful because of its sameness of hills and valleys. The dogs running wild and only checked when some pinnated grouse would arise with a roar and fly for a mile before alighting.

Wanderings in Dakota - "That's Nothing To What You Will See."

A badger stood up inquisitively at one side in a field, and the boys called to me to shoot it. Hastily getting out Frank's rifle, I took careful aim and fired. My friends greeted the result of the shot with a derisive cheer, and I saw that I had overshot Mr. Badger fully six inches. Frank brought the rifle to defend himself against the prospective assaults of gophers, badgers, pelicans and Indians.

We had much fun over that rifle; but Frank insisted he would kill something with it. So he did, for one morning we saw him crawl to the edge of the lake and then heard rapid reports. As he approached the house the ladies exclaimed excitedly: "He's coming! Mr. Frank Leffingwell has made his boast good. It is hanging over his shoulder." We rushed out to welcome the successful hunter and found him carrying his coat over his shoulder, while to our inquiry of what luck? He replied:

"Splendid! I killed it!"

"What?" exclaimed several voices.

"Time!"

And that was all he did kill with that rifle.

Soon the lake was in sight and on its shores, sitting in the grandeur of their solitude, Canada geese were seen in great flocks, while its surface was dotted in patches, acres in extent, with my long-sought friends, the canvasbacks.

We soon reached the house. Night was fast approaching, and while we were unloading our wagons I involuntarily stopped, for there drifted through the open door sounds I little expected to hear, and I harkened delightedly to soft strains of music produced by an artist's hands.

Cordial greetings were exchanged, the evening was passed in sweet converse and music, and in telling of friends of years gone by. A hunt was arranged for the morrow, and then, to our chambers, where I lay and listened, kept awake, then lulled to sleep by the wildfowl's cries which was music most delightful to my ears.

WANDERINGS IN DAKOTA - NO. 2

Editor's Note: This article describes the first hunt in the series. In it Leffingwell refers to the sight of the full moon in October 1892 so we may infer that was the year of the hunts described in these articles. Some of the shooting was on a place named Preacher's Point. When I lived in Devils Lake I knew of a point with that name and if it was the same it identifies the locale in which these hunts took place.

We did not arise hastily on the following morning, for we had much to do before starting out to hunt. And that is where so many hunters err, in trying to obtain immediate shooting without first having obtained the lay of the country. The past has demonstrated to me that in no better way can the old saying, "More haste, less speed," be proven than in a man making great haste in beginning to hunt in a strange country. I have, therefore, always found it better to get the scope of the surrounding land first, in order that I could obtain better shooting the succeeding days. We went to the diningroom and then and there began our ravages on the eatables of North Dakota. This was an easy matter, for with superior cooking and food garnished with witticism which at times made victims of us all, and appetites enlarged by the keen bracing air, we ate and apologized, and our apologies having been accepted, we ate the more.

Considering the limit of space which I intend my articles shall occupy, I trust the reader will bear with me and pardon my not treating the events of our hunt as they happened consecutively. While the trip as a whole was as near perfection as possible, yet at times, when we expected the grandest shooting, something would happen which would blight our anticipations and turn prospective sport into ridiculous disappointment. This was notably the case when one day we marked hundreds and thousands of geese alighting in a field of grain. Leaving them undisturbed we felt sure we would have most excellent shooting the following morning. We were on hand before daybreak. We watched the glittering stars slowly dissolve from view. A fog spread its bluish folds over the earth and we were in joyous spirits, for the wind arose blowing against the direction whence the flight would come and, experienced shooters as we were, we knew that meant easy shots and that we would make a record.

But

"The best laid plans of mice and men," etc.

The first flock swung to the north of us, and as they set their wings to return, making a wide detour, it seemed as if there was a volcano near us, for through the morning air four reports rang out in thunderous tones, and we learned that others had come to that field in the darkness and had dug pits within two hundred yards of us. The situation was so ridiculous that we roared with laughter for we had arisen at four o'clock, driven five miles, and dug our pits only to find others with us. If misery loves company, she was highly entertained that morning, for no doubt our presence was as unwelcome to our neighbors as was theirs to us. We killed six geese; but we marked their flight and vowed revenge. We had it that afternoon, for three of us at that time made the biggest bag of the trip.

A series of articles, to be entertaining to the mass of readers, must contain a fullness of descriptions, with the necessary brevity of space; must contain matter interesting to those of experience, with matter instructive to those who may be considered amateurs. I have therefore no intention of wearying any person by a recital of events which happened in their order, or to treat of them all, but to sift the chaff from the bins of the abundant harvest of shooting we enjoyed and give to the reader the richest and ripest fruits of our trip.

While George, Henry (our host) and myself were prowling over the country investigating lakes and ponds, fields and marshy spots, Frank and Mr. Keener took supreme pleasure in going to a point where the land was high and intercepting the flight of canvas-backs and redheads, obtaining splendid pass shooting.

I want you to know Mr. Keener. He is of medium height and slim, smoothly shaven, polite and affable, brown hair, keen blue eyes, perfect teeth and withal bright and witty. His wife calls him Charles. We called him Jerry. The fraternal tie which binds sportsmen together denies any and all secrecy, therefore you shall know why we dropped the dignified address of Mr. Keener; or said Mr. Keener this, or Mr. Keener that, and called him by the decidedly plain name of Jerry. While we were obstructing the sidewalk on a prominent street corner in St. Paul, a young man hurriedly passed us, and as he did so, he slapped Mr. Keener familiarly on the shoulder and said: "How are you Jerry, old boy?" Mr. Keener looked around in astonishment and said: "Wh—,who the devil was that fellow?" The man had disappeared and Mr. Keener did not see his face. We told him it wouldn't do to plead ignorance, for doubtless he had met the man and had forgotten the time, and wasn't willing to remember the place. But, said Mr. Keener, "My name isn't Jerry!" "It will be for the remainder of the trip," replied George. And so it was.

We could not blame Frank and Jerry for frequenting "Preacher's Point." Indeed we fell in love with it ourselves, and we passed many a delightful hour there shooting canvas-backs, redheads and widgeons as they flew to and from the connected lakes. It is seldom one obtains good duck shooting without positive inconvenience; but here the place was high and dry; a narrow neck of land run to the stream which separated two sections of the lake. This land broadened as it receded and its gravelly bed ornamented with sparsely growing grass, gave scant cover, which necessitated a slight artificial blind to make one's hiding place complete. As the land widened it arose in stature and became a cliff of miniature dimensions, and from its height the soul of the hunter could be satisfied and his eyes feasted with one of nature's most magnificent views; for in each branch of the lakes which were spread before him at the north and at the south, the water was rippled and splashed by the swimming or diving birds, and Canada and Hutchin's geese and speckled brant, and ducks of all kinds from the kingly canvas-backs to the tiny teal or still smaller ruddy ducks, which looked darker in colors as they strayed to and fro between banks of snow geese which forgot their wild chattering while floating on the lake.

No wonder Jerry said: "You go on and wade in marshes; get up at four o'clock in the morning and hunt geese, but Preacher's Point is good enough for Frank and I."

And when we considered the ease of their positions from which to shoot, and knew that from a dozen to a couple of dozen canvas-backs and redheads were daily paying the debt incident to their devotion, we did not blame them.

In Dakota, all places of interest, or which would attract the attention of passers-by, are christened with a name. Four antelope were seen in a slough. The place is called Antelope Slough. Rushes abound in some great marsh. It is called Rush Lake. A peculiar shape is noticed in the formation of some low place where shallow water forms. It is called Spectacle Lake or Horseshoe Bend. A spring bubbles forth with innocent purlings and the water breaks into tiny wrinkles at the foot of some broad, open lake whose shores are as white as snow with crusted alkali. It is named Spring Lake. And so on *ad finem.* Knowing the custom of the Indians to name these places, I felt there was some cause for calling that beautiful spot with its trees of oak and birch and willow,

"Preacher's Point." One evening, after we had related the experiences of the day and were all cosily seated around the parlor and sitting-room, the young ladies favored us with choicest music. Imagine the most difficult sonatas of Mozart, The Wedding March of Mendelssohn, the Tannhauser of Wagner and the entrancing waltzes of Strauss correctly interpreted in this home on the prairies of North Dakota! A lull between a sentence; I cannot say a lull in the conversation, for that never occurred in that witty gathering. But I had the opportunity and improved it, for said I:

"Preacher's Point! Why is it called Preacher's Point?"

"Why, don't you know? Haven't you heard the story!"

"No indeed!" I replied.

"Well, you shall have it, and this is the legend as it has descended to us: The history of Preacher's Point runs back so far that it ought not to be called a story, but rather a legend which gives historical interest to this section. It seems that this point has always been a favorite trysting spot for the Indians, whether they contemplated a hunt or to hold a council of any kind, the reason being, no doubt, that here they could find shade and water in Summer and shelter in Winter. And they met here and sent their searching parties in all directions to locate the bisons, which were very plentiful, as you must have observed by the many deep trails which wind around the different hills, and the wallows which still exist. One day while the Indians were preparing for a feast there appeared before them a white man. He was young and of handsome physique; his face was pale, his eyes the deepest brown, and his great, broad forehead bespoke the intelligence with which he was endowed. The Indians liked him from the beginning. There was that in his appearance which instantly won their confidence. Where he came from or what induced him to forsake civilization, will probably never be known. But he came among them, learned their language and lived with them, and he died and was buried on that point. It is thought that some great disappointment drove him here, for he was unlike most ministers, and seemed fitted for any business calling. But it is evidence the Indians loved him, for that spot is held by them in sacred reverence. This is how the point received the name by which you daily hear it called."

"Well," said Jerry, "that is a romantic story, and the preacher couldn't have selected a prettier spot in which to live and die."

Wanderings in Dakota - Preacher's Point.

"To-morrow!" said Henry, "we'll have a round-up. We'll drive over the country and take in the different lakes and bring home a wagonload of game."

"To-morrow!" exclaimed the ladies, "that is the day for our picnic; but if you will return by four o'clock, you may go."

"Let Henry, Bruce and George go and we will stay with the ladies," said Frank.

That arrangement was made, and early in the morning we started on a trip which will ever be fresh in my mind. The day was grandly beautiful. The sun arose over the eastern hills and seemed to welcome us to the beauties of spring. Our destination was toward the West and the wind blew so gently in our faces that the day and the atmosphere impressed me as the most perfect I ever experienced. We had but one dog with us and he a retriever, although at different times he made points on grouse.

We soon left behind us all signs of human habitation and then we were on the prairies. I was alone in the back seat, and those tireless hunters, Henry and George, talked over other days and chatted about the expectations of the day as if this was the first hunt of the party. How I enjoyed my ride! We traveled all day, only stopping when shooting. Game was too plenty to particularize shots. We had long lost sight of roads and trails, only once striking the trail of some Indians, which was told by the three heavy marks of the poles holding their outfit. A roar of wings and a sharptail grouse would fly a short distance, then alight. The horses would be stopped, our birds selected, and the quick whip-like crack of nitro powder would be instantly followed by drifting feathers and falling birds. Over the hills and valleys! Here the trail of buffalo with grass growing over it, here the places where bulls wallowed and fought—seen for ages by no white man—and here the prints of antelope which came to a spring to drink. The sun shone warmly on us. The heavens were flecked here and there with white clouds which floated lazily along. Great boulders stood as monuments of the years gone by, and then smaller ones in colors of green and white; some moss covered or red and brown; others glittered like diamonds in the sunlight, while before us the hills appeared to meet the sky. At the sides the same, and when I looked behind me the long valley we had passed through reached back for miles and the sea of prairie lost itself in the horizon and into the vault of heaven. No sight of man! No sound of life! No indications that there existed in all the world aught that was not with us and around us! All was grass fair Dakota. The air was delightfully pure and as refreshing to inhale as the coolest draught from the purest sky. Truly this was solitude; and, I love such solitude.

"If *thou* art worn and hard beset
With sorrows that *thou* wouldst forget,
If *thou* wouldst read a lesson that will keep
Thy heart from fainting, and thy soul from sleep,
Go to the woods and hills! No tears
Dim the sweet look that Nature wears."

"Down around this hill is a little lake," said Henry.

We approached it carefully and could see hundreds of ducks on the water.

"No geese here; too many rushes," said Henry.

We scattered as much as possible under the circumstances and then approached. A quack, and then a report, and then hundreds and thousands of ducks darkened the sky. We hastily hid ourselves in the rushes; stragglers circled near us; we fired until our gun barrels were hot, and then the birds, giving one grand wheel, circled away to some other pond. Dragging our load out we began to fill that wagon-box. Henry said we would, and as we were his guests we tried to obey instructions.

There is a peculiarity about duck shooting in Dakota which it will be well to remember. The marshes, with very rare exceptions, have hard bottoms and one can wade almost any distance. This is because the marshes are depressions in the prairies, or places which receive the waters from hills. As the water from the hills comes mostly from snow, many of the little ponds are dry part of the time. Boats are not needed, and duck decoys not especially so. Duck decoys can be used in the long or wide lakes, but in the smaller places a few shots will drive the birds away and they will not come back 'till between sundown and dark, therefore, when a pond is "shot out," *i.e.,* the birds driven away, the hunter should go to some other resort. And here is where the trouble lies, to find that other resort! A stranger would soon be lost; he could not find these places, and unless he is with a man acquainted with the country, he is sure to obtain but indifferent shooting; for in some sections of Dakota it is as a stranger said, "A great big country where nobody lives."

A man to hunt successfully in Dakota must have a dog. Speaking of dogs. There isn't one in a thousand fit to hunt with in that country. Everything is of a yellowish color, even the grass and grain fields, and a dog of any color but a yellowish sedge would be too conspicuous. Most of the shooting is goose shooting, and while a dog isn't a necessity while hunting geese, at the same time a well trained one of the proper color is a blessing.

Henry now started for another lake, and although this land was an ocean of sameness, he knew every pond. We approached one. It was the same old story, a brief period of rapid firing then off again. We had visited perhaps a half dozen ponds when I chided the boys about our promise to return at four o'clock for the picnic. But they were bound to keep up the gait. Of course I had to stay with them, and did. By this time the bottom of the wagon-box was full of birds and I had to kick away a place for my feet, and I tried to conjecture some good excuse to tell the ladies because of our tardiness. It was not necessary, for they said:

"We knew Henry would get after game and not come unless you brought him; and, candidly, we think you and Mr. George Leffingwell just as bad as he."

How we wished Perry was with us! Who's Perry? Don't you know Perry? He is one of my dearest friends and second to none as a shot. He has a weakness. It is jacksnipe shooting, and here he could have got his fill of it. If he didn't, it would be funny. I thought I had seen jacksnipe before, but nothing compared with what it was here. Not only hundreds but hundreds upon hundreds. It seemed as if the marshes were alive with them. We saw them singly, in pairs, in wisps, and in immense flocks. But I must go to the picnic.

As the sun was going down we reached the appointed place. They were awaiting us. A splendid supper was ready. We sat and gorged ourselves and told of the adventures of the day. Geese came over to the lake chattering and screaming, but we were not to be disturbed, and as the moon came up we started for home. The full moon of October, 1892! Perhaps you remember it? But you didn't see or hear what we did! The dew glistening on the grass, the lake silvered with the moon's soft rays, the snow geese in thousands upon the water, the dogs welcoming us home. The night was sublimely beautiful and I chose to walk across the little peninsula, and as I did, I thought:

> "How beautiful is night!
> A dewy freshness fills the silent air;
> No mist obscures, nor cloud, nor speck, nor stain
> Breaks the serene of heaven;
> In full orb'd glory, yonder moon divine
> Rolls through the dark blue depths;
> Beneath her steady ray
> The desert circle spreads
> Like the round ocean girded with the sky.
> How beautiful is night!"

"You did make a record," exclaimed Henry's wife.
"How many birds?" said I.
"Sixty-eight ducks, six prairie chickens, eight geese and one hundred and forty-one snipes."

WANDERINGS IN DAKOTA - No. 3

Editor's Note: This article is a description of goose hunting in stubble fields over decoys. Sheet metal decoys made by the Danz Company were often used in those days. Leffingwell's feelings were expressed as follows: "Fortune may smile on you some day with looks inviting, and southern winds may drift your ship to fair North Dakota, when you will see what we saw, enjoy what we enjoyed, and profit by the truths I have told you."

Luck, if we are permitted to call it by that name, appeared to be strongly against Jerry and Frank obtaining good goose shooting, for whenever they went out they seemed to miss the flight. On the contrary, fickle fortune ever had her blandest smiles for the rest of us, and appeared to send the geese our way. This got to be a subject of comment, and try as they would, Jerry and Frank could not strike a big flight of geese.

"I'm a hoodoo!" said Jerry.

"And my name is Dennis!" exclaimed Frank.

"That's all right," chimed in George, "we will admit you are a couple of Jonahs, but luck can't always be against you and we will try it again this afternoon."

"We won't do anything of the kind," said Jerry. "Today is Friday. I never had any luck on Friday, and I won't go. You three go. Geese will come to you. It always takes a fool for luck, and you fellows haven't missed it yet. But Frank and I will stay at home to-day. See what you do. If you find good shooting we will try it in the morning."

So that afternoon George, Henry and I went after geese. We had noticed the flight in the morning and knew about where to go.

Striking out in a southerly direction from the house, a drive of four miles brought us to a field where we saw a flock hover and then settle. We drove to the field and there found several hundred geese; also hundreds of cranes. The geese did not pay much attention to our approach, only showing their knowledge of it by gathering together and standing still with their long necks stretched to their extreme heights. They were mostly Hutchin's geese, a goose similar in appearance to the Canada's, but much smaller, weighing from seven to nine, and occasionally ten pounds. But our approach seemed to have an electrical effect on the cranes, which showed itself by their uneasy movements. They were apparently not paying any particular attention to us, but every few moments one would jump up a few feet and open its wings slightly as if to ease it, when it alighted. It seemed as if the ground was getting hot, for they began hopping and walking as carefully as a barefooted boy on a stone sidewalk heated by the Summer's sun. Our near approach was too much for their nervousness, and, flopping their great wings, they arose and drifted past us, followed by the derisive "kerr-eh!" of George and Henry. But the geese were impudent enough, for they sat until we were within forty yards of them, and then some Canada's on the outside led the flock, for their leader giving the expected signal, "Ah-unk!" in deep bass tones, the balance got in motion and their cries could have been heard for a mile. Some strange power must have told them we would not shoot then, for many of the Hutchin's swung over us within twenty yards and looked down at us with what some might call curiosity, but to us it was downright impudence. Had we shot at them in the field we might have killed six or eight; but the experienced goose hunter knows better than to drive geese out of a field by shooting at them, if he desires them to return that day. For, driven out in that way, they seldom return. We soon had our pits dug and were ready for the geese on their return, or to welcome any others that had been away making social calls or basking in the beautiful lakes.

The three of us were practical in the art of goose shooting and soon had our profile decoys set out to the best advantage. It is not as easy to set out decoys to make them most effective as the amateur might expect. Advantage must be taken of the direction and force of the wind. At times decoys will be most attractive when placed before the shooter, while again, if placed behind the blinds from thirty to forty yards, they will solicit and bring the better shots. Geese invariably alight against the wind, and if the flight is such that the birds come down wind, unless they are very close, one should let them pass and coax their return by artistic calling; not with artificial excuses, but with the human voice. They will scarce withstand the seductive appearance of the decoys and the beseeching calls they hear. And then comes the trial which tests the coolness of the inexperienced hunter, for as they set their wings and sail toward the decoys, his heart thumps against his ribs till be relieves his anxiety by stealing furtive glances through the stubble which he has placed on the edge of his blind, or by nervously feeling of the safety on his gun, that no negligence may spoil his shot. On, on they come; now with wings set in graceful curves, now with legs hanging down as if to alight; then they flap their wings to gain further motion, and then, swinging to one side, they appear so close with their dark bodies that the gunner feels sure the time has come to fire. The hunter, no longer able to stem the tide of the current of his excitement which is shown in his sparkling eye, aims and shoots only to learn that they were sixty instead of thirty yards away. Every man who has hunted geese knows how deceptive their appearance is while in flight. This is made more so by reason of the hunter being hidden, and forced to remain perfectly quiet while the birds are approaching. Geese fly much faster than is commonly supposed, and proper allowance in aiming must be made when shooting at them. While in some states, especially Nebraska and Missouri, they are shot when coming onto the sandbars of the Platte, the Missouri and other rivers, the generally accepted way of shooting them is from pits or blinds in the fields where they are accustomed to feed. This is a pleasant way of shooting them, for the shooter can always remain dry; besides the sport is best in the morning or in the early afternoon when it is the pleasantest to shoot, of course, excepting the going to the fields before daybreak, for then often times one's teeth will chatter and it takes active exercise to keep one from getting cold. An old toper isn't more regular in going after his drink than geese for theirs; nor a glutton after his meals than they for their food. The birds roost in the lakes and make night hideous with their cries. One night in particular they whooped and yelled so continuously and so loudly that I was forced to lie awake for hours, and I am willing to confess that on the following day I took supremest delight in shooting, for I felt I was getting revenge for my loss of sleep.

At break of day they leave their roosting places and go out to feed. Then is the time when the hunter gets his best shooting, if in the line of their flight, for they travel over the same fields to some objective point where they have been feeding before. They are peculiar in this respect for they pass over grounds equally inviting and go perhaps miles beyond. As they return to the same fields in the afternoon, the hunter should follow the line of their flight until he finds this field, then go away without routing them out and return at about three, or earlier, dig his pit and he will soon see the advance guards coming. At about two o'clock they return to the lakes. In the afternoon they return just before dark. When geese have been roosting in a lake, hunters make a great mistake to try and shoot them in the lake, for here is their haven of rest, and they ought to be left undisturbed. I studied them carefully and learned that while it seemed as if they were never quiet, there was a time when they were, and that was at midday in the lake. During their twice daily flights they fill the air with their coarse or shrill cries. At night the same; but in the middle of the day they float lazily on the lake, some swimming gracefully along, others allowing themselves to drift with the wind, while others seek tired Nature's sweet restorer and drift with head under wing, oblivious to the pranks of their thousands of neighbors. On still days they leave the lakes later and return earlier. But cloudy days breed discontent, and they fly uneasily to and fro, giving the sportsman most excellent shooting.

But I have wandered from the pits where I had led you a most willing captive, and have talked goose lore until I may have tired your patience. If you are experienced in goose shooting, you will pardon me, for I have doubtless recalled pleasant reminiscences. On the other hand, if time, or distance, or opportunity have denied you the pleasure of shooting geese in a stubblefield, Dame Fortune may smile on you some day with looks inviting, and the southern winds may drift your ship to fair North Dakota, when you will see what we saw, enjoy what we enjoyed, and profit by the truths I have told you.

And now the flight began. To the southwest an uncertain line appeared which the moments as they passed brought to clearer view, and a flock of Hutchin's were returning to the field from which they had been driven. They came on perfectly unsuspicious, answering the deceptive cries from the pits, and three fell to rise no more. And so on through the afternoon, Henry's big 10-bore Smith belched out in thunderous tones, or followed in quick succession the spiteful crack of our nitros. George and I were both using 12-gauge, full choke Greener hammerless guns, loaded with 3 1/4 drams of nitro powder, and Henry's 10 ½ 10-gauge Smith was not more effective than ours. And what supreme satisfaction there was to shoot with such shots! No clashing, no claiming of birds; but the stillness of the fields was awakened with the roar of guns, and three, four, five, and at times six birds were killed dead in air, such was the perfectness of aim and the killing power of our ammunition. We hunted much together, Henry, George and I, and I never saw such methodical and effective shooting. Not much was said, but when a flock came over the decoys, the right flank, the left and the center were decimated, showing what coolness and good judgment could do.

We three shot side by side for over two weeks, and I don't recall a single instance where two selected the same bird. As the sun sank behind the hill we went to a little pond and there enjoyed shooting during the evening flight of ducks which came in. The moon lighted our pathway on our way home, and the stars winked at us as if to ask us if we were enjoying the trip. While Henry and I were unhitching the horses Jerry took an invoice of the game in the wagon and said:

"The same old story; twenty-two geese and about a dozen ducks."

"Yes," said Henry, "we struck it fairly well, but the flight was southwest from us, and to-morrow morning you, Frank and I will go to the field where they were dropping in, and you will have a goose shoot such as you have heard tell of."

"And Bruce and I will go together!" exclaimed George.

"George," said I, "let us try the same blinds we had to-day; I don't believe they were entirely shot off, for all did not return that we drove from the fields."

Generally speaking, it doesn't pay to shoot from the same blinds during two successive flights, but we thought best to try it and sincerely hoped that Henry, Frank and Jerry would strike the flight, for George and I had been favored every time with excellent shooting.

We were on the grounds before daylight on the following morning. As day began to dawn the gloaming slowly gave way to the light of the rising sun. Quick and successive reports told the tale of our friends getting shooting, but their shots were too few and far apart. We both noticed it and George said:

"Don't that beat all? They have missed it again."

With us it was different, and as the sun arose, geese came from all directions toward our decoys. They came too fast, for their numbers showed that they had left the lake in a body and we must make hay while the sun shone, or, literally speaking, shoot as fast as possible. The flight was principally Hutchin's and brant, with a few Canada's. I had just remarked to George how pleasant the shooting was to have birds come and no chasing them when one carried his load of No. 3s for a couple of hundred yards. I started for it and then George's sharp "Down!" settled me headlong in the stubble, where I flopped, stealthily, if not gracefully, onto my back just in time to knock a Hutchin's from an almost impossible height.

I started again and repeated the feat, for another goose came down. George was not idle, for I turned and saw him make a pretty double.

"The first thing you know you will strain your gun killing geese so high," said I.

"Don't talk," said he, "you are killing them from sixty to seventy-five yards, and I'll bet you killed one ninety yards. What do you think of this ammunition, anyway?"

"Now George," said I, "you are a good guesser, but I'm not going to commit myself until we are through the hunt."

"All right! Do as you please, but I'll tell you right now that when we used to shoot 'honkers' in Nebraska with our 11 3/4 pound 10-gauges and used six drams of Dead Shot powder and one ounce of No. 2s we never killed them as dead or as far as we are killing them now every day. Just keep up your thinking, but you know mighty well you never shot anything equal to these loads! Here look at this," and he threw me a goose. "That one I killed fully fifty yards. Look at it!"

I did so and found that a dozen No. 3s had entered the breast and gone through it as clean as a bullet from a rifle would have done.

"How does that strike you?" he queried.

"Not so hard as it did the goose," said I, "but I have examined twenty geese at least and noticed this same penetration, showing the terrific hitting power of the guns, and—'kerr-rr-eh!" 'Kerr-rr-eh!"

Down we slid into our pits, each wondering how those immense cranes could approach without being seen or having seen us. "Kerr-rr-eh!" answered George to their repeated calls, and the cranes headed for our decoys. Something aroused their suspicion, for they wheeled to go to one side of us. They presented excellent shots except as to distance, but we arose simultaneously, our guns cracked together, then together again, and the sight will not soon be forgotten, for we each made a double and the air was blue with cranes as the four came tumbling down. Shortly after this three Canada's came in. They gave us exceptionally easy shots. We killed two and the third set its wings and sailed for a quarter of a mile, then dropped like a bullet. A pair of cranes came in a little later and George bagged them both beautifully, for his gun cracked with just the slightest intermission and both birds were killed clean.

Wanderings in Dakota - The Air Was Blue With Cranes As The Four Came Tumbling Down."

We heard no shots from our friends, except occasionally, and George said: "Don't it beat all? I thought they would get splendid shooting, for at least one hundred geese circled and lit in that field yesterday to one here."

The morning was pretty well advanced when we saw the wagon trailing over a distant hill, and we knew what that meant. Henry was marking the flight for the afternoon. As they drove up I said:

"Well, boys, what luck?"

"Same as before," said Frank. "Can't break the spell," said Jerry.

"How was it, Henry?" asked I.

"Oh I don't know; we just missed the flight; but it will come all right. We got no shooting to speak of; we only got five or six. But I see you got in your work."

Wanderings in Dakota - "Kalamazoo! But How We Went Down That Hill."

"Yes," replied George, "I pulled one of my socks on wrong-side-out this morning. Didn't change it, and of course had good luck. We'll go out this afternoon and I will take Jerry and Frank with me and I'll show you that a mascot will protect anyone who is hoodooed."

When we were ready to go after dinner, the boy at the farm hitched up other team. I didn't like the looks of Bertel. Who is Bertel? Neither a man nor a dog, but just a common-looking horse from Montana. Oh! But looks are deceivin'! One could have gazed at that inoffensive-looking horse and admired his patient resignation. Mary's lamb could not have appeared more gentle. But Bertel was too curious to suit me and had the exceedingly bad habit of looking over his shoulder to see what was going on. Now curiosity is all right in a woman, but a horse that gets his oats three times a day ought to strictly attend to business. I ventured to remark to the boy "that Bertel seemed very gentle."

"Don't you fool yourself!" said the boy, "he's jest thinkin'!"

"Have you ever ridden him?"

"Wonct!"
"What did he do?"
"Jumped a ten foot perpindic'lar bank!"
"What became of you?"
"I stuck to the hoss. Can't no hoss get me off till I'm ready. I ain't 'fraid of no hoss!"
"I suppose you have driven him before?"
"Wonct!"
"Suppose he attempts to run?"
"Let 'im run!"
"Suppose he kicks?"
"Let 'im kick!"
"Suppose something breaks?"
"Let 'er break!"

"All right," said I, and I ran over hastily in my mind, $5,000 in Equitable, $5,000 in Accident, $2,000 in—but we were in the wagon.

"Good bye, Frank! Take care of yourself!" said Jerry, and Frank tried to.

Oh, Bertel, you brown fraud! The boy spoke to the horses. Then off one started. Bertel hesitated. He changed his mind when the boy hit him under the belt, Kalamazoo! But how we went down that hill. Bertel had the pole and his mate was crowding him. Would it be a dead heat? We all hung to the wagon. The wagon struck a stone. Biff! Then another. Bang! Then an upheaval at the crest of a small hill, and we all went from five to twelve feet into the air. I just had time to think that someone would be killed and, like the Irishman who went through an experience something similar, "Oi ixpicted to be knocked sinseliss, an' thin to awake to foind mesilf dead," when down we all came into the bottom of the wagon, and the horses kept up their mad run. The heavy sand finally checked them; they were stopped; we inquired who was hurt and then congratulated ourselves that there was nothing worse than one gouged finger, one scratched and one broken gun. Another gun was brought and it was then "On Bertel! On!" And that descendant of one of the fiery and untamed steeds of Montana started again. He was run into the ford and as he struck the soft bottom his speed was checked.

Ah! ha! Mr. Bertel, thought we; this is different. But Bertel wasn't through yet, for when we reached the deepest spot in the ford he just quietly lay down, then gave us that same old familiar look over his right shoulder, as if to say, "Boys, this is the way they do in Montana!"

We tried to pry him out, but he was content. I tried to encourage his mate. He started, then slipped, and I got a spat of mud in my face which filled my eyes. George noticed it and said:

"Wha, honey: yo' bettah take yo' kuhchief an' wipe dat mud offen yo' face." And I did.

We reached the destined fields after an half hour's drive. Frank and George hunted together; Henry and I. Henry and the writer got splendid shooting, and Henry complimented my little 7 1/2-pound gun when he said that in all his years of shooting geese he had never seen birds killed farther, higher or deader; and his gun was at the same time doing justice to itself and its owner. Henry is the equal of any man I ever saw when it comes to shooting ducks or geese.

As we were in our blinds a flock of brant alighted near us. Too far to shoot, yet sufficiently near to decoy moving birds. Slipping in a shell of BBs, Henry stood up and shouted. As they flew he fired. Much to our surprise one came down. I wasn't out entirely for my health; and I shot. Another fell. They jumped from a stubble across a little piece of plowed ground, so we could exactly tell the distance, and we killed those birds just one hundred and five long paces.

That afternoon a pair of cranes came over us. I thought them too high and too far, yet I killed one with each barrel at an estimated distance of seventy-five yards. George and Frank did not get as good shooting as we, but our bags combined counted out over thirty geese and three cranes.

In my next I shall give a comprehensive review of the shells we used, and I doubt if there was ever a more thoroughly practical test made, for the time employed was fifteen consecutive days in calm and blustering weather, and the tests conducted in the most impartial manner, my only desire being to find a powder for my own use which I would consider the best to be obtained.

WANDERINGS IN DAKOTA - NO. 4

Editor's Note: In this article Leffingwell provides details of the guns and powders used. Claims are made of killing geese at what would be thought of as extreme ranges. For example: "George and I killed one hundred geese from sixty to ninety yards....one day....George fired at a flock of geese over one hundred yards from him and brought five down with one barrel." Those statements generated quite an exchange of letters in <u>The American Field</u> by those who disputed their accuracy. Be sure to look for Leffingwell's account of his hunt with the young daughter of Henry their host. By his reference to her as a "sweet specimen of womanhood" we may infer that he had an appreciation of women.

"There was a soft and pensive grace,
A cast of thought upon her face,
That suited well the forehead high,
The eyelash dark, and downcast eye:
The mild expression spoke a mind
In duty firm, composed, resigned."

The reader who has complimented me by reading my previous articles, must have wondered what loads we were using to do such effective shooting. As I stated previously, our guns were Greener hammerless 12-gauges. George's weighed 8 pounds and mine 7 1/2. It has always been a great pleasure for me to experiment with different loads. Guns, like individuals, have their peculiarities, and it takes time and a thorough acquaintance with them to bring out their good qualities, or to learn their hidden defects.

I long since discarded black powder, and think it only fit to use where one cannot afford the more expensive nitros, or at Fourth of July celebrations where noise is desired. In selecting loads for this trip, my desire was to obtain the greatest hitting power with evenness of pattern and absence of smoke and recoil.

An exhaustive test of my gun during a week's outing with my children, showed me that 3 drams of powder, with three black or pink-edge wads on the powder and a thin card on the shot, gave the best pattern obtainable. But I found the pattern almost as good with 3 1/4 drams, while the penetration was far better. I then knew that I required 3 1/4 drams of nitro powder with 1 1/8 ounces of chilled shot. While I am averse to changing an old for a new powder, at the same time I am ever progressive and want the best. I had consistently used American Wood powder for years, but in my many trials I obtained better results from Schultze, and have therefore of late used that powder almost exclusively. The Schultze is powerful; at times too much so, as I have had several 10-gauge guns of 10 and 10 ½ pounds weight thrown open when the first barrel was discharged, and this with 4 1/8 drams of Schultze. Possibly some of my readers may think that 4 1/8 drams is an excessive charge. Surely if a 7 ½ pound 12-gauge Greener will burn 3 ½ drams without racking the gun, a 10 ½ pound 10 gauge ought easily to control 4 1/8 drams. Indeed the comparison as between black and nitro powder is much greater, for the weights and calibers named will stand more than 2 drams of black in the 10-gauge in excess of the charge used in a No. 12-gauge gun.

I had had such excellent results with Schultze in my 12-gauge that I resolved to order all shells loaded with that; but when I gave the matter more serious thought, I concluded to have a great quantity of them loaded with E.C., for having tried that powder, I was in doubt as to the superiority between Schultze and E. C. And then the question of shells arose. I wanted the quickest primers, for quickness of ignition in nitro powder insures greatest propelling power and consequently harder hitting.

After thinking the matter over deliberately and knowing the responsibility of the house, I wrote Montgomery Ward & Co., of Chicago, for prices on 3,000 shells loaded with Schultze and E. C. powder. These were to be for my brothers Frank and George; also for myself. They quoted prices, but much to my surprise, sought to have us try a new powder, the S. S. Now I have had some experience in trying new powders and have lost many an otherwise good day for not sticking to the old and tried. I had no hesitancy in telling them so; but to this they replied that if I did not consider the shells loaded with S. S. equal, if not superior, to any I had ever used, I could return those not used and need not pay for those I had shot. Surely this was an evidence of an abiding faith on their part and I resolved to test their loads of which they spoke in such enthusiastic terms. But I was still shy of getting so many of a new load and going so far to use them. They said the S. S. was a higher priced powder than the others, but that they had recently lowered it so as to meet competition. We gave them the order, divided between Schultze, E. C. and S. S., all shells to be loaded with 3 1/4 drams by measure, a waterproof and two pink-edge wads on powder, 1 1/8 ounces chilled shot, with card wad over shot and tightly crimped, in red smokeless shells with No. 3 primers. Here were three powders to be tried, two of which I knew well, and against them a new candidate for public favor. I liked the looks of the powder, but powder manufacturers have claimed everything except the earth, and I make scant allowance for their claims. As the shells were the same, the loads identically so, and as they were to be given days of trial under circumstances the same, and on birds requiring the hardest hitting to bag, any superiority which was apparent would be rightfully so, and would only be shown after a thoroughly competitive trial. (I wish to disclaim, right here, having any interest in any of the powders named. I paid for my shells, and a uniform price for them.) We, George, Frank and I, shot the S. S. for three successive days; then the Schultze; then the E. C., making note of the effects. There was less smoke and recoil in the S. S. than in the others. It was quicker and far excelled the others in killing powers. So apparent was the superiority of the S. S. shown, that after giving the three an equitable trial, we discarded our shells loaded with Schultze and E. C. and only used them after we had exhausted our supply of S. S. The killing power of the S. S. was astonishing, and we brought birds to bag which seemed impossible and improbable. A man while shooting will frequently make long or high shots, but to do it regularly is the test of the ammunition as well as the shooter's skill; and I think without question, that during this trip, George and I killed one hundred geese from sixty to ninety yards with S. S. powder and No. 3 chilled shot. One day, as a joke, George fired at a flock of geese over one hundred yards from him and brought five down with one barrel, three of them stone dead. A goose fell with its wings tipped with shot; it started to walk away; the boys called to me to try my gun: I did so; and at the report of the gun the bird dropped as dead as if I was only twenty yards away instead of ninety as the measurement showed. A pair of brants came over me high; I got the pair, the second one being fully sixty yards high. It fell dead at my feet. I marked it. The next day we had it for dinner. It was struck with fifteen No. 3s and they were driven through the bird. We were just starting for home one afternoon when a flock of brant came to one side. I raised my gun. "Don't shoot!" said George. I did though, and killed two of them fully one hundred and fifteen yards. Of course a chance shot! It was just such extraordinary shots that made us admit that without any exception the loads used of S. S. and No. 3 chilled shot, were the most powerful in killing power of any we had ever used.

And now come with me and we will wander in pastures where recollections bring the most beautiful sights, and drink with me from the cool spring of nature which refreshes us all. Henry was sick, Frank and Jerry had gone home, George was not to be seen, and I lay in the grass near the house, feasting my eyes on the scenic beauty around me. The day was indescribably beautiful, the filmy haze which o'erspread the lake in the morning had disappeared, the wind which had arisen with the sun was wafted by itself to other climes, and the white clouds which flecked the dome of heaven were shamed at their insignificance and were dissolved, then commingled with the ocean of blue in that ethereal sky. In the west, dark clouds were slowly fading from view, sinking behind the tiny hills in their retreat. And now the flight of snow geese began! Thousands came where hundreds were the day before, and it seemed as if they descended from the sky, so noiselessly did they come in. I watched for them, and while many came in their usual flight, others sank from measureless heights and, like leaves drifting in uncertain winds, or snowflakes from a Winter's sky, they dropped wavering and swerving with their pure white bodies made whiter still in the golden rays of the morning sun.

The surface of the lake was alive with geese and ducks, acres and acres of them.

> "By thousands there the wildfowl came,
> To taste the rich, delicious fare;
> The redhead and the canvas-back,
> The widgeon, with his plumage rare;
> The ruddy duck, the buffel-head,
> The broadbill and Canadian goose,
> Loving o'er placid shoal or cove
> Their flapping pinions to unloose."

Whence came they? From Athabasca or from Hudson's Bay I knew not, but was satisfied that these were the forerunners of the great northern flight.

I was charmed and the naturalness of the scene seemed too perfect, and it seemed as if I was—

"Dreaming?" spoke a woman's voice.

I turned in astonishment and saw the daughter of my host near me.

"Dreaming?" continued she, "I thought men too practical to indulge in dreams. The atmosphere and scenery of fair Dakota must have entranced you, for I have been standing here awaiting recognition while you were gazing into the lake as if you had lost something."

"Yes! I have lost something. Lost it in the lake; lost it in the sky; in the very atmosphere. I have lost myself, for I never saw a scene so calmly beautiful; and it refreshes me, for as I look at it all, it seems as if I were in it."

"In it?" she archly said.

"Yes!" replied I, smilingly, "decidedly so."

"Too bad you cannot go out to-day, for I have marked where the geese are feeding. But Henry is sick."

"You marked where the geese were feeding! Pray where?"

"This morning I mounted my pony and, following the flight, saw the fields they were in, and to-morrow when Henry is himself again, you can go after them."

"And why to-morrow? Why not to-day with you as a guide?"

"Me! Oh, I should be pleased to take you to the fields where I saw them."

"And having taken us there, to partake of the sport in shooting geese?"

"But I have no gun, and nothing suitable to wear."

Well now, if that wasn't the woman of it. Nothing suitable to wear! I wonder if there was ever a woman who did not use that expression when invited to go any place. But George and I with corduroy jacket and cap converted this sweet specimen of womanhood into a modern Diana and we started for the fields. I gave her my son's light 12-gauge, and in a short time I had "shocked" her; that is, had built a blind of wheat sheaves and had invited her to be one of its occupants. I am willing to admit that I did not invite George in with us, for I was just selfish enough to occupy the blind with her myself.

Do you blame me? Of course you don't, and I don't care if you do. We had been in the blind some little time before the flight began. George relieved the monotony of his position by frequently calling for geese which were as yet not in sight. We complimented his voice, for he had a range of several octaves, starting the "Ah' in deep guttural tones and winding up with an "Unk" which sounded like a bullfrog's voice when it jumps into the water. My fair companion and I discussed the habits of geese, on which she was thoroughly posted. Suddenly she turned to me and said:

"Why is it they call a woman a goose?"

Now if there is anything I am deficient in, it is the knack of guessing conundrums; but I looked serious and replied: "Because she decoys so readily." I could not understand what she said, but her looks satisfied me. I had guessed wrong and I apologized. We talked philosophy, discussed books, and then I led her carefully along with questions until I learned that this brown-haired maid aged—but that's a secret—had been burning gas the past Winter translating Homer's Odyssey and delving into the mysteries of Dante's weird writings; that while her home was in North Dakota, she merely spent her vacations there, and for the past three years had been engaged in unraveling the secrets of the kindergarten system at Chicago. I wish the reader could have been with us in that wheat shock. No I don't either. But to have heard the wisdom which that young woman disclosed. I studied her thoughts and expressions carefully and I wondered how so young a head could contain so much knowledge. She stood in the shock, her hair gently stirred by the mild breeze, her corduroy cap set jauntily on the back of her head, her features in profile against the sky, classical in their Grecian beauty.

> "Sweet promptings unto kindest deeds
> Were in her very look:
> We read her face, as one who reads
> A true and holy book."

But geese were coming and near us. I grabbed the bottom of her jacket and gave it a jerk, saying sharply, but softly, "Down!" The tone of my voice was mild enough, but the jerk wasn't, for she wavered for an instant, then one hundred and twenty-five pounds of feminine curiosity came down onto a sheaf of wheat with a concussion which threatened destruction to the shock. But the geese were coming, and I could scarce instruct her for our mutual laughter. Now the great flock

Wanderings in Dakota - "To The Delight Of Us All, Three Fell From The Flock."

was near us. Cautioning her not to shoot until I gave the word, I told her to aim at the thickest of them. She did so; the wind swung the flock near to us; their sides were exposed. "Fire!" said I. She punctually obeyed the word and to the delight of us all, three fell from the flock.

"Good girl! You did that splendidly, Miss Pearl," said I, while six-feet-two arose from George's blind, and a voice yelled:

"Hoopee! Pearline did it!"

"You shot!" said she, turning to me.

"Not I!" I replied, and I showed my loaded gun to her.

And thus the afternoon passed away, she a willing and accomplished pupil, and I with pleasure instructing her in the mysteries of scientific shooting. I refrained from shooting when she did, but gave my attention to her, telling her how to aim and when to shoot. We killed over twenty birds during the afternoon and five of them succumbed to her skill. Five geese isn't many for an older hunter to bag, but where is the other woman whom Nature has given the beauty of her sex, gifted beyond her years, accomplished within the entire range of culture and refinement, whose presence would add grace to the most aristocratic home in the land, who can say that she once shot five wild geese while they were in flight?

It was an experience delightful to her, and one which thousands of her sex would enjoy. The sun beat warmly on her neck and face and I suggested she change caps with me to protect her from the rays of the sun.

"Oh, no! Not for the world," said she, "for when I return to Chicago my tan will be the envy of all the girls, and when they ask me where I got it and how, I will nonchalantly say: "My tan! Oh, yes! That came from North Dakota. I got it one afternoon while out shooting geese in wheat shocks with Mr. Leffingwell. We didn't have very good shooting; just missed the flight, and I only succeeded in bagging five wild geese!" My! But won't the girls look astonished! But I ought to have some proof, for we girls are always joking."

"And so you shall have," said I, and she has the writer's proof, for I sent her a copy of "Wild Fowl Shooting," beautifully bound with morocco, and on its initial page I inscribed words commemorative of that event. What a delightful evening we passed at the house! Henry was much improved and promised to take his accustomed place with us on the morrow.

With the exception of a couple of Hutchin's, the game we

bagged that afternoon was snow geese. These geese are more plenty than any other in North Dakota. They are called there by their proper name of snow geese. In many places they are designated as white brant. In the extreme North and in portions of Minnesota as "waveys." On the Jersey coast as the red goose, a name suggested by the color of their bills and legs. They are plump in form, about the size of the Hutchin's goose, handsome in contour and appearance and most delicious eating. The adult is pure white with wings tipped with jet black. We frequently saw a grayish white goose among them, which Henry called a gray white goose. Others with heads and necks partially colored with a brownish black, and white bodies, the latter evidently being hybrids. Some of these latter ones had very beautiful plumage, with quill feathers a dense black in the center gradually shaded toward the edges in wavering lines, where at the edges it turned to a snow white. Henry was a greater ornithologist than his modesty would permit him to acknowledge, and I don't know of anyone better posted than he on the breedings and habits of geese and the birds and animals of Dakota. Snow geese are really non-residents of North Dakota. They breed farther north, away up in the vicinity of Lake Athabasca, and farther still, at Golden Lake, at Great Slave Lake and in the vicinity of Hudson's Bay. At Hudson's Bay they come in by thousands and furnish the residents in its vicinity with the greater portion of their Winter's supply of meat. The Hudson's Bay Company employ men to shoot them, and the geese are packed in barrels for Winter's use. Hunters are engaged for miles along the shores of the bay. Blinds are built on outjetting points. These points are of artificial construction and extend into the water quite a distance, and equidistant from one another. Then men in boats row in the neighborhood of the blinds and follow the shores, keeping the snow geese in flight. The birds fly over these points and the slaughter continues from day to day. A prominent citizen of Dakota informed me of this, and he obtained his information from one of the officers of the Hudson's Bay Company, who also told him that during the Fall of 1891 the Hudson's Bay Company packed two thousand barrels of geese for the benefit of their employees, for their Winter's meat. A barrel will hold about sixty geese. This would make the enormous quantity of one hundred and twenty thousand geese which were used by a portion of the inhabitants in the vicinity of Hudson's Bay during the past Winter.

Snow geese begin their migration about the middle of October, and they roam through many states on their Southern flight. Their flight usually extends through the Dakota's, down the valley of the Devils Lake and through Minnesota and the states bordering, but west of the Missouri River. Most of them pass through Western Nebraska and portions of Kansas, and they drift along until they scatter through the Southern states, notably Texas, where they are called the snow goose and Texas goose.

Trumbull, in his "Names and Portraits of Birds," speaking of snow geese, says: "They decoy less readily than the Canadian and Hutchin's geese, and fly much higher while passing to and from their feeding grounds." In "Wild Fowl Shooting" I said virtually the same, my conclusion having been arrived at from experience in Nebraska. But this trip convinced me that both Mr. Trumbull and I were wrong, for it was demonstrated to me that snow geese decoy as readily and fly no higher than other geese when going to or from their feeding grounds, and that they will come into a field to feed, flying low and perfectly reckless as to consequences, and many times they would have alighted among the decoys if we had permitted them to do so.

It was a great satisfaction for me to have learned so much about these geese, and I assure the reader I became more thoroughly acquainted with them a few days before we left for home, for we found thousands in a stubblefield which I will tell of in my next and last article of this series.

WANDERINGS IN DAKOTA - NO. 5

Editor's Note: This is the final article in the five-part series. I hope you agree with me that Leffingwell was a true wildfowler and talented writer. In the last days of the trip, William Bruce and his brother George shot 58 geese and they were all Hutchins (small Canada's) and speckled brant (white-fronted geese). His feelings about the trip were summed up in the final paragraph: "I thought then that when I returned home the recollections of my visit would prove almost as pleasant as the happy hours I spent in Dakota...."

We never tired of shooting or eating game, and our four meals a day were partaken of with zest and appetites apparently not being satisfied. Early in the morning before break of day, we arose and hastily took a light lunch and a cup of coffee, and then away after geese. We would return and have breakfast from eight to nine o'clock, then dinner at two, and at night our supper anywhere from eight to ten o'clock. Our long rides in the keen, bracing air ever kept us hungry. How we enjoyed the cakes! And those birds, snipe, grouse, canvas-back ducks and geese, fried, broiled or roasted; and cranes too, for slices from their breasts fried in batter and then covered with cream gravy, were food fit for a king. It actually makes me hungry now to think of it!

But Henry was not satisfied with the shooting; for when we expressed our satisfaction with it, he said: "No you haven't yet had the shooting I want you to have, for I have seen hundreds of geese where we have seen ten, and I have seen them destroying fields of grain."

"Oh, Henry!" said I, "that's the same thing we read of, and I am afraid that's only in one's imagination, for we haven't seen geese enough yet to do any great damage, unless, of course, all should center in one field; then perhaps they might."

"Just wait" replied he, "until the flight of snow geese comes in from the North, as it will with the first storm, and then you will see a flight that will make you open your eyes with wonder and cause you to count the shells you have on hand."

"Well," replied George, "that's what we are here for, and if we can protect some honest farmer's field from being devastated by those voracious intruders we are just Christians enough to do so."

"To-morrow morning," said Henry, "I have a little work to do. If you two can amuse yourselves, then do so, and in the afternoon we will go to a place we haven't been to yet and where I believe we will get good shooting."

That night George said to me: "Are you with me in the morning before daybreak?"

"Preacher's Point?" I replied.

"Yes!" said he.

We were astir in due time and having waded the ford awaited the beginning of the flight. Before it was light enough to see to shoot, canvas-backs and redheads were moving and we awaited sufficient light to begin our sport. Over our heads they shot in their swiftest flight like a dark streak, and the sharp crack of our guns would be followed by a splash or thump as the bird struck the water or ground. Then a single one, coming down wind at a rate of 115 miles an hour, would go past us, never moving its head or swerving one particle from its flight at the report of our guns. There is a satisfaction when one misses a mallard, or most any other duck, to see it "climb" at the report of a gun, but to see a canvas-back go right along, not paying the slightest attention to a double report, as if the shooter was unworthy of notice, makes a man feel decidedly foolish.

We did not remain long on the point, merely taking advantage of the first flight and returned for breakfast with twelve birds, about equally divided between canvas-backs and redheads. Such magnificent birds I never saw; and never plumper ones.

After dinner we took the team and started in the direction of the field which Henry had in mind. As we passed the barn near the house of the man who owned the land, Henry asked him if the geese were alighting in his fields.

"Yes!" said he, "right over the brow of that hill. They have been there for several days, and if I don't get those shocks of grain away before long, they will be worthless."

"Haven't any objections to our shooting in there?"

"Objections! I should say not! Just go in there and kill all you can.

They are doing me great damage, and I'll be only too glad to have you kill every blessed one."

As we reached the field evidences of the destruction caused by the geese were to be seen everywhere. Grain scattered on the ground, shocks partially torn down, and the heads of wheat stripped and ruined by them. We were early on the grounds, and, as Henry left us to take the team to another field, he turned and said: "I know from where they will come. This is the flight I have been after for several days, and to-day we are going to beat our record."

We set out our decoys. Henry soon returned and we were scarcely concealed in the shocks before the flight began. We missed the major portion of it, but we had enough. Great, broad streaks of black darkened the horizon in places. To their repeated callings our soliciting replies were given. Flock after flock came to us and we shot geese as I never shot them before. Henry started after a cripple. He spoiled many shots for us. What of it? For they came on in slightly broken flight. Each shooter had a pile of brant and Hutchin's around his shock. I started for a bird which fell perhaps two hundred yards from me. I made three starts and each time had to run for my blind because of geese coming in. Then I started again and other geese coming, I did not have time to return, but laid on my back in the stubble and killed a pair; then another pair as quickly as I could put in shells. But I run out of shells. So did George. He divided with me, each having two and those loaded with No. 6 shot. George got his pair. I shot one, then held a shell in reserve. A pair of brants came. I let them cross, and at the report of my gun both fell. Henry took a wide detour. George went after several that fell off a good distance, and I beat back and forth between the shocks of grain for a couple of hundred yards. As we gathered the birds up and threw them into the wagon Henry said fifty-eight, and all Hutchins and speckled brant; and George replied:

Wanderings in Dakota - Viewing The Hundreds and Thousands of Snow Geese

"This day we have done much good, for we have saved the farmer's grain."

"Yes!" responded I, "that was what induced me to come, that I might do some good on this earth."

"And you," exclaimed Henry, "came for that alone? Candidly, I never saw two persons enjoy shooting geese more than you and George."

"Well!" I replied, "when I am with the Romans, I do as the Romans do."

We did not expect to find such shooting again; but we little knew what was in store for us, for a few days afterward and a couple of days before we started home, we went after ducks. We felt we had been neglecting the ducks and went that afternoon with the avowed intention of making up for our neglect. While on our way to the big marsh, a flock of snow geese flew over us.

"Henry," said I, "that flock is headed for the place south of where we were the other day. They dropped in there by hundreds."

"It isn't only about two miles over there," he replied, "and we can drive over."

We started, and as we neared a field we saw a sight which will long be remembered. A field occupied by hundreds and thousands of snow geese. We were attracted to them first by their cries, and then we saw them like ridges of snow. When some big flock would hover around them and then settle down, the shrill cries of all could be heard for miles. They utter a peculiar cry, similar in tone to a crowd of men wildly yelling at some political gathering, or sounding more like cheers, when the listener hears the cheers of a vast multitude of people at a ball game when a home run is made. Again, when they arose the noise was perfectly deafening, and shrill cries from thousands of throats sounded like a strong wind whistling through wires, only a thousand times louder.

What a sight we saw! A patch of plowed ground covered with them; the stubble-field alive with them; and then some, more greedy and bold, were tearing the shocks down and destroying what grain they did not eat. We tried to drive them from the field. We hooted at them, "sicked" the dog on them, rattled the iron decoys, cracked the whip, but they would only fly a hundred yards and then alight again, determined not to leave the field. The wind blew a gale and it would drift them over our heads within twenty feet of us, where they fought against the wind and swarmed like bees. George threatened to shoot some of them, but he knew better than to shoot then, so Henry chased them and George and I sat out the decoys.

Finally Henry got them started from the field and, with a roar like a hurricane going through a forest, they took their leave. We were soon in our "shocks." Henry returned, and then we enjoyed goose shooting as we never did before. The geese came stringing back for two hours and a half; to the music of our guns they fell in duets, quartets, quintets, and sextets. As I said, the wind blew a gale, and the birds came against the wind. Our decoys were on the plowed ground and not placed to the best advantage, which we learned when too late, for the birds began to climb before reaching us and then our ammunition was tested, for our little guns and S.S. powder repeatedly and regularly bagged the game at from sixty to seventy-five yards, often farther.

But I must not dwell longer on this hunt. We counted our birds as we filled the wagon box. I held a bunch of twelve on the seat with me, while sixty of their companions in the bottom of the box completed the number we killed.

When I arranged with the editor of *The American Field* to write a series of articles on the feathered game of North Dakota, I intended treating of all the game birds and waterfowl of that State, but time and office duties prevent it. I am therefore compelled to defer writing of ducks and snipes, of curlews and grouse, until, possibly some other time, when, should the spirit prompt me, I will faithfully chronicle what I saw and learned of birds other than ducks and geese while visiting in the land of the Dakotas.

The days were gliding swiftly by and I, lost to the world and oblivious to dates, passed the hours delightfully at this El Dorado where game was so abundant. Now the time was approaching for our departure, and the days were counted, for we had but a few more to spend in that grand country. I say grand, for no other word could better give a proper conception of it. Before visiting North Dakota, I had formed an idea that it was a desolate prairie, with alkali soil, devoid of attractiveness, and whose inhabitants were mostly of foreign nationality, who nearly perished with cold in Winter. I thought to see the prairie with tall, rank grass, coarse and unpalatable for stock, and scenery not the least attractive. But instead of these things, each day the curtain of unbelief was lifted from before my eyes, and I saw and enjoyed a climate beautiful almost beyond belief. The ground is high and rolling. The level monotony which creates a sameness that is tiresome when one views the prairies of Nebraska and Kansas, is not to be seen where we were; but instead the hills rolled with pleasing undulations like ocean billows and followed one the other with a variety and uniformity which made them beautiful to see.

As we drove around some gently sloping hills our eyes would be greeted with a vast stretch of prairie where the buffalo grass grew profusely, or where the prairie hay grew in that wild freedom which was to be anticipated in a country so little disturbed by man. Now the side of a sloping hill suggested a spot where flowers had blossomed in Summertime and wasted their fragrance on the desert air; for the fragrance would be wasted so far as man was concerned. But the birds and the wild animals could see them in their beauty and inhale their odors, even if not appreciated. And then again, tiny lakes abounded. Some lined with reeds and rushes, or with a red weed which grew to a short height and then spread its stems, intertwining the arms of its neighbors.

Our travels brought us to other lakes where the alkali had formed in crusted white along the shores until it looked as if the snow had come from heaven and had selected this romantic spot to purify and beautify it by spreading this mantle of spotless white, verging the waters which were once sacred to the bison and the antelope. Again our drive brought us to higher hills, and I wondered what could be found of interest there. Our rides brought to us scenes of ever changing beauty, and when we reached the highest hill we were at an abrupt elevation of perhaps one hundred feet, and we looked down into Twin Lakes, the waters of which the strong south wind was causing to writhe, and the whitecaps on their surface made the green of their bodies a deeper hue, while thousands of ducks and geese were basking in the sunshine on the shores, or bobbed up and down like corks on the tiny waves which repeatedly threw over them a shower of spray, and to which they responded with repeated quackings, thus expressing their delight.

We drove down around the hill between the two lakes. The day had been warm and as we drove across the dividing ridges which lay between the lakes, I doffed my hat to enjoy the pure breeze which reached us from the water, and we remarked at the change in temperatures, for the winds came to us laden with that delicious freshness which so many of us have enjoyed when at the shore of some large body of water. Occasionally springs were found. Some modestly struggling to escape from the grass which strove to hide them; others murmuring in gurgling tones; while in their depths we saw tiny pebbles in grayish suits, clean and tidy from their constant bathings.

In North Dakota, as in all other states, water is at times scarce and the settler must take his chances of obtaining it. But we saw no scarcity of it, nor heard any complaint. At the shack, where our host had taken a claim, there was without exception the purest and coldest spring I ever saw. We spent two nights there and enjoyed the water as I never enjoyed water before. This spring was known to others than ourselves; others whose ancestors had been coming there for years and years; for nearly every time we went to it, mottled beauties with great big eyes and long black bills darted from us, grating the air with their cries of "scaipe!" "scaipe!"

The most celebrated lake in North Dakota is Devils Lake. It is noted because of its size and the beauty of its scenery. The station on the Great Northern is called after the lake, while on its shore and on the Northern Pacific there is another town named after it, being designated by the musical name Minnewaukan. Devils Lake is a beautiful lake and is rapidly becoming famous as a Summer resort. It is about forty miles in length and from three to ten miles in width. It is called a salt lake, but, while its waters have a salty taste, it is undoubtedly from the effects of the alkali deposits. In the vicinity of this lake at the south and southwest, can be found in season, some of the finest goose shooting in the world.

We had ample opportunity to explore the country and to see of what the soil consisted. Day after day we dug pits for shooting geese, or rode from twenty to forty miles. The country was the same, and the soil the richest I ever saw. It has been a long time since I did much in an agricultural way, but I found that when it came to digging pits from which to shoot geese, that I was decidedly an expert. And such soil! Rich, black loam mixed with a little sand. A spade would readily cut its mellow surface and then when the spade was turned over, a flakey pile, rich and full of promise, fairly inviting seeds to come to it to burst and sprout. It was just such soil as my mother used to send me to get when I was a child, for she wanted only the richest for her flower beds; and here it was, acres and thousands of acres of it.

That their harvests were abundant I did not wonder. How could it be otherwise with such prolific soil? We visited many grain fields and the sheaves bent down with their loads of ripened grain. The wheat was plump and hard and ready to burst in its fullness. Farmers told me it was averaging twenty-five bushels to the acre and they were getting fifty-seven cents a bushel for it at the station. Fourteen dollars and twenty-five cents per acre was enough to make them happy, and the proceeds derived from their grain in the past two years has enabled many of them to pay for their land, while others are, or soon will be, rich.

But the climate captivated me. While undoubtedly it is very cold in Dakota during some of the Winter months, there is a dryness of the atmosphere which lessens the intensity of the weather, and those accustomed to it do not mind it. They know it will come, and prepare for it, and since Dakota farmers have nothing to do but keep warm in the Winter, if they haven't sufficient forethought to prepare for cold and enough activity and ambition to keep them from freezing, they ought to suffer. I can't imagine an easier or more independent life than they lead. Grain is sowed, then harvested in the Fall. After harvest the Dakota farmer does his threshing; then he has nothing to do but take life easy until Spring. Considering the fact that about four month's work each year takes care of a crop which brings them fourteen dollars and twenty-five cents per acre, and also taking into consideration the cheapness of the land, it seems to me that anyone who is struggling along, working hard the year through in other states, makes the mistake of his life by not investing in a Dakota farm, for there he can work one-third of the time and loaf or hunt the balance, as he feels inclined. I have no personal interest in Dakota lands, but simply express an honest opinion, based on what I saw and learned of the country and its climate.

During our entire trip the days were as mild as September in the Middle States, while the purity of the atmosphere was almost beyond belief. Sunshine and days of perfectness. Nights cool and delicious. Every morning the sun would rise above the eastern hill and the heavens would blush like a bride at his approach. Winds would breathe, then gently die away at eventide. The sun would go down in his crimson glory. Night would come on with its myriad of stars, and we saw and breathed and appreciated all these things. My friends told me much of Summer months, a time when canvas-backs forget their cunning and allow their young to be picked up in the marshes; a time when curlews circle in air in flocks of hundreds and come to the decoy of their own peculiar call; a time when the gloaming fights against the approach of night, and silent stars peek inquisitively from the sky as if to see if twilight has taken her departure so they may come out and watch the sleeping world. But twilight is fain to leave on those Summer nights, and they of the household often sit till ten o'clock at night reading by that light which creates the golden link between day and night.

The last night came. We passed it in that same pleasant way we had so many nights before, and I retired to think and dream of days delightful beyond comparison.

A gentle patter on the roof, a mild soughing of the wind, and the veil of years was lifted; for those rain drops banished the present and I was a lad of ten listening to the rain pattering on the roof of the attic where I was so often lulled to sleep by the music of its drops and the soughing of the wind.

We bade our friends farewell the following morning, promising that if permitted to live we would return next Fall. I thought then that when I returned home the recollections of my visit would prove almost as pleasant as the happy hours I spent in Dakota, but—

> "I thought the sparrow's note from heaven,
> Singing at dawn on the alder bough;
> I brought him home, in his nest at even;
> He sings the songs, but it cheers not now,
> For I did not bring home the river and sky;
> He sang to my ear, they sang to my eye."

GOOSE SHOOTING AT MINNEWAUKAN 1901

Editor's Note: *As stated earlier this series of articles is under authorship of Douglas Leffingwell. It is my considered opinion that for reasons unknown William Bruce chose to use that name.*

It was one of those golden, hazy October days that help make life pleasant in this far-off Dakota land. The distant shore of Devils Lake glistened and sparkled in the sun, and above the blue-rimmed horizon long V-shaped lines of geese, flock after flock, swung into view, until the sky was filled with white waving streamers, made up of countless thousands of snow-white geese. On our way to the feeding grounds we stopped at three little lakes nestling among the hills, where the canvas-back ducks usually sought shelter from the windstorms that sometimes sweep viciously across the Dakota prairies. The day was mild, and we did not expect to find any number of birds, but there were certain ones in our party who would sooner bag a canvas-back duck than a cinnamon bear; so, taking our places at the different passes, we started the driver around the lake with the team to stir up the ducks.

There were four of us in the party: Colonel Coldwater of St. Paul, a gentleman close to sixty years of age, and a truer sportsman and finer gentleman I have never met; Billy Turner, Capt. Griswold and the writer, who have hunted together for many years.

It did not take the driver long to circle around the upper lake and soon we saw the birds coming. Two flocks, with about a dozen in each, came swiftly down the channel that connected the lakes, and, skimming the water, swung out in a long skirmish line and came right at us. The sun glistened on their white breasts and seal-colored heads, and I stopped for a moment to admire their beauty as they drew within range, then, swinging in behind the big leader, I pushed the muzzle of the gun in front of him and pressed the trigger. Up went the brown head, but the swiftly moving winds promised to carry him away a cripple, and I went after him with the second barrel, which proved more effective, and I had the satisfaction of picking up one of the largest male canvas-back ducks I have ever seen. Eight shots were fired into the flock and five fine birds was the result.

This performance, as far as the flight was concerned, usually ended the sport for the time being, as the birds dropped in only occasionally during fair weather, so we were soon headed for Pelican Lake, where we were informed the geese would come to rest after their morning's feed.

In the distance, we could hear the geese calling to each other. Answering cries came from the wooded shores and floated down from the far distant sky, as the birds began to congregate after their morning's flight to the wheatfields. Reaching the brow of the hill that overlooks the waters, we beheld a sight that made us pause in wonder and admiration. The surface of the lake for a mile distant was covered with white geese, and white clouds of birds were hovering in the air and dropping into the water.

"Well, boys," said Turner, "it is time to take lunch anyway, so let's make the spread here on the hillside, where we can watch the flight and determine the best place to locate." The recollection of that simple repast, spread out on the buffalo grass of that sunny slope, will long linger among the pleasant recollections of the past. The blue sky, flecked with white lines of geese floating in from the west, the placid water almost hidden with its burden of snow-white birds, with here and there a black patch of Canada geese, the ceaseless music issuing from thousands of feathered throats, and the mellow rays of an autumnal sun smiling over the landscape, made a picture that is seldom seen even in this game-favored land of North Dakota.

Lunch over, we made preparations for the flight that was sure to follow as the day advanced.

Taking the Chesapeake, Turner and the writer made a blind behind a large boulder located half way up the hill, while Coldwater and Griswold entrenched themselves behind a small cluster of trees that bordered the lake. The way of the wild goose is, to say the least, somewhat mysterious. On this eventful day, the white geese rose from the water and flock after flock streamed off toward the north, while the Canada geese headed for Devils Lake, and came straight over us.

He who has ever shot from a goose pit, or sheltered blind, and watched the great birds come nearer and nearer, the metallic Augh Aunk! sounding louder and louder, has experienced a sensation he will endure any hardship to repeat. A big bag of game leaves little impression outside of the few incidents that develop during every hunting trip.

I had just purchased a full-blooded Chesapeake Bay dog, and was very anxious to see what he could do. So was he. He would remain perfectly still until the geese were almost within gunshot, then he developed a strong desire to sit up, in order to see what was going on. At first he had so much confidence in his master's ability to kill his bird that he would bolt after the flock as soon as the first shot was fired, without waiting to see the effects of the shot, but he finally became disgusted and soon settled down like an older campaigner.

I crippled a large white goose that flew off on the prairie about a quarter of a mile, and the dog had finally caught it, after quite a run. He came back toward the blind on a trot, with the crippled goose in his mouth. As he neared the blind, I knocked down a greenhead mallard, breaking its wing, and as it struck the ground it started off at a lively rate across the prairie, with the Chesapeake after him, and the goose still in his mouth. The mallard twisted and turned, and circled around at such a lively rate that I had just started to take a hand in the proceedings, when the Chesapeake landed on him with both feet, and stood there, the goose in his mouth, and the mallard pinned down under his forepaws. It was very prettily done, and I would have given considerable for a picture of him as he stood there waiting for me to come up and help him out. That was about the only time during the day the birds came too thick for him.

As we settled down behind the blind again, Turner whispered: "Here come four honkers. They are coming right at us, and we will give the boys an illustration of how to clean up a flock, and we won't slobber them, either." Crouching low down behind the blind, we waited, with our eyes fixed on the spot where we knew they must appear. We could hear the Augh Aunk! of the leader as they came slowly up against the wind. Another Aunk! and all was still. We waited a reasonable length of time, but they did not appear, and I was just in the act of raising up to see what had become of them, when a warning note caused me to look up, and there, right over the rim of the big white rock, were four Canada geese, and not twenty feet away. We both rose slowly to our feet, and Turner said: "Oh, I guess this is easy! You take the two to the right and I will take the two to the left." Very carefully and deliberately we gave them four barrels, and they went on as unconcerned as if they had no idea they were all four supposed to be dead geese. We sat down, we looked at each other, but we said nothing. However, our friends, located down in the bushes, said something. In fact, they said a good many uncomplimentary things that would not look well in print.

We had noticed Colonel Coldwater hammering away with a persistency that promised he would soon be out of shells, and still no bird fell to the report of his gun. "I don't believe the old gentleman's shells are right," said Turner, and, picking up a box loaded with 3 ½ drams of smokeles powder and 1 1/8 ounces of No. 4 chilled shot, he walked down to the shore and handed them to him, saying: "Your shells don't seem to be doing any execution;

take this box and get in the game." The Colonel soon showed his appreciation by knocking down eight geese with ten shots, which was by far the best shooting done that day. As the day advanced and the shadows began to creep along the prairie slopes and gather in the valleys, the shooting became more brisk. The evening flight had begun, and the birds were headed for Devils Lake to roost for the night. They came in from the north in a steady stream, crossed the lake and passed over us at a height of about one hundred yards. The guns kept going, and the geese kept coming, and now and then a bird would drop from a flock and strike the ground with sufficient force to burst it open.

Great flocks of birds had congregated on the flats back from the lake about half a mile, and as evening came on they left their midday resting ground and flew toward the lake. Thousands of them dropped into the water, and great numbers circled about the lake, vainly calling to the vast throng in the water to follow. The clamor they raised was simply maddening; in fact, if I had been compelled to listen to that music all night long I should certainly have been a candidate for an asylum for lunatics before morning. As the twilight deepened and objects became more shadowy and obscure, the flocks came in lower and gave us plenty of sport. We made no attempt at concealment, but sat on some convenient boulder, listening to the beating wings overhead and watching for the first flutter of white wings, which would indicate that the birds were within gunshot.

When the team started out to make the rounds of the different blinds to gather up the game, Turner and I walked down to Captain Griswold's blind to smoke one of the Captain's good cigars, a liberal supply of which he always carries.

"Well, boys," said the Captain, "what luck?"

"Thirty-six geese," I replied.

"Well," he answered, "that is eighteen apiece, and I guess I have you fellows faded. "There," pointing to his pile, "is a bunch of nineteen."

"What smells so loud around here, Cap?" said Turner with his nose in the air.

"Don't know," said the Captain, reaching for his cigar case, "guess your imagination is working, isn't it."

"Oh, I guess not," said Turner, and walking over to the pile of geese, he picked out a specimen that might have been an eatable goose some days previous, but was no longer serviceable in that capacity. Holding it out at arm's length, he said: "You won't sit at the head of the table to-night, Cap. You can't carry off the honors by bagging game that smells like that. Better give us two geese and we won't tell the Colonel. It would be hard on you, because he thinks he is associating with thorough sportsmen."

The Captain, however, explained that it was a sure enough goose, and, while it had proved to be a cripple, he had killed it as it came skimming over the water just at dark. He refused to part with any of his game, and we finally compromised on the promise of a cold bottle when we again reached civilization. When the game was all counted and placed in the wagon, we found we had seventy geese and ten canvas-backs.

Some readers of this article may think we killed more game than sportsmen will approve of, but the game laws of North Dakota provide that no person shall kill over twenty-five birds per day, so we were well within the limits of the law, and then it was one of those days that come only once or twice during the season, so I do not hesitate to record the number of birds killed.

Everyone was in a cheerful frame of mind that night as we prepared for the long drive home. The moon came up and shed her silver radiance over the hills, the wooded shores loomed grim and shadowy against the slowly fading sky, the prairie slopes lay veiled in the moonlight, silent, somber and indistinct, the lake had taken on its snow-white mantle for the night and the flight was over.

AN OCTOBER DAY AT DEAD BUFFALO LAKE 1901

<u>Editor's Note</u>: *This article describes duck and goose hunting in the vicinity of Dawson. For this article Leffingwell gives his address as North Dakota and perhaps this is why he used the name Douglas. He may have had personal reasons for establishing a different identity. As soon as the Northern Pacific Railroad reached that area, Dawson quickly became one of the most frequented locales by hunters coming from Eastern states. William B. Mershon from Saginaw, Michigan began hunting around Dawson in 1883 and used a much publicized converted railway Pullman car as a hunting camp. It was named the <u>City of Saginaw</u>. Mershon included a chapter "Hunting at Dawson, N.D." in his 1923 book <u>Recollections of My Fifty Years Hunting and Fishing.</u>*

Often during the long Winter evenings, as I sit brooding in the old leather chair before the open fire, with the dogs stretched out before the cheerful blaze—faithful companions in many a campaign against the prairie chickens, ducks and geese—memory steals back to phantom scenes of many a memorable trip on the Western prairies; phantom scenes because they are gone, pleasant recollections from out of the shadowy past to beckon back to life when the mood is on.

The fire burns brightly in the grate; outside the wind moans dismally among the skeleton trees like a soul in distress wandering through eternity. The clock on the mantel ticks away the ever-ready seconds, the fragrance of a good cigar floats out toward the open grate and anon permeates the atmosphere like the golden haze of an Indian Summer day, soothes the fretting brain into an indulgent mood, and summons into being the sportsman's miser hoard, sweet relics of memory to be brooded over in solitude, to conjure into reality once more, but never to be repeated.

The phantom scene that comes back to me to-night may interest the readers of *The American Field*, at any rate I will draw the sketch and if it is not printed it will be because I dream better than I write.

On the morning of October 10, 1898, we pulled out from the hotel at Dawson, N.D. We were bound for Dead Buffalo Lake. A good team, a boat load of decoys, one of the best guides in North Dakota and nothing on our minds but the indescribable pleasure of once more finding ourselves bowling over the breezy prairies of the West.

The air was clear and frosty and it was still dark as we drove past the old Sibley Hotel, which long ago became famous as a resort for sportsmen from many of the larger cities of the East. Billy Turner sat with the driver and, as usual, did most of the talking, while Captain Griswold and the writer occupied the back seat and smoked in silence. After associating with the Captain for many years, it had gradually dawned upon my mental apparatus that when he relapsed into a pensive frame of mind it was dangerous to prod him with conundrums or astronomical observations, and so we smoked on in silence.

Day was beginning to dawn when we reached the old Indian battleground where General Sibley fought the Sioux. Some years ago a government official passed over this historical ground and, on the gentle slope of the hill which overlooks the scene where long ago this savage drama was enacted, caused a sign to be erected which reads: "Battle of Dead Buffalo Lake—Sibley's Command against the Sioux—July 22, 1863."

Down in the valley below the hill traces of the old entrenchments hastily thrown up by the soldiers can still be seen, and away off toward the north, where the blue line of the Dakota hills swings out bold and clear against the sky, you can gather the outline of a cross, and farther back among the silent hills, little piles of stone gathered here and there in the yellow grass mark the line of retreat and the graves of Sibley's soldiers, fighting where they fell. I never look upon the scene but I feel that I, too, had I been an Indian, would have fought for the lands which they so fiercely defended. A hunter's paradise to-day, what must it have been during the days of the buffalo before the white man drove the great herds across the Missouri never to return?

As we approached an old abandoned tree claim a mile or so beyond the hill, Charles suggested that if we wanted to bag a few grouse we should get out and walk through the claim three abreast. Pulling up the team at the edge of the wood, we got down from the wagon and were soon pushing through the stunted undergrowth about a gunshot apart. The sun was beginning to give out a little warmth and the birds lay well, so well, in fact, that several grouse got up behind us after we had passed them! Nearing an open spot in the claim, an old bird dashed out of the clover and gave us a fair shot. We let her go, as it has always been our custom to spare the old birds when we could detect them from the young ones. With a whir and a roar a dozen grouse flashed out of the dry grass within ten yards of us. Out over the stunted trees they went and for a moment the air was alive with whirring birds. In three seconds it was all over; and four ruffed bodies lay quivering in the grass. Gathering up the game we pushed on. About a hundred yards further on, and when we were almost through the claim, another covey rose out of the low brush and, loath to leave the protection of the grove, turned in a circle and gave us quartering and side shots. One bird flew directly over my head and I turned and cut it down by a chance shot as it flashed in among the trees. Turning quickly, I saw Griswold and Turner each make a double. While standing there wondering why I had been foolish enough to take a chance shot at a single bird when there were a dozen within easy range, a single grouse jumped up within fifty yards of me and, covering it as quickly as possible, I pressed the trigger. At the crack of the gun it dropped its legs and fell fluttering among the branches. I realized I was in pretty fast company and was congratulating myself on being fortunate enough to hold my own with my two friends, when Turner shattered my aspirations by calling to me to pick up the bird he had just killed, when I came to it.

"Did you kill that bird?" I asked, my spirits sagging away to the freezing point.

"I have the honor," he replied. "A great shot, wasn't it?" he added, "fully a hundred yards from where I stand."

Whenever our conversation happens to drift onto the subject of long shots, my friend refers to this almost impossible shot with considerable pride, and says he would not have the nerve to relate it were it not for the fact that I had been a witness to the deadly execution of his gun, a weapon which my friend reluctantly laid away last Fall for a new one, and which he always claimed was a world-beater at one hundred yards.

We reached Buffalo Lake about 10 o'clock in the morning, and after putting out the decoys beyond a point of land jutting out into the lake, took to the tall grass and proceeded to make ourselves invisible to the naked eye of a duck. The wind came in gusts across the white-capped waters, and flocks of canvas-backs beat their way slowly up against the wind, and others went skimming down the lake at lightning speed.

"Mark, down!" called Griswold, and peering over the rushes I saw a long string of birds coming in low over the water and headed straight to the decoys. On they came, their wings gracefully set and with just sufficient motion to keep them in the air they swung over the decoys. We raised up together and cut loose. Four birds let go and struck the water in a bunch, and another left the flock with a broken wing and finally toppled over in the middle of the Lake.

"Somebody missed that time," cried Turner.

"Not me," said the Captain, "I made as pretty a double as ever happened on this pass."

"Well, I got two the first shot," replied Turner, "so where does Leff come in?"

"That crippled bird out there in the lake looks a little like his work," said the Captain.

I was not prepared to argue the matter, for when my two friends put on their shooting clothes they were a hard team to beat.

"Look out! Here's a lone boy coming in again," called Griswold.

It was a canvas-back, and he pulled up toward the decoys with a confidence that made us admire his nerve. Right over the bunch he came, hovered for a moment over the painted dummies bobbing in the water, and then Turner gathered up his old 12-gauge and went after him with both barrels. Mr. Canvas woke up, shook himself, spread out his tail feathers and started leisurely off, and then the Captain rose up out of the sere and yellow rushes and went after him with his new gun; and still he did not seem to be much offended, just rubbered around at the Captain and came past my blind with measured beating wings. Making allowance for the wind, I pulled a little ahead of him and let go, so did the duck, and the boys generously gave me credit for bagging a bird that was all shot to pieces, only he did not know enough to know when he was dead.

While we were discussing the manner in which the bird had accidently come to grief, we were startled by the familiar aunk, augh, aunk, sounding somewhere back upon the prairie. Not a goose was visible, but we rightly concluded they were coming down to the lake from Bill Little's wheatfield, where they had been feeding all the morning. We were some forty feet below the surface of the prairie and if they came over us we would have a splendid shot. Judging from the racket they made, I concluded that an army of geese would soon darken the sky. All of a sudden they burst into view, flying low down over the prairie. Up over the hill they came and dipped down the bank that sloped gradually away to the lake.

Head on they came, and I knew something was going to happen to that particular flock that had probably never happened before. Fifty or sixty Canada geese and all gabbling together and looking almost too big to fly with such ridiculous ease. There was no hurry, we were good waiters, and had been fooled too often to bungle this job. We waited until their bright, black eyes were plainly visible in the white patches on the sides of their heads, then we rose up out of the tall prairie grass and got busy. With a great clattering and beating of wings they rose in the air and gave up the opportunity we had been waiting for. What a sight and what a shot! The great birds, stricken in their flight, collapsed over our guns and came rushing through the air in their downward course like meteors bolting from the heavens. Four honkers was the best we could do, but that was enough to satisfy even an Indian.

"Are the pits dug, Charlie?" inquired Griswold of the driver.

"No, but it won't take long to dig them," he replied.

"I'll pass," said the Captain.

Here Turner cut in and suggested that as I was the best all-around pit digger in the party, I should tackle the pit and the geese and he and the Captain would linger where they were and dally with the canvas-backs.

This was agreeable to me, and after a drive of some two miles we pulled up in a wheatfield that had never been cut, and were soon busy digging a couple of round holes in the sandy soil. It was a good hour's work to dig the pits, obliterate all signs of the fresh earth and put out the sheet-iron decoys. The wind had died down to a gentle breeze, the sun shone bright and warm, and the blue waters of the lake rested the eye to look upon. Overhead white clouds drifted with the breeze, their gay shadows flitted across the sun-baked plain and darkened the purple hills in the distance. Without a sound a sandhill crane passed over us as we lay stretched out in the wheatfield. At the crack of the gun he doubled up and pitched forward, and I remember thinking as he came down that he reminded me of a folded umbrella thrown out of a third story window.

About 4 o'clock we got into the pits and waited for the geese to come in to feed. It was 4:30 before they put in an appearance. Some three miles away, and far below us, a black, disjointed thread crept across the prairie. I could just make it out in the distance. The flock crossed the lake and then for a time were lost to view behind the range of hills that skirted the shore.

"Here they come," called Charlie; "keep well down now and don't shoot until I give the word."

A peculiar cackling sound that is hard to imitate reached our ears, and immediately it was repeated from the driver's pit, a call so clear and natural that the geese turned from their course and cackling and babbling away lined up toward the decoys. Peering out through the spears of wheat I could see the flock coming up the slope and apparently getting ready to alight just beyond the decoys. A series of calls from the driver's pit urged them on, and when he yelled "burn 'em" the entire flock was hovering over our pits in a state of utter bewilderment. We dropped four mottled breasts out of the flock, and although we hastily reloaded and gave them four more barrels we did not succeed in doing any further damage. Some half a dozen flocks came down through the field during the next half hour, and we managed to bag five more geese. The flight was about over, so gathering up our game and decoys we drove back to the lake.

Turner was standing on the shore watching Griswold paddling vigorously away down the lake in pursuit of a crippled duck.

"You must have had great sport," he said, as we pulled the nine geese out of the wagon and added them to the bunch of canvasbacks. "I heard you shooting and it made me nervous listening to those four shots ring out every few minutes. But just wait until Griswold gets back; look at him down the lake there about a mile; he is chasing a crippled spoonbill I shot, and I told him it was a canvas-back. He will be red-headed when he gets back and no mistake."

"Well, he will know what it is in a minute," I replied, "he is getting ready to shoot."

A faint report reached us, and the Captain pushed forward and we saw him reach out in the water and gather something in. He surveyed it for a moment and then carefully stowed it away under the seat. Putting the boat about, he paddled leisurely back to the blind. His hat was off, his flannel shirt was open at the throat and the perspiration was dripping from his face. He was certainly hot, but he did not look mad, at least not yet. Pulling the boat well up on the muddy shore, he reached under the seat and drew forth the most dilapidated specimen of a spoonbill I have ever seen, and, calling to Turner, asked him if he knew what kind of a duck had he been chasing for the last half hour.

"A big canvas-back, wasn't it?" said Turner, grinning at the Captain over the rushes.

"Yes, and I'll make you eat this one, feathers and all," and stooping down he rubbed the bird into the soft, slimy mud and then went after the conspirator. The Captain's heavy boots, however, soon put an end to the chase, and hoisting his handkerchief on the end of a reed, Turner demanded a parley, and under the protection of a flag of truce peace and harmony were soon restored.

We lingered on the pass for an hour or so, but the evening flight was over. The sun had gone down behind the Western hills and twilight was fast creeping over prairie, lake and the distant hills. When night settles down over the Western plains, it brings with it a spirit of desolation, a vague feeling of sadness and depression. Perhaps it is the wandering spirit of Manitou brooding in sorrow over the land of his vanquished people. A wolf across the lake howled, and somewhere back among the hills another let out a series of mournful yelps.

Gathering up our decoys we made ready for the homeward trip.

Twenty-six canvas-backs and redheads, thirteen geese and ten grouse were the fruits of as pleasant a day's sport as I have spent in many years. This was our first day out and we were booked for a ten days' shoot. Every day we changed our route and every day was a story in itself.

Some readers of *The American Field* have spent many pleasant seasons in this Dawson country, and I wish to inform them that while the crops are usually a failure, the settlers still raise enough wheat to feed the wild geese when they stop over on their migratory flight in the Fall.

North Dakota.

THE ECHOS OF LAC QUI PARLE
1901

Editor's Note: Leffingwell provides a good description of Lac Qui Parle when its ecology was still in a natural state before a dam was constructed. Wild celery was a premier food of canvasbacks in many lakes in the eastern United States. Leffingwell relates an experience that most duck hunters have experienced at some time. It involved shooting behind the bird and stopping the swing. They must have shot fairly well as the bag for the day was 49 and all canvasbacks and redheads.

The days are now far away and the Autumn leaves have been falling many years since last I stood upon the shores of Lac Qui Parle (the waters that speak) and looked down upon its blue but treacherous waste of waters.

Sunken rocks lie hidden beneath the surface, and on stormy days when the foam lies thick along the shore and the white caps rise out of the bosom of the lake and, driven by the wind, go riding boisterously down the channel; when you hear the wash of waters as the white caps rise and fall, and see the white spray lashing the great rock in the channel, then it is far more safe to be on dry land than to venture out upon this inland sea. But on a still Autumn day, when the wind has died away and the water ripples gently along the shore, it is a very peaceful scene to look upon. One is never alone on these echo-haunted shores. The report of your gun rings out across the water and rolls away down the rock-bound shore in hollow sounding waves. Send your voice out over the lake, and faint and far away the echo calls to you from the farther shore.

Winter or Summer the echoes never sleep along the shores of

Lac Qui Parle. They linger forever among the hills, boisterous, defiant, unconfined; they cry out among the prairie solitudes when disturbed, but sleep peacefully enough among the hills and ravines when their haunts are free from human sounds.

Many years ago a friend of mine got tangled up with the echos, and the experience he went through left him with the morbid impression that the vicinity of Lac Qui Parle was haunted by mocking spirits that hovered among the hills and tried to lure him to destruction among the rocks where they make their home.

Lac Qui Parle lies in the valley of the Minnesota River in Western Minnesota, and at the time of which I write it was one of the greatest resorts for canvasbacks and redheads in the Northwest. Wild celery grew here in abundance and the shore was lined for miles with the drifting celery stalks, and the white, delicately flavored celery bulbs could be picked up along the shore almost at random. In the center of the lake several large rocks rise to a height of twenty or thirty feet, and one group covers about an acre in extent.

On windy days the canvasbacks fly up and down the lake in great numbers, passing directly over or within gunshot of the "rock pile," as it was generally termed. Chris Engebretsen's farmhouse stands on the east shore of the lake, and although Chris had a house full of hunters at the time of our arrival, he promptly told us to dump our baggage and he and his wife would take care of us if we cared to put up with such accommodations as they had to offer. We cheerfully acknowledged our intention of accepting anything in the shape of an accommodation that could with courtesy be construed as such. Our baggage was soon stored away, and as it was quite late when we arrived, we turned in for the night, after giving Chris instructions to wake us up for an early start. It seemed as though I had hardly closed my eyes when a heavy pounding on the ceiling downstairs (which was the signal agreed upon) roused us from our slumbers and brought us back to the uncomfortable realization that the room was very cold, the wind blowing a gale and that it was very dark outside. My two friends from St. Paul—Dave Campbell and Tom Marshall—unanimously agreed that Chris must have had a nightmare; that it could not be later than 2 o'clock in the morning. At any rate they both declared they had families and relatives at home who were interested in their future existence and they did not propose to commit suicide in a manner that might leave grave doubts as to the quality of the gray matter contained under the arched dome of their skull plates; and thus agreed, they promptly went to sleep again. The pounding was renewed shortly, and wondering why we never fully appreciated a comfortable bed at home, we put on a bold front and were soon dressed and ready for breakfast.

A steaming cup of coffee put us in a better humor, and when we struck out from the landing for the "rock pile," we were ready for almost any kind of a proposition that old Dame Nature might have up her sleeve, and we got all that was coming to us before Orion again pushed his crimson rim above the eastern horizon. Campbell and Marshall pulled away down the lake in a heavy rowboat, while I followed in a light skiff which could be propelled only with a paddle, the boat being too narrow to permit the use of oars. The morning mist still hung like a veil over the lake as we drew up to the island and secreted our boats in the little bay that extends in among the rocks.

Climbing out over the boulders we waited for the fog to lift. The sun came out and soon the mist began to melt away. We could see the banks on either side and the lake stretching away to the southeast for ten straight miles.

The wind freshened a little and the birds began to stir about. They came from one direction only, flying against the wind. We knelt behind the sheltering ledges and for two hours the birds came up over the rocks in such numbers that we were often undecided as to which flock to shoot at. Very often a great flock would split up as it approached the island and, beating up against the wind, pass by on either side at a distance that appeared to be within easy range of our positions.

Shot after shot we poured into the flocks as they passed, but not a bird exhibited any signs of distress. Finally Marshall laid down his gun, declared we had a bum lot of shells, and started out to enumerate the various things that were going to happen to a certain dealer when we returned to the city. While my friend was ruminating on the uncertainty of life and the disappointments he had encountered from his early youth, a flock of redheads swept past us. Marshall refused to salute the bunch with his old 10-gauge, and called out to me in sarcastic tones to pick off the leader. I had plenty of shells and an intense longing to shatter the hoodoo that hung over us, and went after the red-headed dandy that was leading the bunch with a confidence that was magnificent.

I covered him quickly; at least, I figured it out that way, and my imagination pictured him doubling up with folded wings as the chilled shot smote him, and I had even marked the spot where he would fall; then I pressed the trigger and shot the tail feathers off the last bird in the bunch. Marshall was on his feet in a second.

"I know what the trouble is," he yelled. "We have been shooting behind them all the time."

The air was very clear, and the birds were really from twenty to thirty yards farther away than they appeared to be, and then, instead of continuing to swing our guns on the birds when pressing the trigger, we had evidently stopped the motion in the act of shooting.

The birds had been shot at for weeks and had grown very wise. They would come down the lake on an air line for the rocks, then, as they drew near, would swing out over the channel from seventy to eighty yards distant. We were using chilled shot, sizes Nos. 2 and 3, and by leading the birds from twenty to twenty-five feet, we were able to cut out a couple from each flock. A bunch of five canvasbacks came down the lake, swung out over the channel, then turned, and beating up against the wind, worked their way diagonally across the island, about twenty yards high. Marshall and Campbell fired together, and three birds dropped from the flock. The remaining pair wheeled into the teeth of the wind and came down the line like the fleeting shadow of a thirteen-inch shell. I dropped one with each barrel, after they had passed me, and then explained to my friends that I could perform this feat regularly without a break, only I did not want to kill the limit in an hour or two, and then be tempted to cut into the next day's allowance, and so brand myself as one of the much-detested game-hogs that infest the country.

Marshall listened patiently to this explanation, said he believed it, then offered to bet me ten to one that I would not make another double during the rest of our hunt. I never carry money in my shooting clothes, which custom, I figured, saved my friend quite a lot of coin, as I was known to be quite reckless with money when I had a dead sure thing.

The sky clouded over in the afternoon and the wind freshened to a gale. We dropped a couple of birds some distance from the rocks, and, against the earnest pleading of my friends, I pushed the light skiff out from the little bay and went out to retrieve them. I did not realize what I had done until the boat swung clear of the rocks, then a great wave struck me in the back, between the shoulders, and I knew that I was up against a combination that had sunk many a craft and a more skillful boatman than I. Shifting my position a little forward, I paddled on with my eyes over my shoulder watching each wave as it struck the gunwale, and balancing the frail affair as the water surged up on either side of me, I picked up one of the birds as the boat drove by it—picked it up because I had gone after it, and not because I ever expected to eat it. A realization of the peril I was in came over me with crushing force. The sky was growing darker every minute and the wind drove the stinging spray into my face with a fury that benumbed my flesh and bewildered and confused me. Every moment carried the boat farther away from the island. The black water stretching away for eight or ten miles was filled with sunken, jagged rocks, and if the boat should strike one of these it would be all over in a few minutes, as no one could live long in the icy water. If I could succeed in turning the boat about without capsizing it, I felt that I could drive it back in safety to the rocks.

Watching for a favorable opportunity when the big rollers were smothered by the wind, I succeeded in putting the boat about. I found myself distant some two hundred yards from the rocks, my two friends standing on the highest point of the island watching my progress. I have always had a secret understanding with myself that whenever I went after anything that it must be got. I went after that island good and strong, and it was not long until I began to realize that my cherished ambition was in danger of being shattered. My arms ached as I drove the paddle desperately through the water, and the wind shipped the breath out of my mouth before I could draw the air into my lungs. Inch by inch the boat crept back toward the rocks, and when it seemed that I must give it up after all, I found the force of the wind partly broken as the boat drew into the lee of the island, and at length my friends waded out and drew the skiff ashore. We laid aside our guns, and, sheltered from the wind by the projecting rocks, we watched the canvasbacks go over us in thousands, ten, twenty and thirty yards away.

It was growing colder, the wind increasing, and to add to our discomfort, it began to snow. Night settled down over the scene, blotting out the low-lying landscape, and the lights in the distance farmhouse faded from view. We tramped up and down for hours in the driving snow, trying to keep warm. We joked each other, but a black cloud hung over us and could not be easily dispelled.

Along about 10 o'clock the wind eased up and we decided to make an attempt to reach shore. Marshall and myself took the larger boat, and cautioning Campbell to keep close behind, we pushed off. Campbell was one of those fellows who always found something to do at the last moment, and for some reason he did not put off promptly, and we were soon out of sight of the rock pile. Once or twice the boat struck heavily against a sunken rock, but we finally reached shore without accident. Thinking that Campbell had perhaps landed his boat farther down toward the farmhouse, we walked along the shore in that direction, but he had not yet come ashore. Marshall sent a long "hello" across the lake, but we heard no answer. After calling repeatedly and getting no response, we decided to go on to the farmhouse, thinking our friend had perhaps arrived before us. It was midnight when we reached the house, and Chris was just starting out with a party to search for us. We tramped down the lake for a couple of miles, swinging lanterns to light the way, and occasionally discharging a gun to guide our belated friend in our direction, providing he still inhabited the land of the living. Finally a gun flashed out away down the lake, then two more flashes followed in quick succession. "That's Campbell," said Marshall, "but it is a mystery to me how he ever landed over on that side of the lake." We hung the lanterns up in the trees and fired a shot occasionally to guide the wanderer home. After awhile a faint "hello!" came drifting in to us in answer to our signals, and soon the prow of Campbell's boat loomed out of the shadows and grated on the shore.

"Boys," he said, as he pulled himself together and leaned back against the side of the boat, "this infernal lake is haunted and no mistake. I got lost out there when you fellows pulled away and left me, and after awhile I heard you calling, but you were away over on the other side of the lake. I followed the sounds and called to you from time to time, but your voices sounded fainter and farther away and finally ceased altogether. Now what I want to know is, how did you fellows manage to get over on this side of the lake?"

"Say, Willie," said Marshall, "you want to get this pipe dream out of your head or the robins will be roosting in your belfry before morning. We have been on this side of the lake all the time, so what kind of a fairy tale are you giving us, anyway. "Here," he added, handing him a small flask, "take a pull at this and wake up."

"I think I can help your friend out some," said Chris. "You see, there is an echo over there among the rocks, and when you are out on the lake you hear the echo first, and sometimes when the wind is blowing you hear no sound at all save the echo in the hills."

This explanation was a revelation to us all, and Campbell admitted it was a relief to him to know his intelligence bureau was still working in harmony with his surroundings. It was after 3 o'clock when we again returned to the farmhouse, and after partaking of a light lunch which Chris furnished, in the shape of a collection of hard-boiled eggs and cold ham, we retired for the night, weary and worn out with the day's work.

The next day being Sunday, we did not make our appearance until almost noon. Our game had been hung up on the outside of the barn during the night, and after dinner we went out and took stock of the day's bag. Forty-nine specimens hung there to our credit, and every bird a canvasback or a redhead. The wind had blown itself out during the night and all nature seemed to be in a repentant mood. The sky was free from clouds and the lake stretched its shimmering miles of treacherous waters far to the southward. Sea gulls loafed lazily about the lake, dipping here and there in search of food, the only signs of life in motion. A great bank of ducks were feeding on the celery beds, the splashing and puttering sounds being plainly audible from the porch of the farmhouse. Cattle lay sunning themselves on the hillside, and a Sabbath stillness brooded over the valley.

Lac Qui Parle is still in existence, and on stormy days, when the wind drives cold and raw, and the white caps shake their hoary heads above the sunken rocks, the canvasbacks fly up and down the lake and frisk about the rocks as of yore. The echoes still sport among the prairie slopes, eager to mingle their mimic voices in the shadow of the hills, or join in any tragedy that may be played along the rockbound shore, and if any of my fellow sportsmen find life dull or uninteresting, I would suggest that they make a journey to Lac Qui Parle during the open season, and if they do not find something of interest in the vicinity of the "rock-pile" to stir their blood, then the place is sadly changed since the good old days.

Fargo, N.D.

AMONG THE BARLEY SHOCKS
1901

Editor's Note: This article details good mallard and goose shooting in grain fields near Minnewaukan. A rainy fall had prevented the harvesting of shocked barley and any hunter can imagine how attractive that was to waterfowl. When the article was published in 1901 the level of Devils Lake had been falling from high levels in the 1870s when the steamboat Minnie H ran from Minnewaukan to Devils Lake. In 1901 the water's edge was three miles from town.

The autumn tints had faded from the landscape, and the charm of the melancholy days was tempered by the approaching frosts of Winter. The trees that skirted the Northern lakes had shed their flaming banners, and stripped of their radiant foliage tossed their rugged arms to the breeze in solemn protest of the storm-laden winds that swept down from over the Dominion line. The Autumn days, reluctant to leave the scenes of their withered beauty, lingered on for a time in defiance of the warning blasts that heralded the dread approach of Winter.

For weeks the sky was o'ercast with leaden clouds, and week after week the rain came down on thousands of unthreshed fields. Cold weather set in and the prairie lakes were covered with a thin coating of ice. The shocks of wheat and barley froze solid in the fields, the threshing crews disbanded and the machines were hauled away. The wild geese and ducks still remained, however. All day long they fed in the unthreshed fields, even roosting among the shocks at night, and saved many a farmer the trouble of threshing his grain when the weather finally permitted.

Billy Turner sent me a wire from Oberon, North Dakota, in

which he explained the time was ripe for a farewell crack at the birds before they pulled out for the South for the Winter, and suggested that I take the Great Northern "Flier" to Leeds, make connections with the Northern Pacific and he would meet me at Minnewaukan on the following day.

The train reached Leeds about midnight, and as I would be obliged to be on deck bright and early, I went to the nearest hotel and promptly retired. During the night a heavy snowstorm set in, and when I stepped out of the hotel office in the morning, I found the street covered to a depth of six or seven inches with drifting snow. It looked very much as though I had had my trip for nothing, but it was not cold and I consoled myself with the thought that we would at least have an opportunity to shoot the tail feathers off the last stragglers as they came down from the North.

The combination train pulled out of Leeds over the Northern Pacific line about 7 o'clock in the morning. We had proceeded but a few miles, when my eyes were gladdened by a sight such as I had never seen before and never expect to see again. As far as the eye could reach, the fields of unthreshed grain stretched away to the slate-colored horizon, and the wild geese and mallards swarmed over the stubblefields and covered the shocks in such numbers that it seemed as though all the web-footed game in North Dakota was feeding within sight of the car windows as we sped by. Open water showed in many of the prairie lakes and sloughs, and about these water holes the mallards congregated in thousands. The train pulled into Minnewaukan after a two hours' run and I found Turner standing on the platform rigged out in his old moleskin clothes and looking like a steer roper from the sage-scented slopes of the Bad Lands. Whenever I see my friend decked out thusly, I wonder why he never gives his hair a chance to grow, and keeps the little bunch of buckbrush on his chin from developing into a goatee. His makeup always left me with the impression that a Wild West show was the tamest combination he would care to handle outside the big tent. On banking days, Turner usually looks like a Wall street manipulator of bonds and stocks, or a promoter with a map of the lost Aztec mine and a couple of clean shirts in his alligator grip. He has, however, the happy faculty of grappling with a jest without the aid of a chest protector, and as long as I do not refer to him as the leader of "The Anvil Chorus" I still have the privilege of borrowing money from him, providing the collateral is equivalent to a sum that would make the principal figures look like interest money.

After talking matters over, and comparing notes, we concluded to put in the balance of the day prospecting, and the following day we decided we would get an early start and drive back along the railroad track ten or twelve miles, where I had seen the greatest number of birds feeding in a barley field.

There was a time not many years ago when the town of Minnewaukan stood on the shores of Devils Lake, and steamboats landed at the docks within a block or two of the hotel. The lake has gradually receded until now the shallow water is some three miles distant from the town.

In the early morning the geese come out of the west end of the lake and fly directly over the town, and although it may seem incredible, many a goose has been brought down from his early morning flight from the porch of the hotel, and while the court house was in course of construction last Fall, the contractor took his stand on the tower of the building every morning and, gun in hand, waited for the geese to come out of the lake, and while he was not always successful, he managed to bag several geese from this unique position.

The popular and genial Fred Snore, who makes a specialty of fitting out hunting parties, furnished us with a fine rig and a team of horses that looked like prize-winners at a county fair. Fred's chief ambition in life is to give the boys a good time, and he always sends you off with the warning to "bring in the game," so that his competitor, located down the street, will not think he is being patronized by a kindergarten syndicate. Fred has the finest residence in the town, the broadest smile, and a heart that palpitates with good-will toward all men and sportsmen in particular. On this occasion Fred loaned me an oxskin overcoat that had probably served time as a skin boat on the Big Muddy during the palmy days of that great fakir and gourd-rattling medicine man, Sitting Bull. However, Fred apologized for the garment, saying he had loaned all his buffalo coats to a party of traveling men the day before, and as he insisted that I looked quite as comfortable in the blanket as Turner did in his sheep-herder's outfit, we gave him the high sign and drove away. We headed for the south, and after a drive of some six or eight miles, left the rig and climbed upon one of the numerous strawstacks that dotted the kopjes to the south of the lake, and proceeded to put in the afternoon telling stories and watching the great flight of geese as they came out of the lake for their afternoon's feed on the stubble. Owing to the heavy snow that had fallen, the birds came out high, and instead of feeding in the vicinity of the lake continued their flight for thirty or forty miles before alighting. A great flock of snow geese circled about in our immediate vicinity and finally settled down about two hundred yards from the stack. We motioned to the driver to make a circle and drive them over us. Making a wide detour he drove in behind the flock. They did not seem to be much afraid of the rig and allowed the team to drive almost within gunshot. Then, without an effort, they rose like a great white sail and came straight for the old strawstack standing apparently deserted on the prairie. We had a splendid view of the white-winged beauties as they crossed the swale and came directly on about twenty yards high. The snow in the background appeared a dusty hue compared to their pure white plumage, and their black-tipped wings looked as though they had been dipped in ink. We made no sound as they drew near; in fact, I think I forgot to breathe as I shoved the safety lever up on the old 10-gauge and burrowed a little deeper in the yielding straw. As the flock drew near, they seemed to become suspicious of the monumental silence that reigned in the vicinity of the stack. They ceased their clattering and slowly and cautiously pulled up toward us. Our nerves were tingling like live wires as we crouched at the base of the old straw pile, and with our eyes riveted on the bristling ridge of this monument of the harvest time, waited for the magic picture to be traced against the blue canopy above on which our eyes were narrowly trained. In the twinkling of an eye a row of long, white necks shot out over the straw line, and the great birds, with their long hammer heads, were looking directly down upon us. Their wings were fanning the top of the stack as we scrambled to our feet, and the birds piled over each other in their wild endeavor to get away. Such a tumult of surprised cries, and the contact of the huge wings beating against each other, rather disconcerted me, but I held back until I was quite ready and, covering the bunch nearest to me, fired both barrels in quick succession. The birds continued their flight for a moment and I experienced that humiliating sensation of realizing that I had ignominiously missed a beautiful shot. Then two geese dropped from the flock and my confidence was restored before they struck the ground. In the meantime Turner had unlimbered his "Long Tom" and was burning up ammunition in a manner that looked promising for the overstocked cartridge factories. Three geese fell victims to the rapid manipulation of his well-lubricated rain-maker.

We returned to town at an early hour and made preparations for the trip for the next day. Charlie Maxwell, a lumberman from Minneapolis, expressed a desire to accompany us, and a right good fellow he proved to be. By 4 o'clock the next morning we were sailing along the road that borders the railroad track at a ten-mile clip, and when the first streaks of gray appeared in the East, we struck the barley field we were in search of. As we drove into the field we noticed the snow was covered with black patches covering several acres. In the uncertain light we could not make out the nature of the phenomenon. We were soon enlightened, however, for upon driving a little nearer the black patches rose in the air with a roar, and 5,000 mallards let out a flood of duck language that was simply appalling. They flew two or three hundred yards and settled down again. Upon driving a little nearer the whole bunch got up with a roar that sounded like the thunder of a cataract and made off in the darkness in the direction of the lake. We set out the goose decoys and, making blinds of the barley shocks, waited for the geese to come out to feed. The birds had apparently changed their minds during the night. They evidently wanted a change of diet, or the morning air was so fine they preferred to take a long promenade. The flight passed to the south of us about half a mile. For almost an hour, a continuous stream of geese trailed across the sky, flying low, but they had mapped out a safe course, for not a gun cracked during the morning's flight. A stray flock circled over us at long range, and I managed to pull a goose down as they passed over. I did not go after it for some time, and when I did it raised its head, walked out into the stubble, shuffled off a few shuffles of the Virginia reel, then spread its wings and flew away toward Turner. The bird was flying about six feet high and on a direct line between us. Neither Turner nor myself dared to fire for fear of shooting each other. The goose did not seem to be at all awed by the Shakespearian attitude which my friend had assumed. Possibly it mistook him for one of those draped figures which the farmers erect during harvest time to shoo the birds away from their ripening fields. At any rate, the goose flew directly over his head, looked down at the black tube that had been following its flight, and Turner promptly shot its head off as clean as though it had been cut off with a hatchet.

We were destined, however, to have better sport than goose shooting. We visited several small lakes within half a mile of the barley field, bagged a few mallards and then returned to our blinds about 2 o'clock in the afternoon. We had hardly reached the edge of the field when a flock of mallards came out over the low range of hills that encompassed the field and, flying low down over the barley shocks, swept through the field about thirty yards away. We cut three birds out of the flock, and then, running to the top of the hill, we saw flock after flock flying low over the prairie and coming straight for the barley field. We hastily repaired to our blinds and, opening up the shell cases, so that we could get at our ammunition promptly, cleared the deck for action. The day had been warm and the snow had disappeared. The air was fresh and clear and the brown fields, dotted with countless thousands of wheat and barley shocks, rolled away over the undulating prairie to the sun-kissed horizon. A church of the Advents stood at the edge of the barley field, and the congregation was beginning to arrive in all kind of conveyances as the mallards began piling in over the hill. We got out our duck calls and began squawking as the ducks swarmed into the arena. In swiftly moving circles they swept around the field until they located the place where we were vigorously working the squawkers, then a dozen flocks would make a quick turn and come for us from all directions. The birds swarmed into the field in such numbers that we deliberately started in to pick out the greenheads.

The sun hung low in the west, the south wind fanned the withered fields, loosened the frost-bound shocks and gladdened the hearts of the Advents in the little church on the prairie. The sun sank away to the horizon, the organ in the little church pealed forth and from the open windows came the strains of some old-time melody brought from over the seas. Strange music floated up to us as we knelt among the barley shocks and cracked away at the swiftly moving birds. The sun dipped behind the cloudless horizon; the dull, red light lingered for a moment on the summit of the distant hills and touched the spire of the little church with its mellow light; the barley shocks stood out in bold relief against the yellow background, like bronze figures on a copper plate. Discordant sounds were wafted in to us from over the prairie, mingled with the distant jangle from the great flight of geese returning to the lake far to the southward. The mallards squawked and circled over the low range of hills in ever narrowing circles; the musician in the little church still pedaled away at the organ, the congregation chanted some weird melody in a foreign tongue, the guns cracked away and the shadows gathered, and still the birds swung round the field in ever increasing numbers. Very strange it seemed to be, carrying death and destruction to the webfoots of the marshes almost under the shadow of a church and within sound of the organ. But we did not seem to be disturbing the ceremonies on this Saturday afternoon. Probably the farmers were glad to have us drive the birds from the fields, which certainly saved them part of their crops. Flock after flock of mallards in full plumage passed over our blinds. Their green heads glistened in the sun, their broad, gray bellies, with the rich brown trimmings at the breasts, making beautiful marks to look at over the shining barrels.

We picked out the greenheads as they passed over, making doubles more often than we missed them. Before the sun went down we had some fifty birds spread out in rows in the stubble and most of them greenheads. A lone mallard passed over us in the gathering twilight. A wild tumult of calls from the shocks wheeled him about, and, making a circle within sixty yards, he turned and came directly back, squawking in low, inquiring notes as he came on. Turner fired as the bird loomed up before us, and a greenhead mallard dropped with a thud beside the blind. I do not advocate shooting ducks after dusk but these birds were certainly trespassers and should be treated as such.

It was growing too dark in the hollow to see well enough to shoot, and I took up my position on the hill, where I could outline the birds as they came in against the red light in the western sky. Maxwell was out on the plowed ground near the church, and the peculiar clicking sounds produced by the mechanism of his pump gun, as he rapidly worked the loaded shells from the chamber of the magazine, reminded me of the racket engineered by Eddie Foy during his desperate attempt to scuttle the ship while on his theatrical cruise with Sinbad the Sailor. Turner was still down in the hollow, and his old bell-muzzled smoke-consumer had caught fire and was vomiting baleful forks of yellow fire, felt wads and chilled shot at a rate that would make a Fourth of July celebration look like A Midsummer Night's Dream. The guns cracked and lanced the darkness with red jets of flame and the thud, thud of the birds as they struck the ground indicated we were not wasting many shells. We started out to gather up the birds before it became too dark to find them, and upon counting up the result of the day's sport, found that we had seventy-four mallards and over sixty of them greenheads.

As we drove into town that night, Fred was standing in the office door ready to give us the glad hand as we pulled up. I can see him now as he stood there with the lantern held high above his head, peering into the wagon at the game piled up high under the seats. "Say," he exclaimed, in his slow, hesitating way, "those 'pikers' over at the hotel have been stringing me about you fellers. That guy with the weak lamps and gold spectacles brought in a couple of squaw ducks and said he would sell them to you cheap, if you wanted to send some game down to the old folks." "Tell him to come over, Fred," said Turner, "and we will make him a bid." Fred started across the street to the hotel and told the sport with the weak lamps that we had had hard luck and wanted to buy his game if he would smuggle it over to the barn on the quiet. The fellow evidently "tumbled," but he came over, and when he saw the big bunch of ducks stacked up on the barn floor, sailed in and began to count them, As he waded through the bunch he began to grow excited. Seventy-four, seventy-five seventy-six, he counted, with a threatening accent in his voice as he threw the last bird on top of the pile.

"Gentlemen," he said, straightening himself up and pulling back his coat, displaying a star on his vest. "I am a deputy game warden from Grand Forks, and I arrest you on the grounds of shooting one bird over the limit." Fred walked over and gripped the fellow hard by the collar.

"Say, my fine goslin," he said, "my driver can kill more birds on the wing with his whip that you can shoot with that lead-slinging harvester of yours, if you had the birds hobbled out there on the prairie. We don't care whether you are a deputy game warden from Grand Forks, or the head pilot on a pickle boat," and escorting the fellow to the door by the collar of his corduroy coat, advised him to take to tall timber when the moon rose over the reservation, and while the murky waters of Devils Lake glittered under its phosphorous effulgence.

The church of the Advents still stands upon the prairie, but the mallards no longer circle in countless numbers above the barley field, as they did on that bright October day. Benson County remains the greatest resort for feathered game in the Northwest; and when the geese begin to come down from the North in the Fall, and the sportsmen gather about the hotel office of an evening, Fred invariably tells them about the big bag of mallards, the remarkable performance of his driver in cutting a swiftly moving mallard out of the air with his bull whip, and how the deputy game warden from Grand Forks took to the tall cottonwoods and was seen no more.

THE LAND OF THE DAKOTAS
1903

<u>Editor's Note</u>: *One can sense the excitement that Leffingwell felt as he traveled westward from Jamestown on September 20, 1902. He gave a good description of the land and the appearance of Dawson in those early days. The observation of "Too much water" influencing the lack of ducks at Lake Isabel and the 1863 battle ground at Dead Buffalo Lake being under six feet of water shows how deep water can prevent heavy use by waterfowl. I have noted this in many former premier waterfowl hunting lakes in Kidder County with high water levels that began in 1995 and continue to 2001. On the other hand, other wetlands that had not held water since the 1950s are now good seasonal and semi-permanent marshes.*

Away out beyond the range of hills that marks the western boundary of the valley of the Jim lies a country famed from the historical days of Lewis and Clark for its famous hunting resorts. The native buffalo grass still mantles the Dakota hills and spreads its luxuriant growth over the endless, rolling prairie. This is a land of wondrous sunsets, of desolation, of peaceful contentment, and when the sun has sunk low in the west and the winds are lulled to sleep, and the evening shadows begin slowly to gather over the dun-colored buttes and veil the silver lakes with twilight's softening shades, it brings back something to life that dies with each succeeding year, that dies when the Autumn leaves begin to fade and unfold their crimson colors in acknowledgment of Autumn's melancholy courier. Indian Summer days, when the winds sway the brown billows of prairie grasses and the shadows go creeping across the plains like old memories of haunted, forgotten days, mellowed by time and hallowed by eternity's creeping shadows, that steal into the sportsman's heart, softening and subduing many a sympathetic nature that the relentless forces of civilization have forged into callous and sordid creations, that overshadows for the time being the pitiless pursuits of commerce, or the endless strife for existence or wealth, and, unconsciously, irresistibly draws one in closer communion with nature, closer than the chimes inspired by some distant cathedral bell or a loved song of one's native land.

As yet the fair surface of this country has not been subdued by the encroaching hand of civilization, but the time will come when to the sportsman's eye the scene will lose its charm, when the freedom of the plains will be hedged with endless miles of fence, the gentle undulating prairie furrowed with seams of toil, and houses, barns and stacks stand like sentinels on the plain. When this time comes, I think the sun will cease to shine as brightly on the silent hills and the silver lakes, and when this change takes place, then I shall be sorely tempted to lay aside my gun and hunt no more.

At least so ran my thoughts as I looked from the window of the palatial North Coast Limited as the train sped westward on the morning of September 20, 1902. Jamestown, Crystal Springs, Tappen, Dawson. Dawson, lying there in the middle of the windswept prairie, could hardly look interesting to the average traveler. The little brown station, the big frame hotel built years ago by an enterprising individual in anticipation of events that have never developed, two or three stores, a water tank, a dusty, gravel-strewn street, and the polished steel rails of the Northern Pacific stretching away like a silver needle to the westward. All this could hardly be expected to arouse any sentiment of interest or curiosity in the mind of the casual tourist, but to Turner and myself it told a different story. There were our dogs standing in the door of the express car looking wistfully about for their masters, and well we knew the hills south of town were alive with grouse, and that almost every lake within twenty miles teemed with myriads of ducks.

Old Comley Rhodes, the proprietor of the Sibley Hotel, who has not been out of the state of North Dakota for twenty years, was there to greet us. Lee Pettibone, the czar of the short-grass country, waved a welcome from the door of his real estate office, and we were soon inside our old clothes and hobnailed shoes, ready for any proposition our genial landlord might have down on the program.

And so it happened that the first day out developed into rather a prospecting trip. The waters of Isabel, the queen of the prairie lakes, the home of the canvasbacks and redheads, lay unruffled under the clear rays of the Autumn sun. A flock of Canada geese, sunning themselves on the sandy shore, raised their curiously hooded heads, walked leisurely to the water's edge and then took wing.

The lake was deserted, not a duck was visible, where before at this season of the year countless thousands could always be seen feeding and roosting on the drifting celery beds. "Too much water," replied our driver, in response to our disappointed inquiries. We will try Buffalo Lake, but we did not get to Buffalo that day. When we reached the scene where General Sibley gave battle to the hostile Sioux, we found the old battleground covered with six feet of water and a flight of ducks coming in from Buffalo Lake that offset any disappointment that we may have experienced at Isabel. Our arrangements were perfected that night, and early the next morning when the flight came in from Buffalo Lake, if the noble red man from the realms of the spirit land could have come galloping back on his spotted pony from the "happy hunting ground," decked out in his war bonnet, with his eagle feathers fluttering in the wind, he would not have seen the swiftly moving band as they circled about the Sibley command, nor heard the eerie cries of the hostile Sioux which broke upon the prairie solitudes that faraway Summer day in 1863. Instead he would have found the scene of his former triumph turned into a rice lake, and a short man in rubber boots, reaching to his armpits, plodding patiently through the reeds, and a tall man with a long paddle, poling a canoe through the thick rushes.

I have seen many a flight of ducks, dead shots and poor shots, but for a winning combination that day certainly carried off the bunting.

Without mentioning any names, I will state that the short man in the rushes belongs to a syndicate that never misses a shot, and when an unsuspecting flock of gadwalls lined up within a range of forty yards, the head and shoulders of the short man would suddenly emerge from the tangled growth of rushes, the sun would glint for a moment on the shining barrels of his Greener gun, two reports, two rags collapse from the swiftly moving flock, and then the short man would subside into the grass like a muskrat. The tall man in the boat was not making a record that he could hang his hat on. The canoe was a little unsteady, the birds were forever coming and going on the wrong side, and the light twelve-gauge gun was always shooting behind its intended victim. At last, disgusted, he poled the boat to shore and changed the twelve-gauge for the old ten-gauge, and with pockets loaded with shells, came creeping back through the rushes with confidence in his eye and faith in the old ten-gauge that was prophetic. A big bunch of gadwalls came boring in from Buffalo Lake, the tall man gathered up the ten pounds of steel and walnut, drew the combination to his shoulder and the big flock swept by minus six of its number. The first fleeting sense of exultation over, a feeling that the shot was hardly to be commended appealed to him strongly. He concluded to shoot only at single birds thereafter, but the old ten-gauge had fired its last salute for the season. A death grip had settled in the breech and the gun refused to open. A peculiar click in the lock, when the lever was thrown over, indicated that she was out of service. And now it seemed that all the ducks in the country were pouring into the lake. They crossed and recrossed over his head, but he sat there with the gun resting across his knees, the water gently lapping the sides of the canoe, watching the short man cutting birds out of every flock until he was out of shells, and while he was not naturally a selfish man he concluded he was glad of it and that the birds were entitled to a rest during the noon hour.

When we picked up the birds we found we had killed the limit for the day, so we pulled the boat up to a convenient haystack and spread out the lunch. We were hungry and tired, and the short man was wringing the water out of his clothes, out of his necktie, and out of his hair, and expressing his general satisfaction of the day's sport. The tall man reached for a piece of fried chicken and sat silent and moody, musing on the uncertainties of life, and watching the sandhill cranes as they circled far above against the blue dome of the sky.

Early the next morning we found ourselves hitting the trail away to the southward, bound for the sandhills, the home of the grouse and the prairie chicken. It was getting late in the season, the weather was fine and the dogs went beating among the hills with a vim and energy that was encouraging. We found the birds pretty well scattered through the sandhills, but found no large covies. The sandhills are the miniature Bad Lands of the West, mere warts humped up along the slope of the foothills. Small trees and clusters of bushes were scattered about everywhere and the birds would single out this shelter and find a cooling retreat under the shade of the trees. It was not long before the dogs caught on and began to hunt the scattered clumps of bushes, instead of ranging out in the usual way. Very often when one of the dogs was on a point we would walk close in behind him and there, under the shade of some protecting branch, sat a full-grown grouse, and we had to "shoo" him out before he would take wing. Toward evening we worked out of the hills and headed for a wheat and flax field which we had figured out would tempt the grouse along about the feeding hour. We were there in time to witness a flight that put an end to the argument as to whether the birds were in the habit of running or flying from their distant retreat to their feeding grounds during the day. While we were discussing the matter we noticed a lone grouse flying low through the hills, headed for the fields. On came the bird, flying over the wheat, and dropped in the corner of the flax field. Then another, and another, and then a continuous stream of birds from the hills, one at a time, came in over the wheatfield and dropped into the flax. Probably one hundred or one hundred and fifty grouse flew into the field as we drove down from the hills, but they did not come in for the purpose of being exterminated.

The flax stubble was about three inches high, and when we tried to work in on them they stood up on the breaking, looking as big as turkeys, and then took wing before we could get within range. We marked down one bunch of about fifty, which settled on the prairie, and went after them. Here I saw Turner make some of the longest shots I have ever witnessed. In one instance he started out to pace the distance, but the birds got up all around us and when we got through we were a little mixed as to the identical birds referred to. I believe that two of the birds were killed at a distance of ninety yards. I have never seen birds killed outright at a greater distance.

And so the days ran on, the nights grew colder, the sandhill cranes came down from the north in numbers, and an occasional flock of Canada geese came trailing out of the northern sky, their clear, melancholy notes floating down from their trackless path in the heavens, like the challenge of a bugle call. Under the shadow of the clouds the landscape began to take on a somber, forbidding appearance, the twilight lingered longer in the hollows, the silver lakes were rimmed with ice, and the silence of the plains seemed shrouded in gloom when the sun hid his red shield behind the barren hills. And so we said good-bye to Dawson from the platform of the observation car—Dawson lying there in the middle of the wind-swept prairie, with its shabby little cluster of houses, the big hotel sketched darkly against a blood-stained sky, and the steel rails of the Northern Pacific gliding away into the West like a silver serpent.

THE PLATEAU DU COTEAU DU MISSOURI
1903

Editor's Note: This is my favorite article of those that Leffingwell wrote about hunting in North Dakota. That is because it places him right in an area that I have hunted in for the past 30 years. His base was the ranch of James D. Marston that was located on the south side of Chicago Lake which is north of Chase Lake National Wildlife Refuge. The history of the Marston Ranch is well detailed in a book "Pettibone 1910-1960" that was produced by two able historians, Mrs. G. B. Stuart and Mrs. Henry Luehr. James Marston came to Dakota Territory in 1865. In 1893 the Marston family settled on the ranch which they named for their native home of Chicago. In the article is stated: "After breakfast we drove over to a chain of lakes located some three miles to the westward." That would have to be Brock Slough and DeKrey Slough and others with passes in between them. Those are places where I had many fine hunts in my duck boat with a spread of decoys and black Labrador retrievers. It is interesting to read about details of James Marston's home. The furnishings were luxurious and a library contained hundreds of books. The Pettibone history states that in 1893 the only other settlers were the Col. Springer family and the D. W. Scott family, both living in what is now Weiser Township, and Joe Williams and his parents, the Jeremiah Williams, who lived in what is now Lake Williams Township. The David W. Scott homestead was one mile east of my hunting camp where I am working on this book. He came to Dawson, Dakota Territory, in 1883 from New Hampshire. The homestead was staked in 1893 and Mr. Scott became a prominent citizen in the area. In the Pettibone history it is stated that Mr. Scott was a broad reader and the library in his *ranch home contained about a thousand books. Such was the environment that existed at the time when Leffingwell was in this area to hunt.*

Sometimes when the winds come moaning down through the barren hills, and the waters of Isabel Lake are sending their restless volumes against the sandy shore and twilight is weaving its sable garments over the shadowy plains, blotting out the Autumn banners that float forever in the western sky when the sun has sunk to rest; they bring with them a spirit of depression, gloved with sadness, that makes the hunter stand in silence watching the brilliant curtain fading to ashes against the western sky and brooding over memories of old forgotten days long ago veiled in oblivion. Nature, the great pervading spirit of the universe, wooing in silence the cankered spirit of civilization, brings one to the realization that God made the country and man made the city.

Somewhere among the Dakota hills, where the short grass reigns supreme from the line of dawn to the western horizon, lies the property of the N. W. Cattle Co. Strange settlers are gradually pushing into the outer hills, and lonely cabins perch here and there on some distant butte, the only signs of civilization in this land of silence and desolation.

We were bound for the ranch of the N. W. C. Co., located forty-six miles from Dawson on the main line of the Northern Pacific. Dr. D__, George W__, of Minneapolis, and the writer rode patiently along behind a team of horses belonging to my old friend, Comely Rhodes, who has not been out of the state of North Dakota for twenty-three years, and at the rate we were traveling it is doubtful if the horses would succeed in getting across the line during the same length of time. James T__ of Michigan and Stephen D__ of Ohio, who were shooting at Dawson, had accepted our invitation to join the party, and they proved themselves to be thorough sportsmen and the right kind. May their shadows never grow less.

We reached the ranch at Marston Moor about 1 o'clock, and while spreading out the lunch on the prairie Mr. M__ introduced his son, who came out of the ranch house carrying in his arms a small black and white animal with a long, bushy black tail. This special breed of animals has a national reputation and is usually given a wide berth by judicious persons and people of mature judgment. We did not shake hands with the young man, but held our ground and looked as cheerful as possible under the circumstances. After lunch Mr. M__ asked us to take a look at the storehouse, as he termed it, and we were very agreeably surprised upon entering the building to find ourselves surrounded with all the luxuries of a modern city home. The walls were covered with costly pictures from Rome, Venice and many foreign cities, curios from all over the world lay scattered about in profusion. The bedrooms were fitted up with brass bedsteads, India rugs and lace curtains. The library contained hundreds of volumes of books, letters from many prominent men and an accumulation of relics that must have required the effort of a lifetime to gather together. The atmosphere was laden with the smell of mold. Dust lay heavy on the contents of the rooms and an air of depressing desolation pervaded the place. Mr. M__ told us afterward that he had left the rooms just as they were when his wife died some six years ago. He also informed us that he had lost some three hundred head of four-year-old steers during the severe blizzard of the previous Winter. He had traveled all of the world, and here we found him living contentedly with his son, on a lonesome ranch twenty-five miles from the nearest railroad station. We left him standing in the door of his "storehouse," his pipe in his mouth, looking away across the prairie, where the sky line swings in a circle and the buffalo grass fills in the balance of the picture.

Shortly after leaving Marston Moor we let the dogs out for a run. Away across the prairie they went like the White Squadron steaming across the tranquil bosom of a Summer sea. Upon over the hills they raced and disappeared from view. The trail wound its tortuous way down through the valley and up the distant slope, and when we reached the top of the hill there stood the dogs, all three on a point; Dewey with all four feet spread out and his head twisted to one side as though he had just been spilled out of the wagon, and the other two dogs backing him.

"Well, this looks like Old Missouri," said Doctor, who hailed from the state bordering on the Big Muddy.

Five men lined up abreast and three dogs standing like carved statues outlined against the dun brown hill seemed like taking an unfair advantage of this poor little covey of chickens. We walked up behind the dogs and urged Dewey on gently, but he stuck his claws into the short grass and refused to navigate. In a second, in fact, in the fraction of a second, a great white jack-rabbit flashed out of the grass and bounded away on three legs.

"He's crippled," yelled Doc; "I'll just catch that boy and take him home with me," and he started on a run after the bundle of steel springs gently bounding over the prairie.

"Get a little closer," I called to Doc, who immediately put on a little burst of speed which somewhat widened the distance between himself and the object of his pursuit.

"Now you have got him," we all yelled together. The Doctor planted a hobnailed shoe against an ant hill and fired both barrels in quick succession. Just then the white pointer went by him like the fleeting shadow of a thirteen-inch shell, and the other two dogs went thundering past, scratching up the gravel and throwing up little clouds of dust and yelping in wild delight, as they closed in on the crippled rabbit. Mr. Jack finally looked over his shoulder, put his fourth foot down on the soft buffalo grass, and then things began to grow dizzy.

Far up in this land of the Plateau du Coteau du Missouri the hills rise abruptly and the valleys slope away in graceful curves to the next grassy butte. The jack was going now, and even to the untrained eye it was apparent that he was moving and moving fast. Just a long gray streak flashed across the yellow background of this vast prairie solitude as the rabbit hit the tops of the highest hills and vanished in the blue and hazy distance with a mere slip of his tail that did not even ruffle the atmosphere. The dogs stopped, looked at each other in a confused sort of a way and then went to work hunting chickens as though nothing had happened. The Doctor gathered up his gun, and as he mosied back to the wagon, said with a grin:

"Well, boys, what would you think of that?"

We had all been there before and told him to cheer up, that perhaps, after all, it might not be true.

Nothing of particular interest happened on the way to the ranch. Occasionally we would get out and bag a few grouse when the dogs came to a stand; otherwise the trip proved uneventful. Mile after mile we pounded along through the short grass country, not a living thing was seen save now and then a gopher sitting upright on a little mound of earth beside his den, or a buzzard circling far above against the blue vault of the sky. Along about 6 o'clock we came in sight of the buildings of the N. W. C. Co., perched on a range of hills to the eastward bordering a beautiful sheet of water, at least we would so consider it in North Dakota.

A bell, suspended from a framework just outside the ranch house, was ringing as we drove into the corral, and indicated that we were just in time for supper; and notwithstanding we had nine members in the party and were entirely unexpected, we were promptly taken care of without much confusion.

There is something about ranch life that has always appealed to the writer. Here far away from the nearest railroad station no sound reaches you from the busy world beyond. Of the cares, the strife, the selfishness, the petty jealousies of civilization, no echoes reach you in this land of silence and sunshine. Out here one has time to think, to get in closer touch with nature, from which civilization too often lures us away like a mirage to the thirsty traveler, only to find the vision disappears and his feet are treading the sands of a desert waste. To me there was always a fascination in watching a thousand head of cattle come trailing over the northern slope at sunset, to watch the evening shadows gathering on the distant buttes and the flight of ducks over the lake lying like a silver sheet embedded in the prairie.

We were up early the next morning. It was very still and clear, and thousands of wildfowl were feeding in the lake. Several flocks were puttering about almost within gun range of the ranch buildings.

After breakfast we drove over to a chain of lakes located some three miles to the westward. Great numbers of birds were flying up and down one of the larger lakes and crossing over to neighboring ponds. Jack (the driver) and the writer pulled the duck boat off the boat wagon and running it into the water pulled across to the opposite side of the lake; put out some three dozen decoys and then pushed the boat into the rushes.

It was one of those still September days when everything seems at peace with the world. Not a reed rustled or a ripple broke upon the quiet surface of this prairie lake. Only the shadow of a cloud falling on the silent hills and the warm breath of Autumn were lying like a benediction over the land.

The boys were scattered out over the pass. Mr. T__ and Mr. D__ located at the north end, while the genial Doctor and Rhodes planted themselves about a gunshot to the southward, which proved to be the natural pass between the lakes. Presently the birds began to come back in singles and doubles. For a time not a bird got over the pass. Rhodes and the Doctor cut them down as fast as they came over. They had picked up about a dozen birds, and so far we had not fired a shot. We could hear my medical friend talking to Rhodes and commenting on our efforts in driving the birds out of the lake for them to shoot, and speculating whether we would get any birds or not. A moment later a bunch of five redheads came skimming across the water and lit among the decoys.

It is not considered sportsmanlike to pot birds, but the instinct of the pot-hunter apparently lies dormant in the human breast, and then our reputations were at stake.

"Jack," I said, "you take the three swimming to the right in the clear water and I'll get the other two when they get up from behind the rushes."

Jack waited until the birds were in line and then gave them one barrel in the water and the other as they rose. The remaining two birds flew in toward the shore, but the rushes were so thick I could not get a shot at them. The three birds Jack shot at were apparently uninjured. They flew directly over the Doctor and Rhodes, who promptly knocked them down, all three of them.

Someone laughed and then Rhodes called out to us and wanted to know if we had injured any of the decoys; then they all laughed. We said nothing. There is a time in the affairs of men when silence is a virtue and sometimes it does not require any great amount of intelligence to know when it is clamming time. But soon the birds began to come in flocks of from fifteen to twenty. Almost every flock headed direct for the decoys. They were within easy range, and after about two hours shooting we figured we had about killed the limit and started around the lake to gather the birds.

We picked up forty redheads while circling the lake, gathered up the decoys and rowed across the lake and joined our friends. The boys had thirty-five redheads and mallards, making a bag of seventy-five birds for six guns.

We were satisfied with the day's sport and gathering up the game we drove back to the ranch. The cattle came pouring down over the hills at sunset as usual, and high up on a distant hill, outlined against the crimson light in the western sky, motionless and silent, sat a cowboy on his pony like a statue carved in bronze. The shepherd dogs were rounding up the trailers, and soon the whole herd was taking an evening drink at the lake.

The sunset in this western land defies description, defies the painter's brush, and leaves one with the vague idea that he has seen the golden gates ajar. A thousand hilltops raise their yellow heads in the burnished light and the valleys are veiled with the shadows. The sun dips his red shield behind the western hills and slowly the silver lining of the clouds turns to lead and the crimson fades to ashes.

It was a merry crowd that gathered that night in the ranchhouse. The Doctor entertained us with a story of a shipwreck, and his description was so vivid that we could actually feel the house rock on its foundation. One by one the boys dropped off to bed, and the Doctor and the writer strolled down to the corral and sat down on a rock among the great bunch of cattle. The moon was up and shed a silver radiance over the scene. The great herd of cattle were lying down quiet and contented; the moon threw a weird light over their great hulks, and not a sound disturbed the silence of the night save the heavy breathing of the steers. The lake lay like a liquid shadow under the twinkling stars, and the prairie stretched away in the moonlight, dim and gray and vast, until lost in the obscurity of night.

Suddenly from away up among the hills came the curious melancholy cry of a coyote. A curious mixture of cackle and laughter penetrating through the night and then dying away with a mournful note and all was still again. Several of the steers got up and walked about in a restless manner, but otherwise the herd remained undisturbed.

It was quite late when we returned to the ranch house that night. The moon had tilted far to the westward and her yellow disk still shone down on a sleeping world, so calm, so bright, so still.

LONG LAKE
1904

Editor's Note: This is the last of 12 articles in the Leffingwell series about duck and goose hunting in central North Dakota between 1892 and 1904. From the careful observation and classic writing we are able to learn of how wildfowling was in those halcyon days when the land was new and birds abundant. Just as in the present time it is apparent that congenial relationships were formed between Leffingwell and his friends and local farmers and hunters. In the last paragraph he shares some useful philosophy with his readers.

The Autumn tints had come and gone. September frosts had sapped the oak of its life blood and on the listless foliage painted in gold and crimson colors their tribute to the passing Summer. October, with its cold gray storms, came moaning out of the far Saskatchewan and tossed the withered leaves to their annual Autumn graves.

The flight of blue-winged teal had long since passed to the southward and the croaking cry of the sandhill cranes no longer floated down through leagues of space from their undisputed realm among the clouds.

As the season advanced the gray storms that for days swept through the lonely sandhills spent their force, and the balmy breath of Indian Summer came hovering over the landscape like a ghost of the departed Summer. Day after day, long waving lines of snowwhite geese came trooping out of the northern sky and passed on in silence to the sandbars of the distant Missouri.

In the early morning and afternoon the geese leave their roosting grounds or water holes and go out to feed on the stubble fields, often flying twenty to thirty miles to their feeding grounds.

Mr. T__, of Chicago, who is known among his friends as the "Greek philosopher," had never been fortunate enough to bag a goose that he could identify as being the victim of his own individual efforts. So our mutual friend, Comely Rhodes, volunteered to get us under a flight of geese, and further guaranteed that the event would be pulled off within a mile of town. We were on the grounds at the appointed time (about 2 o'clock in the afternoon) and after an hour of honest work succeeded in digging a couple of pits in the sandy soil that reflected no particular credit to the "man with the spade."

The goose decoys we located some forty yards from the pits, and then proceeded to obliterate all signs of the fresh earth, by pulling quantities of stubble from the wheat field and arranging it in rows along the sides of the pits, so as to leave no suspicious signs which the wary eye of the wild goose is quick to detect and avoid. Mr. Rhodes suggested that he would "batch it" in the single pit, while Mr. T__ and the writer arranged to make ourselves as comfortable as possible in the double dugout.

We have never been able to settle among ourselves, in a satisfactory manner, who was personally responsible for engineering these excavations.

The party who owned the land was heard to remark afterward that the larger of the two pits bore a close resemblance to a cyclone cellar, and that the party or parties who made his wheatfield resemble the architect of the ancient mound builders were evidently delegates to the irrigation convention then holding forth at Bismarck.

At any rate, on the particular day referred to, we were in the pits and there was no one about to question our excuse for living. Only a band of sheep, feeding on a distant hill, and the shepherd and his dog stretched out on the sunny slope at its base. A light breeze was blowing from the north; the Autumn sun shown down through the clear, pure air with a drowsy warmth, and far away across the plains the North Coast Limited came crawling out of the hazy west. No sounds floated up to us from the little prairie town sleeping peacefully in the sunshine, only the faint tinkle of a bell from the distant sheep herd and the murmur of the North Coast Limited, as it crept out across the sunlit plains. Silence and sunshine, peace and contentment, and so we waited for the geese to come out and stir things up.

"Listen, boys!" said Rhodes; "can you hear them?"

We listened. There was something in the air and coming our way, as the music seemed to be growing louder each moment. "Sounds like a lot of Chinks at a chop suey banquet," dryly remarked our Chicago friend. We could see the birds now, as the flock came winging its way up over the low-lying hills, flying low over the prairie. To our surprise the geese made a wide circle about the decoys and settled down about one hundred yards distant from the sheep herd.

"We will have to drive them out of that roost," said Rhodes, "or they will decoy every flock that comes in and spoil our shooting."

Climbing out of the pit he started on a run for the wagon, which the driver had pulled in behind a deserted building some two hundred yards away, and instructed the boy to drive around to the westward and start the geese over toward the pits. Rhodes then started back toward us, but before he reached the pits several more flocks came in and, cackling and gabbling away in anticipation of a good feed, settled down among the first arrivals, near the herd of sheep. There were now probably about five hundred geese in the field, and the driver circled almost within gun range before they finally took wing. The great bunch of birds made several circles of the wheatfield, each time drawing nearer and surveying the sheet-iron decoys with evident distrust. Finally they swung out in a long, waving line and headed straight for the painted dummies standing bold upright on their thin steel legs. The entire flock had ceased their cackling and came slowly up the slope, as silently as a passing shadow. The sun glinted for a moment on their snowwhite plumage and black tipped wings as we peered cautiously through the rows of stubble bristling about the pits. Suddenly the leaders let out a series of shrill, startled cries, the great flock bunched up and we knew that we were discovered.

We rose together and poured in six barrels as the birds went towering skywards. Five great white bodies collapsed in the air and came tumbling to the ground from a height of eighty yards. The big flock went clucking and chattering away across the prairie and finally disappeared in the distance. It was now the usual feeding hour and soon we could see geese coming in from every direction in flocks ranging from two hundred to one thousand. They called to each other from the prairie slopes, and answering cries came floating down from the far sky as the birds came circling in from their long flight. One bunch of about a thousand geese passed almost within gun range, and while we were deploring our hard luck a gun cracked over near the deserted shack and the whole bunch swung gracefully around and passed directly over the decoys. What a picture they presented as we looked up and saw the great white birds with their long hammer heads looking down upon us and within easy range.

"Now is our time!" cried Rhodes, and springing quickly to his feet cut down two geese with the first barrel, but missed with the second.

The writer fanned the atmosphere with the first barrel, apparently shooting behind the mark. Leading the line about six feet, I succeeded in bringing down two birds with the second barrel, and then throwing out the empty shells, called to Mr. T__ to lead the flock about six feet, and when the gentleman from the "Windy City" brought down a goose with each barrel he expressed his pleasure in the performance with considerable emphasis, stating that the world's greatest wheat pit was a tame affair compared to such sport, and that he would willingly journey all the way from Chicago any time if he could repeat this exhibition of his skill.

The flight set in so strong now that we hardly had time to pick up the game before another flock came heading in toward the decoys.

It is difficult to make a big bag of these birds, as they band together in great numbers, and often the hunter may estimate a flight of 10,000 birds and include them in ten or fifteen flocks which come and go with a rush and leave the man in the pit with about as many empty shells and usually a smaller number of geese.

The flight lasted about an hour, and when we gathered up some twenty-odd geese, we were well satisfied with the afternoon's sport.

As we drove home that night in the early twilight we could hear, far overhead, the beating of huge wings and the occasional guttural cry of the Canada geese as they passed on in the gathering darkness.

Often at the evening hour I have remained on the wooded pass above the famous Isabel Lake, waiting for the flight of ducks that was as sure to come as the flight of twilight out of the furnace fires smoldering in the West. At such a time I have often noticed a silver thread of water stretching leagues to the westward. Reality or mirage, it is there at twilight, but fades into vapor under the rays of the noonday sun.

This lengthy body of water, according to the map of the state of North Dakota, is recorded and is known to the natives as Long Lake.

This was our destination on a particularly bright and sunny morning in the latter part of October, 1903. After a four hours drive, and after knocking about over some pretty rough country, we came out on a high range of hills bordering the western shore of the lake. Mr. P__ took out his field-glasses and, after surveying the lake with the binoculars, reported that the shore was lined with both black and white geese and mallard ducks, as far as he could see. We drove down to Rancher Blake's place, where we watered the horses and then moved on to the range of hills bordering the lake, where we could get a better view of the country. We spread the lunch out on the sunny slope of the hill and proceeded to take stock of our surroundings. On either side of us the lake stretched its shimmering miles of water as far as the eye could reach. The Autumn sun shown down on a scene little changed since the days of Red Cloud and the buffalo. In days to come the inventions of civilization may furrow the virgin sod with seams of toil, and from the fertile plains the sugar beet and the festive cabbage spring forth to gladden the heart of the vegetarian and testify to the ingenuity of man. But now the scene belongs to nature. All day long the geese go streaming down the lake and myriad flocks of mallards feed in undisputed security among the rich sedge beds that border the shallow shores of this great alkali lake.

After lunch Rhodes and the writer waded out through the rushes and located about a quarter of a mile from shore. Mr. P__ and Mr. T__ still lingered in the vicinity of the lunch basket, but when our guns began to wake the echoes and the birds commenced to return to the feeding grounds which we had taken possession of, our friends crawled into their waders and were soon splashing through the mud, weighted down with one hundred shells to the gun. It usually requires a windy day to drive the ducks into such an open marsh as we were located in, but the fixed habits of birds will always be open to argument, and on this particular day thousands of mallards came pouring into the rich feeding grounds in such numbers that we deliberately picked off the greenheads as the birds piled into the sedgegrass beds.

We were not shooting for the market, nor were we there for the purpose of breaking any records. We devoted a large share of the time in gathering up the dead and wounded birds in preference to increasing the bag. As it grew dark some of the guns were silent for lack of shells. I stood on the shore after lugging in about twenty mallards and watched the birds come boring in from the open water. There was a steady roar of wings as the twilight thickened, and thousands of ducks came sailing in with wings set, and plumped into their favorite feeding grounds in absolute indifference to our presence. Mr. P__ and Mr. T__ came splashing through the water, loaded down with ducks, and, upon counting the stack of game piled up on the shore, we found we had seventy-six birds, the greater number being mallards, which figure is well within the limit according to the statues of the North Dakota game law.

We stopped with Rancher Blake that night, it being too late to return to town. We were up early the next morning, and after breakfast drove out along the range of hills bordering the lake. We were out on a reconnoitering and pleasure trip and had no fixed designs against the numerous wildfowl that sported among the sedgy marshes.

For hours the white geese came streaming down the lake, flock after flock, as far as the eye could reach, until one could trace the thin waving lines far away in the dim distance, and back beyond the range of human sight the birds came creeping into view like an endless chain.

It was very still and clear and we lingered about on the bluffs, reluctant to take leave of a scene that is seldom witnessed even in the great game resorts of the West. Autumn days are wont to linger in the memory like the perfume of some favorite flower in the senses.

The human heart has its calms and storms, and sometimes, like a great ship at sea, goes throbbing on with measured pulse beneath a tropical sky and favored winds. But sometimes we awake from our fancied security to find the great ship in distress, storm-stricken in its flight. Fateful sounds come echoing from some dark abyss and danger lights flash out their timely warnings. But sooner or later the great ship will swing at anchor in some peaceful harbor, storm-worn and battered, but ready to continue the voyage of life as the forces of Nature and destiny may prescribe.

Minneapolis, Minn.

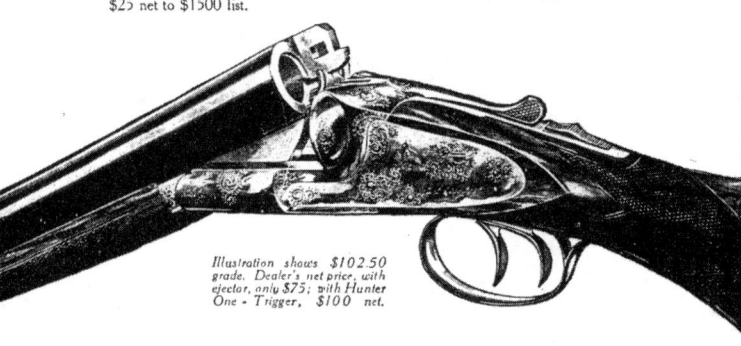

Advertisement from Outer's Book for August, 1912. Many early day wildfowlers used L.C. Smith shotguns with praises for their workmanship and shooting qualities.

PART 2
(The American Field)

DUCK SHOOTING IN NORTHERN DAKOTA
By Pin Tail
1884

St. Vincent is situated in the extreme northwestern corner of Minnesota, upon the banks of the Red River of the North. It is a lively little town of about five hundred inhabitants, and is the terminus of both the St. Paul, Minneapolis and Manitoba and the Canadian Pacific railroads. Better than all, however, it is surrounded by as fine a game country as one could possibly desire.

Twenty-five miles from here, in Dakota, is the Big Slough, where, in the month of September, 1883, I spent two very successful days among the ducks—days which I shall always remember with pleasure.

Our party on the occasion referred to numbered eight, named respectively: Masher Joe; Tom, his partner; Ike, who is pretty good at slinging type, but an indifferent shot; Jim, who does not care much for shooting, but always likes to be with the boys; Jack and Phil, two jolly good fellows; K., the driver, the handsomest man in the party, and lastly your humble servant, of whom more anon.

Much time was occupied, after getting the party together, in loading our wagon with the boat, plenty of provisions and all the other articles necessary for comfort and convenience, but finally, at two o'clock in the morning, we drove down to the ferry, which we found waiting for us on the Minnesota side, and we were soon across the raging Red, safely landed on Dakota soil.

Jim was perched upon the front seat with the driver, as he was the only one who knew the way, and it even puzzled him sometimes, for it was pitch dark. Nevertheless, we enjoyed the drive very much, for not only did Tom amuse us with his imitation of his team calliope, but Joe also, who is an expert with the harmonica, entertained us with some choice selections, among which were those old favorites, "Home, Sweet Home," and "The Mocking Bird." When he became tired of music he told us of some of his wonderful shots, which, let me assure you, are indeed wonderful, for Joe is a remarkable shot. I have seen him break, with his Winchester rifle, fifteen beer bottles straight, when thrown in the air at forty yards distance. I have also seen him make a double on two bottles thrown in the air at the same time.

Time passed rapidly, and almost before we were aware we had reached the half-way slough, which is about twelve miles from our starting point. It then being light enough, we all decided to get out and give our team a rest, while we made a grand charge upon this slough. Each of us had taken a different direction, but I happened to be near Joe, who was working his way through the long grass to the edge of the slough, when suddenly there was a great fluttering and quacking in front of us, and as Joe brought his gun to his shoulder and the two reports rang out upon the still morning air, two mallards fell fluttering into the marsh.

"A double, by Jove," I exclaimed.

"Yes," said Joe, "and the easiest double I ever made."

The continuous shooting in the direction of the other boys told us plainly that they were not idle, but we concluded that we had spent time enough here if we intended to reach our destination, so we called the driver and had him bring up the dogs, which retrieved the birds, and we returned to the wagon with seven fine, fat mallards.

When we were about ready to start, Phil called our attention to the dog Turk, which was on a point some distance to the left of us. We supposed he had found prairie chickens, but on coming up to him we made the discovery that it was not prairie chickens, but skunks. We immediately beat a retreat to a more distant and safer standpoint, and concluded that this variety of game required a chokebore gun and five drams of good powder. We had both, and used them, too, but that skunk seemed to bear a charmed life. However, after we had fired half a dozen shots a well-directed one from Jack put him to sleep, and the problem was solved—we had been shooting at his tail, the only portion visible above the tall grass. After this little episode we were soon again rattling along the road, and the half-way slough was quickly left in the distance.

We had determined not to stop again on the way, but after passing several promising stubble fields we came to one so tempting that we could not resist, and the dogs were cast off. They soon found game, and we had some very nice shooting, and after making in all fifteen shots we returned to the wagon with twelve fine prairie chickens, which we considered very fair shooting.

On arriving at Story's we were greeted with a hearty "Good morning, gentleman," from the old man himself.

"How are the ducks, Mr. Story?" I asked.

"Well," he replied, "there are more than you can carry in that wagon, and from the looks of your guns you will, no doubt, get your share of them."

His two daughters now came out to welcome us, and Joe, who had succeeded in working his way to the front, was soon on a point, but the game did not flush worth a cent.

After bidding them good morning, and getting permission from the old gentleman to use his boat, we drove on to P__'s place, where we were soon busily engaged in unloading our wagon. P__, who was living in town at the time, had kindly given us permission to use his shanty during our stay. The building was provided with a stove and cooking utensils, and all things necessary to camp life. While K. drove over to Story's to get his boat before he unhitched the team, the rest of us began preparations for breakfast, which were completed by the time he returned, which he did speedily, in order to be in time to help us dispose of it.

The slough, distant from the shanty but a quarter of a mile, and over which we could see the ducks flying in great numbers, is a body of shallow water about three or four miles long, from a quarter to half a mile wide and from one to six feet deep. Its shores are covered with reeds and swale grass four or five feet high, making the very best of blinds; some places the reeds extend completely across the slough.

Breakfast over, we donned our corduroys and left K. in charge of the camp with instructions not to get any dinner (it being already 9 o'clock A. M.), but to have a good supper ready for us when we returned, with a little hot toddy handy in case any of us should get wet. Joe meanwhile having strapped on the medal of the champion wingshot of Manitoba, led the van, and the procession moved on.

Arriving at the slough, the boys with the muzzle-loaders agreed to remain on the shore as it was more convenient for them to load, and they were soon snugly ensconced in their blinds; we with the breech-loaders, however, took the boats—Joe in one and Ike and myself in the other—and endeavored to make it interesting for the boys on the shore. We finally arranged ourselves in such a position that when Joe fired at a flock they would swing around to the boys on the shore; they in turn would blaze away and Ike and I would get a crack at what was left, but when they came from the other direction we had the first chance.

We did not have to wait long, for the ducks were flying, and we were soon hard at work. Presently the magic phrase: "Mark right!" from Ike, drew my attention to a single mallard coming straight toward our blind.

"He's mine," said Ike; "no; yes," and on he came, and then Ike opened on him and scored one of the prettiest misses on record, and as the duck sailed away, Ike called after him:

"Go it, you gay and festive old cuss, you are doomed to die anyhow, and I know it."

And so it proved, for as he swung around over the boys on shore, a well directed shot from Jim's gun brought him fluttering to earth.

Again it was, "Mark left," and this time there came a flock of teal, and I have just time to exclaim:

"This is a side shot' aim three feet ahead," when with a "whizz" they shot past us. At the crack of our guns, however, we had the satisfaction of seeing two drop.

"That's all pure luck," said Ike, "a fellow might as well try to bag a streak of lightning as those birds."

"Yes," I replied, "I think they are the hardest of all to shoot."

I had scarcely time to finish my sentence when I heard: "Mark straight on." This time a flock of sandhill cranes were seen jabbering and slowly working their way toward our blind. We were in the act of changing shells for those loaded with BB, when a shot was heard from Joe's blind, and on looking up our cranes were seen swerving off to the right of us, completely out of range of our guns, having been frightened by the report of Joe's gun.

It was now getting dark; the ducks were pouring in by the thousands, and we had excellent sport for a short time, but presently, on looking toward the house, we saw K. beckoning us to come to supper, and calling Joe, we gathered up our game and returned to camp. Upon counting up we found that our bag numbered thirty mallards and sixteen teals; as many more perhaps were lost in the tall weeds of the marsh.

We had not eaten anything since breakfast, and consequently very much surprised K. by the rapidity with which we caused the supper to disappear, and we began to fear that the poor dogs would have to go to bed hungry that night, until K. set our fears at rest by informing us that he had taken the precaution to feed them first, when we went on and cleared off the table effectually and quickly. After supper we cleaned and oiled our guns and loaded more shells for the morrow, and then filling our pipes with fragrant Vanity Fair, we sat down to a little game commonly called "poker," using gun wads for chips.

> "In the scene that ensued
> I did not take a hand,
> But the floor it was strew'd
> Like the leaves on the strand
> With the cards that Joe had been hiding
> In the game he did not understand."

Finally, when bed-time came, we spread some clean wheat straw on the floor, and laying ourselves down, with buffalo robes and coats for covering, we were soon in dreamland. Nothing occurred to disturb our peaceful slumbers save now and then a growl from the dogs, and occasionally Ike, who had retired before the rest, was heard to mutter something about sandhill cranes.

Next morning we were again up before daylight, and busily engaged in preparing breakfast, and that finished, we again repaired to the slough and were soon in our blinds, anxiously awaiting the light.

Our sport on this, the second day, was similar to that of the first; now a hit, now a miss, and every little while a duck would come tumbling down. I stood in my boat hidden from the birds by the tall reeds and rushes, and as the ducks came into my decoys, set out in an open place, I got many fine shots, and the great majority of them proved fatal to the ducks.

When we returned to the shanty and counted up our bag, we found that it was somewhat larger than that of the previous day, and numbered sixty birds, about equally divided between mallards and teals. We had expected to find geese here too, but I am inclined to think that we were a little too early for them.

As it had been determined at supper on the previous evening that we should return home this day, we began preparations for leaving; the boat was again loaded upon the wagon, the blankets, ducks, and what little provisions remained were packed away, and we moved off upon our homeward journey. We chose a different route going home, in order to stop at the Iceland Cooley, where we increased our bag to the extent of nine mallards. But our sport was not all over yet; when within three miles of home some one suggested looking for prairie chickens, but the most of us thought that it was too near town for them, and that it would be useless to look for them; Joe thought differently, however, as he had been here before. The dogs were accordingly cast off, and Curly was soon on a point, but you may be sure we were somewhat backward in going up to flush, as the adventure with the skunk on the preceding day was still fresh in our memory. We stood for some time admiring the dogs; the remaining two having now come up and backed Curly, and at last summoned courage enough to come up and flush the birds, and I distinguished myself by missing with my first barrel, but did good execution with my second; Joe, however, bagged two and Jack one. We marked them down a little ways off, and continued to pound our shoulders to our heart's content, bagging in all eighteen birds, and leaving the rest for breeding purposes.

It now being 9 o'clock p.m., and too dark to hunt further, we drove on our way and soon found ourselves again waiting for the ferry, refreshed both in body and mind by our trip.

In conclusion, I wish to say to those who may be seeking for some relief for their tired minds and bodies: Let them rough it for a few days among the ducks of Northern Dakota.

Grand Forks, D. T.

NORTH DAKOTA NOTES
(Mandan, Dak.)
1885

To the sportsman North Dakota presents a field which will probably compare favorably with almost any other portion of the United States. From Fargo to Medora, along the line of the Northern Pacific railroad the country fairly swarms with game of all kinds. On the uplands are to be found pintail and pinnated grouse, several different kinds of plover; the ponds, sloughs and lakes are alive with all kinds of geese, ducks, cranes and snipes, while in the "coulies" or ravines and in the timber along the streams black and white tail deer are plentiful. Antelopes, too, are numerous, while in the famous Bad Lands are found elks, deer, mountain sheep, bears and antelopes. Besides these, for the lover of the chase are found numerous wolves, coyotes, foxes, swifts and jackrabbits, sufficient to try the mettle of the best hound.

When I came to this country I thought I had seen geese in Iowa, Minnesota and Nebraska, but when in Kidder County, fifty miles east of here, I saw a million geese (more or less and rather more) rise off one stubble, I began to think I knew nothing about geese whatever. One of the most celebrated and best places for ducks and geese is Long Lake, which is in Burleigh County, about twenty-five miles southeast of Bismarck. It is some twenty miles long, and from three hundred yards to a mile wide, and in the Fall and Spring is a favorite stopping place for ducks and geese. There is fine feed in the lake itself and smaller ponds around it, while the immense grain fields around it also give most excellent feeding grounds.

A party of us left here one bright morning last October, and crossing the Missouri on the ferry stopped for a short while in the lively city of Bismarck, and then struck out for the lake. We arrived there about four o'clock in the afternoon and while some of the party put up the tent and made camp at the foot of a high butte which stands at the east end of the lake, the rest of us put on our rubber boots, took our guns and waded out in the lake to see if we could get a shot at some of the many geese and ducks, which, frightened by our approach, were circling about and making a great racket. I waded out about one hundred yards, and concealing myself in a patch of tall grass, prepared for active work. I did not have to wait long for soon an old greenhead came within easy range, and an ounce of No. 4 shot, backed by four and a half drams of good powder in my ten-bore settled him. From then until dark I had fine sport and came into camp with some fifteen ducks and two geese. The rest of the boys had equally good luck and we ate our supper in high spirits over the success of the day and prospect of the morrow.

Daylight the next morning found us at our posts, Joe H. and I on the south side of the lake, and the rest scattered out in different places. There did not seem to be a bird in our end of the lake when we took our stands, but about sunrise the geese began to come in, and for an hour or more as far as the eye could see there was one continuous flight of geese. Geese to the right of us, geese to the left of us, honked and occasionally tumbled. I was in the line of flight, but three of the fellows were ahead of me, consequently when the geese got to me they were a trifle high, but my gun throws shot well and occasionally one "took a drop," and once two came down. Five drams of powder, three wads and one and one-quarter ounces of BB shot in a ten-pound full-choke gun is hard to resist if held right.

After the flight of geese the ducks came in, mallards, widgeons, sprigtails, all kinds of teals, bluebills, a few redheads, and I killed one canvasback and saw several more. It turned cold during the day and a strong wind came up, which made the shooting fine. The next day we shot until ten o'clock, then packed up and came home, which we reached safely, much pleased with our trip. Our bag consisted of about three hundred ducks and fifty geese to eight men, which was fair considering five out of the eight were new hands entirely at the business, four of them never having shot at a goose or duck before. We could have killed a great many more geese had we had decoys, and gone to the stubbles and dug pits and set the decoys, as that is the best way to shoot them out here. None of these birds were wasted, but were divided up and distributed amongst our friends here and in Bismarck.

I am sorry to say that the game laws out here are almost a dead letter and are constantly being violated. It is the intention of a few of us to form a game protective association soon, engage a competent lawyer and endeavor to enforce the law in this county at least. There are some few good dogs owned here in town, but the best are yet puppies. Herter's Irish Sam and Gordon Frank; Jos. Hager's Irish Champ and Doyer's Irish Bird are all good ones. I am the owner of a five-months-old white, black and tan that I expect great things of, for he is certainly the brightest and most precocious puppy I ever saw.

Cow Boy

SHOOTING WILDFOWL IN DAKOTA
by White Crane
1885

Mr. Frank Bowe and the writer having business in Barnes county, Dakota, packed our grips with shells, rubber boots and loading tools, and with our Parker guns took the train at Brandon, Wisconsin, Monday afternoon en route for Sanborn, a smart little town about seventy miles west of Fargo, on the Northern Pacific Railroad.

We reached our destination the following Wednesday at noon, and found Mr. A. A. Booth awaiting us with a good team and double buggy to take us to his farm, twelve miles north of Sanborn. After dinner we purchased a good supply of ammunition and started out. Before reaching Mr. Booth's place it began to rain, and continued until after dark. Nevertheless, upon our arrival we immediately changed our clothes, loaded a few shells and drove out two miles to shoot geese as they came into the lake. We were a little late, but came in with three fine geese and four ducks, and well satisfied with the first night's sport. After supper and smoking our pipes we loaded our shells and planned for the next day. We were up at four o'clock next morning and went to a large slough about two miles distant. The morning was foggy and mallards looked as large as geese. We stationed ourselves around the slough, while the ducks flew around lively with now and then a flock of geese. The shooting was splendid for two hours and when we came together we found we had bagged four geese and forty mallards, which was quite a load for three of us to carry two miles.

The afternoon was occupied in shooting ducks with abundant success. Saturday we drove twelve miles north in search of better goose shooting; but we stopped for a few moments at a large slough to shoot ducks, and found them so plentiful that we unhitched the team and took our stations. At about four o'clock it commenced to rain, but we were having such fine shooting that we did not mind the wet. Just at dusk a few geese came in, and finally when we stopped shooting our bags contained four geese, thirty ducks and three grouse. We were then wet to the skin and had twelve miles to ride in the wind and rain. During the day we found where thousands of sandhill cranes and white cranes were feeding upon a piece of grain in the shock. We, therefore, planned on Monday to get a white crane. They are very difficult to obtain; at least the sportsmen in that section say so, for it is nearly impossible to build a cover that they will not detect.

We were on hand Monday morning before daybreak and concealed in the shocks of Dakota's "No. 1 hard." The ducks came first, then a few flocks of geese, but they were too high; next followed the cranes. It was amusing in the extreme to listen to the cranes, geese and ducks just at day break on a large slough about one mile distant making their preparations to fly out after their food. It was one continual quack, quack; honk, honk, and co-r-r-, co-r-r-r. The first flock of white cranes made directly for me, and when I thought them in fine range raised upon my knees and fired both barrels, but without success. Mr. Bowe was stationed at one side and could tell the distance, which he claimed to be one hundred and twenty-five yards. This I find to be characteristic on the prairies; the distance is far greater than we calculate.

I had not long to wait before I saw three white cranes coming directly for me again. Waiting this time until I could see their eyes, I arose and downed one with each barrel, killing them dead. Mr. Bowe then placed one of them near his station and I the other near mine for decoys, when we again waited the approach of more. Soon a fine flock of them were coming directly for Frank, when one of the party fired at some geese fully one mile high; this of course scared away the cranes. Again one came for Frank and just as he was preparing to shoot the same party fired again and spoiled his shot the second time. Had one of our party stayed at home, we surely would have bagged five white cranes. By the way, however, we had some little bets upon who should down the most white cranes and the party above alluded to was on hand in the morning with a Winchester rifle and a breech-loading shotgun loaded for bear. We made up our minds no one would get another shot at white cranes, so we drove to a little slough about a mile away where Frank killed a goose and each of us bagged several ducks. Thus ended the hunt. We bagged, in the four days, fourteen geese, two white cranes, one hundred and fifty ducks and three grouse. The white cranes are magnificent birds measuring seven and one-half feet across the wings. One of them was left with Mr. Seagerford of Sanborn to mount and place with his collection. I think a better place for goose and duck shooting cannot be found in Dakota than in the county of Barnes. There are plenty of small lakes and sloughs. We were a little too early for the best goose shooting. Any sportsman happening that way to hunt will find in Mr. A. A. Booth a genial sportsman and a gentleman, looking only for the welfare and enjoyment of his guests. He is farming a whole section of land, has good buildings and is in a beautiful country swarming with game.

Brandon, Wis.

JAMESTOWN, DAKOTA - A SPORTSMAN'S MECCA
By James Whitman
1886

Jamestown, Dakota Territory, on the line of the Northern Pacific Railroad, is 367 ½ miles west of St. Paul and 1548 ½ miles east of Portland, Oregon, one of the *termini* of that great railway thoroughfare—for such it has now become. The passenger travel this season, both for pleasure and business, has been unprecedented in its annals; whilst, as I am credibly informed, its traffic earnings for August last showed an increase of over $200,000 compared with those of the corresponding month of 1885. The little "shacks" on the prairie have been, and are being, replaced by huge establishments, with acreage under tillage, running up into the thousands—some into the tens of thousands, of which the great Dalrymple farm is a specimen. This famous farm is stated in the guide books to consist of 25,000 acres under cultivation; but this year, I am told, Mr. Dalrymple has cut over 30,000 acres of wheat alone. The station at Dalrymple, Dakota, on the line of the Northern Pacific Railroad, 75 miles east of Jamestown, marks the site of the farm, and from thence in the distance may be seen some of its red-colored buildings; but the great bulk of the land stretches away out of sight for miles to the north and the south of the railway.

Seldom does nature prepare so beautiful a site for a city as that which Jamestown—"the gem of the prairie"—presents in its charming valley with the living arms of the river caressingly circling its cradle; for Jamestown is a baby yet—in years. Six Summers since the census showed less hundreds of people in Jamestown than could be counted on a single hand; now, the number of thousands it holds requires both hands to tell their figures on. The streets are broad, rectangular and adorned with solid, substantial and, in many cases, striking structures. Nearly every state in the Union and every nation in Europe seems to be represented here, and seemingly to come from the more intelligent, industrious and enterprising classes of the states and countries they represent. The educational advantages are great (Dakota already possessing more than 2,000 schools), as the law makes liberal provision for the support and perpetuation of public schools, free throughout the territory, by reserving two sections of land in each township for their maintenance; while there is a college in operation which affords the opportunity of the higher classes of study. Besides the four schools in Jamestown, there are seven churches; but whether the same seven mentioned in the Revelations is scarcely to be esteemed a fair subject for inquiry.

Branching north and south from Jamestown, there are two lines of the Northern Pacific Railway Company—the former to Minnewaukan, on the celebrated Devils Lake—if one devil can be said to be more celebrated than another. At any rate, this lake is very celebrated for its sport. The distance to the lake is 90 miles from Jamestown, and on the road a short line of railway branches off to Sykeston, near which is one of the two very large tracts of land in Dakota owned and farmed by Messrs. Sykes & Co.— English capitalists of Manchester, who also own another very large and beautiful farm in the state of Iowa. The Northern Pacific branch hence to the south now runs to LaMoure, 48 miles, intending to connect with a railway rapidly reaching it from Yankton, on the Missouri, the southern boundary of Dakota, near its confluence with the James River, which latter, though it seems so little known, is over 1,000 miles in length. There is an impression in England that a law has been, or is about to be, passed in the United States to interfere with the ownership of land by foreigners. The fact is, that in every state in the Union, except New York and Vermont, an Englishman can buy and hold land as free as an American can buy and hold land in England. The Northern Pacific Railroad Company holds immense and valuable blocks of the best of farming lands which, to encourage settlement, are offered for sale at exceptionally reasonable rates—though the choicer country is fast being taken up. Still there is an abundance of free land to be had in Dakota, and second-hand purchases of excellent quality can be made at $4 to $8 per acre, according to situation and proximity to towns and railroads.

With these great railway arteries from east, west, north and south, Jamestown must soon become one of the chief headquarters for the many sportsmen who will undoubtedly flock to this region when its immense resources of fish and game shall have become better known. Among the numerous lakes in its vicinity, the Spiritwood lakes, a chain of five or six, stand pre-eminent for the sport, both in fishing and shooting, which they afford. These lakes lie about fourteen miles distant from Jamestown, and abound with pike, mascalonge and thunder-fish—the latter sometimes running up to eighty pounds in weight. It is said that a cart-load of fish can be caught in a couple of hours. Before the lands were plowed grouse were in great abundance; and now, by their retreat from the wheat stubble, the prairie chickens have succeeded in equal numbers. Wild geese in enormous flocks come right after the chickens leave. These geese are so plenty that you can sometimes see whole sections (640 acres to the section) black with them for miles. After the geese come the ducks—the mallards last. The season for ducks is just commencing and lasts till about the first week in November. After the ducks comes frost. While there are numerous deer, the antelopes are more abundant—especially in the neighborhood of the Coteux Hills, about twenty miles from Jamestown. I am told that tents for camping out can be obtained from the livery stables here, and all kinds of sporting goods from O. St. C. Chenery, a dealer in guns, ammunition and fishing tackle. This would relieve the sportsman of a great deal of trouble in lugging along his heavy equipage and ammunition, as he can get both almost upon the spot.

The hotel accommodations at Jamestown are not surpassed along the route of the Northern Pacific Railroad, and this, after the splendid hotels I have mentioned at Detroit and Moorhead, in Minnesota, is saying much. The sketch which your artist presents herewith of the Gladstone Hotel at Jamestown reveals no less external architectural attraction than is presented by the comfort of its internal arrangements provided by that popular manager, Mr. Sam Mathews, as the landlord. Your artists herewith, also presents a sketch of Jamestown as viewed from one of the adjacent hills, by which, as like a line of stalwart Roman wall with the river for its moat, it is surrounded. The North Dakota Hospital for the Insane forms the subject of the concluding sketch. By the kindness of its eminent resident superintendent, Dr. O. Wellington Archibald, who has made an envious reputation for his successful treatment of this unfortunate class in the neighboring State of Iowa, the writer and your artist were shown by him all through the institution, which has only been opened this season. It is one of the two public insane hospitals in Dakota Territory, the other being located at Yankton, in South Dakota. This one of the north stands upon the broad plateau on the summit of the hill encircling Jamestown to the west, from whence there opens a most magnificent view. The land appertaining to the hospital, erected at a cost of $115,000, embraces a whole section of 640 acres; while all the vegetable gardening, with other kinds of work, is performed

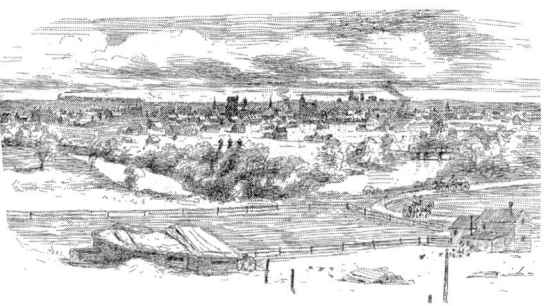

The City of Jamestown, N.D., From The Hills Overlooking The James River

by patients in the institution. There is an unfailing supply of water which, both cold and hot, is forced by steam-pump throughout the building. Steam heat and the electric light—the incandescent of Edison's system—is furnished all over the buildings, where, although some of the 125 patients therein contained are considered dangerous, there is not a single iron bar to be seen upon any of the windows; nor, as the Doctor assured me, since he has taken charge,

Jamestown, N.D.

has a single pane of glass been broken by any of the patients and only one of them has taken French leave—he, a former convict, being paroled for church. Upon the superintendent's stating the Government's intention to erect more buildings and my consequent inquiry whether the ratio of insane persons to the whole population of the territory was large, he informed me that such proportion was the smallest in the Union—being only 1 in 1850 persons, while in California it has reached the ratio of 1 in 350. The whole system speaks as highly for the management of the superintendent as it does for the liberal humanity of the territorial government. Dr. Archibald is a Canadian from Nova Scotia.

Division into two separate states and admission into the Union are now the ruling questions of this region; but as they are questions on which it would be extra-judicial in your correspondent to offer an opinion, he leaves them in full confidence that the near future will see this rich and fast-growing territory, now containing over 400,000 souls, emblazoned among the stars that, along with the stripes, float over the broad expanse of the whole United States.

Jamestown, Dak.

DAKOTA GAME NOTES
(Menoken, Dakota)
1886

Editor *The American Field*:—I feel it incumbent on me, in part payment for the benefit and pleasure which I receive in perusing the pages of *The American Field*, to try and interest some of the readers with an account of the sport to be had in this part of Uncle Sam's domain. The writer having had the misfortune to lose the only dog of any value for hunting purposes owned in this neighborhood, did not have any prairie chicken shooting the past season to speak of, but from what I have seen and from reports, I judge that they were quite plentiful. G. P. Miller, a sportsman of Bismarck and a gentleman, reported some good bags, ranging from thirty to fifty. Since cold weather came on I have seen large flocks of fifty or more. Ducks and geese have been here in the most astonishing numbers. The early Fall rains filled all of the slough places, so that good shooting could be had in almost any direction at water birds of all descriptions, from the diminutive rail to the stately mallard.

The best good shooting was on the stubble-fields over decoys, where some large bags were made. The largest bag reported for one day's shooting was made by W. B. Bell and another gentleman, of Bismarck, which was sixty-two. The geese were shot within two miles of the railroad station of Menoken, on a stubble-field of over six hundred acres in extent. That same stubble-field during the latter part of November was the resort of the greatest number of ducks and geese that the writer ever saw or heard of. To speak within bounds, I think I have seen five thousand ducks in the vicinity of that field at one time, and I think they were nearly all mallards. I did not visit that field for the purpose of shooting for the reason that I did not have the time to spare, and besides I could shoot all the ducks that I could make use of within one-fourth of a mile of my house, and I did not have to go over a mile from home to get good goose shooting. My partner and I usually shoot together and we would get from three to eight geese in about one hour's shooting, commencing at daylight. We usually had our blinds about eighty yards apart, with our decoys, which number just five, set out half way between us, and the geese coming in from the "big slough" would see the decoys and pass between us, when we would open on them with our 12-bore Colt guns, which seldom failed to bring one or more to the ground, with a thud that would send such a thrill of pleasure to the shooter as only a true lover of the sport can understand. One thing noticeable in the goose shooting this Fall was the large number of yellow-legged geese; fully one-half of the geese that we shot were of that kind. One year ago this Fall we did not shoot one of them.

 The writer witnessed quite an interesting scene on one occasion this past Fall. Dike and I started out one morning for a stubble-field where we had seen a number of geese flying around for a day or two. We did not get around as early as we intended, consequently when we stepped on one edge of the stubble-field the geese arrived on the opposite side. On seeing us they took a short circle around, while we made a dive into a straw stack near by. The geese soon came around, but being suspicious that the straw stack was not entirely what it seemed, they alighted on the grass ground just out of gunshot. There were at least two hundred of them, and such a racket as they did make. They puttered, scolded, hissed, and I think they swore some, but I am not well enough versed in their language to speak positively as to that. The deep bass of the Canada mingled with the shrill tenor of the yellow-legged geese made one continual roar. We watched them with great interest for some time, but as they showed no disposition to come within gunshot we crawled out of the straw and sent them off with a grand rush. The geese remained here quite late this Fall; I saw a flock December 5.

One year ago this time, there was quite a number of deer made their headquarters in the creek bottom within a few miles of this place, but this Fall very few have been seen, owing, in part, to the fact that they have been scared out by hounds and the prairies having been burned over in the north for a long way, which keeps them from coming down. Dike shot a very fine buck about the middle of November; it was the largest and had the finest and best-shaped set of antlers that I have seen. Deer have been quite plentiful in the timber along the Missouri River, and a good many have been killed. Charles Russ of this place, in company with two other gentlemen from Bismarck, has recently returned from a thirty days' trip in the Upper Missouri country, where they killed forty-two deer. Whether that was sport or slaughter I leave to the readers of *The American Field*, but I feel confident if a vote should be taken the verdict would be murder in the first degree.

During the cold weather a good many antelopes usually come down into the settlements, but they have not appeared yet this Winter, and whether they will get down over the burned district or not remains to be seen. If they do we are ready for them and will entertain them in true sportsman style.

W.T.T.

WHERE TO GO TO GET GOOD GOOSE SHOOTING
By Dr. J. L. Williamson
1893

With the permission of the editor of *The American Field* I will answer H. T. H., of Springfield, Mass., and many others who have inquired of me where to go to get good goose shooting, the time to go, what to take along, what can be done with the overplus of game that may be secured, and also some other questions pertaining to the sport.

In the first place, I believe North Dakota offers perhaps the best inducement to goose hunters, although northern Minnesota is in some respects better, especially for those who are anxious to get large numbers of Canada geese. The goose hunter will notice that Canada's frequent mainly fresh or sweet water lakes—a little point worth knowing and bearing in mind, as I have never seen any mention made of this in all my extensive reading upon the subject. The white geese, white-fronted, blue, and even the Hutchin's geese seem to consider alkali water good enough for them; but the Hutchin's, I have noticed, prefer the sweet water lakes to the others. For all varieties, however, save the exceptions above noted, North Dakota from the Red River west to Bismarck and beyond, is one vast goose pasture. There is, however, a strip of country that seems to be a favorite with them, that extends from a point about half way between Fargo and Jamestown on the east, to a point of from twenty-five to fifty miles west of Dawson on the west, and over this territory the geese pass annually in vast numbers in their southern migration. In the spring of the year they seem to spread out more, and are found scattered over a much larger space, but as we are interested only in their Fall flight we will consider that only.

Devils Lake, Stump Lake, Jim Lake, Arrowwood Lake, Long Lake, Goose Lake, and all of that country from one hundred to one hundred and fifty miles in any direction from Devils Lake, is a good place to go for geese, cranes, swans, pelicans, ducks and antelope. A few black-tailed deer also are to be found west of Devils Lake. Now, as to the time. I should say, any time after September 25. There is a small flight of geese usually about the first of October, and a large flight of cranes. About October 16 occurs the first really large flight of geese. The geese stop and feed, and their numbers are constantly being augmented by fresh arrivals from the north. About October 25 to 28, as a rule, the birds come in hordes, in multitudes. The air is filled with the gyrating, honking seekers of a warmer clime, and they remain until driven south by severe weather. They feed in the stubble-fields until the fields are covered with snow, and are loth even then to leave if there is any open water to be had. They must have water twice a day. They are voracious feeders. They do not stop to pick up kernels of wheat, but swallow the heads of the grain entire.

Again, as to what is necessary to take along. Besides a strong shooting, heavy gun of large caliber and suitable ammunition, a good Allen goose caller should be taken. That one article of a goose-shooter's outfit I consider almost indispensable in the successful pursuit of these large birds. One can perhaps call well with the mouth, but it is extremely difficult to make oneself heard at any considerable distance calling that way, especially if there is much wind, and that condition of affairs obtains almost continually during the latter half of the month of October. Learn to call well with the artificial caller, and get one with a stiff reed; one that can be blown at the full strength of the lungs and not have the tone "split," as I call it. When you notice that an approaching flock of geese are attracted by the call, do not continue blowing, for that would be a fatal blunder. Duck your head down in the pit and call a few times, but in a much gentler and subdued manner. Cover the end of the call with your hands; call once or twice when the birds are close to your blind, and then suspicion on their part will be well nigh disarmed and they will set their wings, drop their legs and come in well over the decoys. All the goose calls that I have seen have one great fault; they are nickel-plated and one must be extremely careful not to allow the flickering, glancing light to be so thrown off that the geese will notice it and pass a much disgusted, would-be goose slayer far to one side and out of range. The goose calls should be painted or japanned some dull, neutral color, and this trouble would be obviated. I am very much surprised that the manufacturers of goose calls have not "caught on" to this. We might just as properly have nickel-plated gun barrels and expect to succeed in approaching game as to flourish those highly polished callers in the sunlight and hope for success.

Now, as to provisions. One need not tote them around for any great distance. Strong & Chase, of Jamestown, can furnish you with everything you may need, clothing of all kinds for that climate, canned goods of all varieties, leather and rubber boots, coats, blankets, shells—10 and 12 gauge, empty or loaded in any quantity—and all these articles at metropolitan prices or cheaper. They are splendid men to deal with and will send goods to any part of North Dakota on the shortest possible notice, and, being very fond of goose shooting himself, Mr. Chase knows just what is required.

You speak of a tent. I hardly think you will require one, especially if you go late in October, for you can find good accommodations at a farmhouse or at any of the little towns or villages. A team and driver can be had at from $2.50 to $4 per day; and you will enjoy the advantage of being with a man who knows the country well, and that counts for much up there. It is very easy to get lost on the prairies after dark, as our party found on more than one occasion. The people are glad to have goose hunters come out there, as thousands of bushels of grain are destroyed annually by both geese and cranes, and anything that will kill or scare the birds away from the fields will be appreciated by the farmers. One man told me that our party was worth ten dollars a day to him in the saving of grain. The geese not only feed in the stubble but get right on the wheat shocks, knock down the cap sheaves and break off and destroy lots of grain besides what they eat, which is no inconsiderable quantity.

Do not allow the fear that you will kill so many geese that you cannot dispose of them in any way cause you any uneasiness, especially if you are inclined to use a light or small bore gun. If your stay should be prolonged to two or three weeks, you may have during that time splendid shooting at short range, on two or three, possibly on more occasions than that. Do not expect to get good shooting every day, if you do you will be disappointed. You may strike a good flight or you may successfully shoot to-day, for instance, from a stubble-field pit and to-morrow the geese may feed five or ten miles away from that locality. One can never tell in advance which direction they will go when they leave the lakes. It depends very much on the strength and direction of the wind. They almost invariably fly against the wind except when migrating, and then how they can go! Just try shooting at a few single geese coming down wind that is blowing a fifty mile gale, and decide for yourself as to the "hold on" or the "hold ahead theory."

It was the custom of our party to guard jealously the feeding grounds of the morning flight and to see that no other shooters anticipated us and took up their stands there for the afternoon flight, for as a rule, the geese return to the same grounds in the afternoon if not disturbed in the early part of the day. We were on more than one occasion much chagrined by allowing geese to feed unmolested in the afternoon and then getting up early in the morning before daybreak, and, after driving perhaps six or eight miles, find other parties just ahead of us and insisting that those very geese were the ones they were after, and that they proposed to stop right there and shoot. In such an event one of us had to leave, and usually the other fellow got the shooting. We would then be obliged to drive away a distance of a mile or so and pick up what few stragglers happened to come along. As likely as not we would not get a half dozen good shots between us; but in the afternoon it was far different. We would drive out leisurely to where we saw geese pitching down in the morning, take our lunch along, wait until the geese left for the lakes of their own accord, then drive on to the grounds, dig our pits, eat our dinners, set out the decoys and have everything in readiness when the first flock showed up, which, late in the Fall, is as early as 1 o'clock p.m., and from that time on until sundown we would have excellent sport. And by watching the morning flight we got morning flight shooting and afternoon pit shooting every day of our stay.

Now as to blinds. Perhaps you have had but little experience in this kind of sport. Let me give you a few pointers. Do not, unless you have an abundance of time, spend from half an hour to an hour in digging a pit—the hardest kind of work even if you have lots of time. Do not pile the dirt high up around the excavation. You must not have a heavy or solid appearing blind or bank of dirt about you; and if you throw the earth far back of you, be sure and cover it over well, but lightly, with straw, stubble, weeds, etc. A poorly constructed blind is fatal to good decoy goose shooting. One of the very best and most easily constructed blinds, and a convenient and cheap one withal, is to take a net, such as can be had from all net or sail makers, in six feet long sections, eighteen or twenty inches wide, with meshes of one-quarter inch. Take two or three such sections, roll them up and put them in your pockets or shellbox or bag until you are on the feeding grounds, then dig a shallow pit and around it stretch the nets in an oblong shape, fasten them to the ground by a few little stakes or still reeds, having the nets lean in over the pit so that at the top the opening is about half as large as at the bottom. Then get your gun, shells, coats, spade, etc., in the pit, jump in yourself and you are ready to receive calls. It would be well to weave into the meshes of the nets a few weeds or bunches of grass. From such a blind you can see the approaching geese all the time and they will not notice you. When the flock is over you or to the side, which will depend on the way your decoys are set, rise to your feet and shoot. In South Dakota the large tumble weeds make good blinds and answer the purpose of the nets in North Dakota.

The idea is, to be able to keep the geese constantly in view and yet to be hid from sight of the birds. Very few hunters seem to be aware of how prominently a man's face looms up in the grass or weeds, especially out on the prairies. That white face, perhaps partly covered by a black beard, frightens more geese than many would at first suppose; but I have noticed this thing so often that I am sure I am right in this respect.

A very good way to overcome this difficulty is, to wear a large, coarse, brown veil, or a piece of brown or dirty colored mosquito netting over the face; or one can take a child's parasol of the proper color, cut off the handle to about ten or twelve inches, and hold that over one's face. This can readily be carried in one's pocket, and the geese can be clearly seen through it when it is spread open. When you see a flock of geese approaching, drop on your back, get your feet and legs under the thick grass or stubble, have your gun cocked and lying diagonally across your body, hold the little parasol over your head and face, and if you keep your body and legs still, you can turn your face in any direction in watching the coming flock and need have no fears of alarming them. When the birds are directly over you, drop the parasol, and also drop as many of the geese as you can. Another good way is to take a lady's fan, cut off the cloth and paste a veil or piece of cheese cloth of brown color over it. This held in front of the face will do well also; anything to effectually hide the face.

Now, as to decoys, Messrs. Horne & Danz of St. Paul, Minn.,

make a very beautiful one in profile, of metal. They are rather expensive, and fifty of them weigh a good many pounds. Our club boys have about two hundred fine decoys, but they are made of wood. We went to Sheboygan, Wis., and from a paper pattern which we sent them, had a goose body in one piece and a head and neck of another cut out. We had them make us about one hundred and fifty of these, cut from maple and whitewood veneering such as is used in street car seats, chairs, etc. We then riveted the pieces together and painted them in good imitation of the birds we were after, and we now have a very fine lot of decoys. They are light, strong and stiff; do not rattle in the wind nor in the wagon as do the metal ones, and give complete satisfaction.

 Well, suppose you have only a dozen decoys, that is a very small flock. You should have as large a flock as possible. It is more essential than it is to have a large flock of decoy ducks when shooting those birds. You can do this in case you have but a few. Set your dozen decoys in a circle with heads pointing in all directions. In the open space you can put paper decoys made after this manner: Take a newspaper and roll it up into a large funnel or cornucopia; stick a pin through it to hold in place, leaving a tail-like projection on one side. Now place this paper cone over a bunch of stubble and have the projection of the paper point in the direction from which the wind blows; throw a couple of handfuls of earth on it so the wind will not blow it over, and so continue until you have three or four dozen decoys. These paper counterfeits will answer the purpose nearly as well as dead geese. As fast as you can put out your dead birds. Take you knife and cut a slit under the head and push the pointed end of a stick or reed well up into the head of the goose and run the other end of the stick down into the ground to the proper depth. These make really the best kind of decoys, as the wind ruffles up the feathers and causes them to look rather more lifelike. When we went out only a short distance from camp we usually threw a few of the dead geese into the wagon to use as decoys. These geese, which we had killed on the day previous, when returning to camp we would give away to the farmers, and keep those freshly killed for ourselves. We would thus have fresh birds all the time for our own use and none were allowed to go to waste.

Finally, if one likes shooting and is desirous of having one good goose shoot before he dies, I would say, go to North Dakota, step out from tent or house early in the morning, dilate your nostrils, throw back your shoulders, take deep, full inspirations of the purest ozone just fairly brimming over with health-giving and life-prolonging qualities. You will feel, my word for it, like an untamed mustang or a wild Indian. You will feel like the bridegroom mentioned in the good book: "He rejoiceth like a strong man to run a race." You will probably shy your castor on the grass, waltz up to the nearest man and seductively try to persuade him that you are the most harmless being in the universe, and at the same time secretly wish and even openly aver, that in your humble opinion, if he dares to lay even so much as one little finger upon you, in one short half minute thereafter you will not vouch for his anatomical integrity. You will even go so far as to declare that if any of your companions will step forward, not more than two or three at a time, you will undertake to lay them individually and collectively sprawling upon their backs. In fact you will know what it is to live, to breathe, and to have your being. You will find that every organ of your body will work in entire harmony and accord with every other piece of bodily mechanism. You will be unconscious of lungs, stomach, nose, throat or kidneys. In short you will be in the enjoyment of perfect health. Your wife will tell you when you return home that you are ten years younger; you will be able to make more money in a week than you had previously done in a month; the interest on your debts will not seem half so burdensome nor large; you will be willing to mortgage your household furniture even for a modern ejector and feel assured that no matter how expensive the gun you will have no difficulty in paying for it. For every man who neglects or allows his business to suffer owing to his love for field sports, there are twenty men who are ruining their health, becoming a burden to themselves and friends for the lack of such recreation. This I verily believe, and I base these remarks on personal observation.

Another thing, dear reader, which I nearly forgot to mention, and that is, take clothes of generous proportions with you. Do not think that because you now weigh 160 pounds you will return weighing only 161 pounds. You will find that you will be obliged to let out the strap about a notch every day. Would you believe it? I am afraid you won't, but it's a fact, that ten of us, after a day's tramp ate sixty-five snipes for supper!

Although it may be a trifle inconvenient considering the present price of provisions, do not, I beg of you, fail to bring back with you your recently acquired appetite.

Milwaukee, Wis.

GAME IN DAKOTA IN OLDEN TIMES
By A. Wall, M.D.
1894

Editor's Note: This is a noteworthy article because of the amount of information it contains about the wildlife that was in the Red River Valley prior to white settlement. The author, A. Wall, M.D., was with the command of Lieutenant Colonel Abercrombie who established a military post that was named after him. The date was 1857 and so the land was still in a mostly pristine state as when it was occupied by Native Americans.

At the time it was published I was much interested, as I have no doubt many others were, in the perusal of Mr. Leffingwell's graphic narration of his shooting trip to North Dakota, my pleasure being enhanced by the fact that he was shooting over ground that I often traversed thirty years ago with horse and hound, gun and pointers; and thinking that an account of the fur, fin and feather of that locality as it existed at the time I speak of might prove of interest to some of the many readers of *The American Field*, I will give it as concisely as I can.

In the capacity of assistant surgeon I accompanied the command of Lieut. Col. Abercrombie of the Second Infantry to the Red River of the North in the Autumn of 1857, that officer having orders to establish a military post on the banks of said river for the purpose of restraining the hostilities of the Indians of that country (the Sioux and Chippewas), and also for putting a stop to the operations of the trappers and hunters of the Hudson Bay Company, who were rapidly thinning out the game and furred animals of that part of Uncle Sam's farm. At the time I speak of the valley of the Red

River constituted the boundary line between the Chippewas on the east and the Sioux, or more properly, Lacotahs, on the west, so that these Indians seldom visited that locality for fear of encountering one another, the war between them having lasted so long that neither party knew when or how it originated. As a consequence large game, with the exception of buffaloes, was still abundant there. The buffaloes had been pretty well thinned out through the efforts of the employees of the Hudson Bay Company, and were only found in detached and diminutive herds at some points east of the Missouri River. Elks, however, were very numerous. As an illustration of the latter fact it is only necessary for me to state that upon one occasion a pack of timber wolves chased a herd of elk right through our encampment, and after running them a short distance beyond succeeded in pulling one down. Upon observing this, a voyageur, who was quietly mending his birch bark canoe on the outskirts of the encampment, ran into the midst of the wolves with his ax and succeeded in driving them off and securing their quarry. I subsequently asked him whether the wolves offered any resistance, and he replied that "one feller he growl a little" I will here digress so far as to remark that I am firmly of the opinion that there has been more wilful and downright lying upon the subject of wild animals having a propensity to attack human beings, than upon any other subject, save, perhaps, that of angling. But more of this hereafter.

On the Wild Rice River, which runs for some distance parallel to Red River, and at a distance of about five miles, the elk were particularly numerous, being attracted by the abundance of wild rice that grew upon the banks of that river and of which they are very fond. I seldom failed to secure a fat elk in that locality during the proper season. Owing to a lack of timber, bears and deer were not numerous in our immediate vicinity, but on the eastern side of the river, in the wooded lands of Minnesota, they were very abundant. So abundant were the deer at the period I speak of, that upon one occasion, as I was credibly informed while in that country, a band of Chippewa Indians, headed by Pug-o-na-ye-gick (a famous warrior and hunter of that tribe), killed four hundred deer in one day by surrounding a piece of woods. Large game was particularly abundant in the vicinity of Devil's Lake, for this spot was seldom visited by the Indians, as they entertained the idea that it was the favorite place of abode of his Satanic Majesty, and they were consequently very cautious about monkeying around that locality. The dread the Indians entertained of this lake was probably based upon the fact that in times of drought, when its water is low, it assumes a greenish hue and has a bad smell and taste, qualities imparted to it in all probability by the copper contained in the rocks which line its shores. But I am slipping away from my subject.

Of furred animals, such as the beaver, otter, mink, marten, muskrat, ermine, wolves, foxes, etc., the woods and streams were full, excepting the first named, which had been much reduced in numbers. In fact this section of the country still offered a fine field for the skill and enterprise of the trapper. Our interpreter, a half-breed Indian, was a most skillful trapper, and I frequently accompanied him when he went the rounds of his traps in order to while away time, of which I had an abundance, so that in the course of time I became, under his excellent instruction, an expert at the business.

Wolf and fox shooting at night during the Winter constituted one of our favorite and most exciting amusements. The way we went about our work was to dig a pit about five feet deep and large enough to hold four or five persons, fill this partly with straw on account of its warmth, then gather the offal that had been left from the cattle slaughtered for the use of the troop and place it upon the lowermost limbs of a tree near our pit, and at night we would repair, with guns and blankets, or buffalo robes, to our pit, and usually it would not be long before the fun would begin. The animals which usually came to our bait were two species of wolves and three of foxes, viz.: the timber or gray wolf (*Griseo-Albus*) and the coyote; the Arctic, cross fox and kit—the latter a most beautiful little animal. When undisturbed the big gray wolves would help themselves first, then the coyotes, and after these were satisfied the foxes would come in for their share, the little kit fox bringing up the rear.

When the animals would come to our bait we would give them a volley, and those that were not killed or too badly disabled to travel would scamper off to the woods, where they would howl and bark the remainder of the night, creating a most infernal din. The hunters, also, were not long in getting back to their huts and warm stoves, for they could not long endure a temperature of thirty or forty degrees below zero, which was the usual Winter temperature of that hyperborean clime. My companions commonly used double-barreled guns loaded with buckshot, but I always stuck to my Colt five shooters, carrying twenty-four round balls or fourteen long balls to the pound. This gun, I will remark, *en passant*, had been recommended to me by Major (afterward General) R. B. Marcy, who was the best civilized hunter and woodsman I ever had the pleasure of meeting. Our interpreter got his pelts far more comfortably and easily than we did ours, for he had a pitfall in which he was sure to secure some kind of a varmint every morning.

When the wild rice was ripe the wildfowl came down from the North in innumerable multitudes, the mallard ducks being by far the most numerous. The white or snow geese were not as numerous at the time I speak of as they are at present, according to the account of Mr. Leffingwell. That was probably owing to the fact that there was no grain raised in the valley of the Red River at the period I speak of, for the only human beings in the country at that time were a few soldiers and Indians, with here and there a wandering trapper. Swans, also, were scarce and difficult to get a shot at, for they were smart enough to keep in the middle of the lakes in the daytime, coming to the shore at night to feed. After the prairies were burnt off, an event which usually happened sometime in October, golden plovers would visit them in vast flocks. My favorite mode of shooting wildfowl was to drop quietly down the river in a birchbark canoe manned by a voyageur, the most skillful of oarsmen. I would thatch the prow of the canoe with rushes, and then, lying on my back, my expert companion would let me float into the very midst of the wildfowl, and I would given them one barrel on the water and the other when they lifted their wings to fly, and then my superb oarsman would send the canoe like an arrow among the crippled birds, which he would soon dispatch with his paddle. Thus we would pursue the sport until we had our canoe filled to repletion with geese, brant and ducks, and an occasional swan. Of all the rivers I had then ever shot over the Red River of the North was the most uniquely convenient, for, owing to its wonderful tortuosity, I could float upon its surface for hours and then upon ascending its banks find myself only a short distance from the point of departure. As to the plovers above alluded to, they were in the habit of coming to a slough about a mile or two below our encampment, from about 4 o'clock, in the afternoon until sundown, for a supply of water. These birds, as is well known, do not like to venture into brushwood or tall grass, and as the weeds and rushes along the shore of the slough in question had been well trodden down by our cattle, it afforded them an admirable watering place. At one end of this slough I built my blind so as to get an enfilading fire upon the ranks of the birds. At the hour indicated above the plovers would commence coming in in vast flocks, and so thirsty did they seem to be that they apparently cared very little for my presence, for I would at times fire both barrels of my gun at them when they were standing along the margin of the slough and they would merely fly up in the air a few feet and then alight in the same spot. Upon one occasion I remember killing one hundred and forty-six of these birds without leaving the blind. This may appear like wanton slaughter to some, but there was a mouth in the garrison for every bird I could kill. This shooting was done with an old-fashioned muzzle-loader. How many I could have slain with the modern breech-loader it is difficult to image.

Northern Dakota is the home of that most noble game bird the sharp-tailed grouse, and at the time I speak of the prairies were filled with them. As I had with me an excellent pointer and little or no opposition, my sport, as may be easily imagined, was simply superb. My only regret was that I did not have with me, to help enjoy the royal sport, some of those dear old shooting cronies I had left behind in "Ole Virginny," and with whom I had often trodden the stubble-fields of that dear old state.

As the dog I owned at that time was the best one that has ever been in my possession, I hope my readers will pardon the common weakness of old sportsmen who are inclined to descant upon the merits of famous dogs they have once owned. He was a pointer and his name was Nat, he being named after the abbreviated Christian name of Nathaniel Burwell, Esq., of Clarke County, Va., who gave him to me when a puppy. He was rather above the medium size and of faultless physical conformation. In nose, speed, bottom and intelligence he was unexcelled, and perhaps unsurpassable by any of his kind. He was not only an "all day" dog, but an "everyday" dog, and seemed to be a stranger to fatigue. To see him, with head erect and waving tail, all day long topping the tall prairie grass with the ease and speed of a hawk, was a sight calculated to gladden the heart of any true sportsman. He always gained the unqualified admiration of everyone who saw him perform. I was once hunting with an English gentleman and sportsman of wide experience (the late Sir Francis Sykes), and upon my inquiring of him whether there were many finer dogs in the "Old country" than my Nat, he replied: "No, nor could there well be." From my imprudence in allowing him to retrieve wildfowl, he ultimately contracted rheumatism in his shoulders, which much impaired his efficiency. At the breaking out of the civil war I gave Nat to a gentleman living near Ft. Ripley, Minn., and have never since heard either of the dog or his progeny. Perhaps the lapse of years has erased from the minds of those I once knew in that vicinity—if there be any of them left—the memory both of the dog and his master.

I am sorry I cannot share Mr. Leffingwell's enthusiasm regarding a permanent residence in Dakota. I have "been there" and prefer not "taking any in mine." Although it is true that a part of the year, say from the beginning of September until the advent of cold weather, it may well be looked upon as an earthly paradise, yet from the beginning of Winter until the disappearance thereof, that country presents climatic conditions which are quite otherwise. The swelling and bursting of the trees of the forest from the effects of the fearful cold, producing sharp reports similar to those of revolvers during cavalry action, and the terrific blizzards, making it dangerous for one to venture out of sight of his house, are some of the Winter attractions of that clime which, I ween, will not be much sought after by ordinary folks.

Bloomery, W. Va.

AN OUTING AT DEVILS LAKE
by M. L. Shover
1896

September 22, 1896, I left Chicago for my annual outing at Devil's Lake, North Dakota, where mallards, redheads, brants or snow geese, and honkers, and sandhill cranes come in great numbers in their flight south.

September 24, at 3 a.m., found me at Devil's Lake. After a few hours' sleep and a hearty breakfast I hunted up a liveryman, engaged a team, and was soon loading up dog and traps for a nine-mile drive to my friend's, F. A. Chisholm, on Sweet Water Lake. We had hardly got out of town when I saw a small covey of prairie chickens on an old strawstack. We endeavored to get close enough for a shot, but the birds did not seem to like the looks of us and flew to a wheat stubble probably a quarter of a mile away. It was only a few moments until we were where we supposed they had gone down. Doc, the setter, was anxious for the fray, and while he had never seen a prairie chicken he well knew I was out for blood. I had counted them as they flew from the stack, and they numbered nine. Up rose one, now another, then another, all out of range. I kept walking on, keeping the dog well in hand, when up went another twenty-five yards away. My 12-gauge Parker went up to my shoulder in a jiffy and one and one-eighth ounces of number seven chilled shot, behind which was three drams of E. C. powder, started after it, and it doubled the bird up in fine style. First shot and first blood. Hardly had this bird struck the ground until another took wing fully as close, but on this one I scored a clean miss. Before I could put in other loads the last bird had gone.

An hour more brought me to the front gate of my friend

Chisholm, one of Dakota's pioneers, he having settled where he now lives in 1882, and for weeks had no other company than his dog and team; and it will not be out of place here to say that the same dog is still living, and his master says when he dies he shall be buried with all honors.

Mr. Chisholm married in 1884 and has now ten children—one pair of twins—and has as many hundred acres of land as he has children. After a hearty handshake all around, he informed me there were more ducks this season than had been seen in Ramsey County since he lived there, and that only a few hundred yards from the house was a slough, where I could get shooting all the afternoon. This slough had for three years before been dry.

As I was getting on my "togs," a Mr. Ordist was introduced. Mr. Ordist I found an all-round sportsman, a genial companion, and a good shot. Mr. Ordist consented to accompany me to the slough, and as he had been shooting there for a week, he knew the lay of the land. He placed me in a position so I could get good shooting, while he waded out in the tall grass to raise the ducks and possibly get a few shots when the ducks rose enough. I had told him how I expected to make doubles if they came as he said they would. I had hardly got located before a flock of teals came down by me at a hundred-mile-an-hour gait. Now for a double, I thought. I waited until they got nearly opposite me and then turned both barrels loose, expecting to see at least four ducks fall, but not a feather was harmed. I looked to see what Ordist was doing, and noticed that he seemed to be looking for something close to him, as he was looking down and walking very slowly. Soon a lone mallard came insight. It came directly over me. I allowed it to get twenty yards past me, and then with a quick glance along the barrels of my gun I pressed the trigger and Mr. Mallard stopped as though it had hit a stone wall. By this time Mr. Ordist had begun to raise ducks all over the slough, for the next hour and a half both of us were kept busy. It had now commenced raining and we concluded we had enough for one afternoon. We compared notes and found we had twenty-one ducks, five mallards, three spoonbills and thirteen teals.

On Monday, September 28, we pulled out for the Black Coolie, sixteen miles away, as we learned there were a great many sandhill cranes feeding near the edge of the settlements. We arrived at John McBride's at 4:30 p.m. He informed us that cranes were plenty and that we were welcome to make his home our stopping place as long as we cared to remain. We had succeeded in bagging a few prairie chickens on our way over, so after a hearty supper of prairie chicken, cooked by Mr. McBride's daughter (who, by the way, we found a fine cook), we retired, pondering on how we were going to slay the cranes the next day.

Five o'clock found us up and at the breakfast table. Mr. McBride directed us to a point, not four hundred yards from his house, where he said the cranes flew over every morning as they went out to feed. The air was very crisp and the ground was covered with a heavy frost. I was soon concealed in a bunch of pigweeds. The sun was just peeping up, when away to the north we heard the well-known and never-to-be-forgotten call of the sandhill. Some twenty or more prairie chickens alighted within close gunshot, but we were not tempted to shoot, for nearer and nearer came the cranes. "Look out!" came from Ordist, who lay concealed two hundred yards beyond, as a flock of six cranes came in sight, but they passed us away out of range. A pair was now heading for us, and to the east of us hundreds seemed to be passing. I chanced a shot at the pair, but scored a miss, as they were at least ninety yards away.

A flock of twenty or more settled down several hundred yards away, and were soon joined by pairs, threes, sixes and up to flocks of fifty. Now, if we could only sneak up within gunshot what a chance; but we knew it was impossible to do this. Hark! Off to my right I heard a call, and I looked and saw three not a hundred yards away, heading for the large flock on the ground, and saw that they would pass nearly over me. What magnificent birds they were, with their long necks stretched out, all unconscious of danger. Now they were nearly over me, not more than forty yards away. I jumped to my feet. The leader took in the situation and gave his warning call, but too late, for a load of No. 4's doubled him up in grand style and a load from the left barrel tumbled another, and both lay not twenty yards apart. I looked around for my friend Ordist. He lifted his hat and dropped out of sight in the weeds, for the large flock had taken wing, alarmed at the report of our guns. We carried our birds to the house and found that together they weighed twenty-nine pounds, which was rather a disappointment, as we supposed when we picked them up they would weigh twenty-five pounds each.

We went out early in the afternoon, hoping to get in the flight, as they came back to feed, but the disturbance in the morning changed their course and we found they were going out a mile east of us. Ordist went back to the house after our pony and buckboard, and I went to a lot of straw lately thrashed and hauled out and left in bunches. In this I concealed myself, for I could see a great many cranes feeding half a mile away. As they did not see fit to come my way I concluded to start on, when a hawk that had been sitting near, on a bunch of straw, made a dive at something twenty yards away in the straw, which proved to be a prairie chicken. A load of No. 4's from the right barrel and a load of No. 3's from the left barrel stopped both of them not ten feet apart, as nice and clean a double as one could wish to make.

The cranes proved too smart for us and we turned back, when we saw a flock of brants, or white geese, feeding in a wheat stubble. Ordist proposed that he sneak up and take a shot at them. I laughed at the idea. But he called my attention to a field of oats which had not been cut, and which was not more than fifty yards from the geese. Soon he was down on his hands and knees, crawling toward the oats, which he reached and crawled to edge next to the geese rose up, up went the geese, and two loads from his Greener stopped four of them, the first geese we had killed.

Next day we pulled out for home, stopping at some of the sloughs, and went in with fourteen ducks, three prairie chickens and two jack-rabbits.

Then for a few days we had fine shooting on ducks and prairie chickens, which were more plentiful than at any time since I have been going to Dakota, now four years.

On October 10 Mr. Ordist left for Buford, N.D., for a few weeks' deer shooting, and afterward wrote me he had good shooting and got several deers and wolves.

October 12 found me on my way back to the feeding grounds of the sandhill cranes, accompanied by Mr. T. J. Keogh, a native of Dakota, a whole-souled, genial gentleman, and a fine wing shot. Five o'clock found us at McBride's, who informed us there were more cranes than I had found before. As we had a little daylight left we drove to a rise in the ground about a mile away. When we reached the top of this rise we beheld a sight that sent the blood tingling through our veins with a rush. Only a few hundred yards away, in a barley stubble, were congregated thousands of sandhill cranes. Never before had the writer beheld anything like it. We at once began to figure how to manage to get at them, when they took wing and went north to their roosting grounds.

My friend proposed that we go on until dark overtook us, camp for the night, and get close to the roosting ground by daylight; but we thought better of it and went back to McBride's, where we held a council of war and arranged to get between the barley-field and their roosting place by daylight and do our shooting as the birds came out to feed.

Next morning we were up early, and as soon as we could see a trail in the grass we were away. After driving as close to the feeding grounds as we dared to we unhitched our team and got in line. Soon a heavy fog settled down and one could see but a few yards. It must have been 7:30 a.m. when out in front of us we heard the call we were longing for, and we then knew the cranes had started for their breakfasts. We were probably fifty yards apart, concealed as best we could in the prairie grass. Some of the cranes came so near us that we could hear their wings flap, but on account of the heavy fog we could not see them. The whole country seemed to be alive with cranes. A flock of three came out of the fog right in front of me. I pulled on the leader and made a clean miss, but doubled up the middle one with my left. By this time they were nearly over Keogh, and he made as clean a double as one ever saw. Soon we had three birds each. The fog then cleared away, and we went back to the wagon, fed the team, and ate our dinner. We then secured some sticks from near an old abandoned shack, fixed up two of our cranes for decoys, and then fixed ourselves for the afternoon shooting, which resulted in our getting two more cranes, one of which the writer crippled and captured, much to the amusement of Keogh.

The next morning Keogh, on account of pressing business, pulled out for home, leaving the writer to do all the shooting, and on this day I broke all my previous records. After digging a pit and putting out my goose decoys, consisting of fourteen, made of thin sheet-iron, and painted to resemble honkers, I waited until the sun was half an hour high before a goose saw fit to pay any attention to my decoys. Then a flock of twenty honkers came in sight and decoyed in good shape. I scored a miss with my first barrel, but killed an eleven-pounder with my last barrel. After a few minutes I heard a crane call, and soon three came in sight and passed within sixty yards of me. I made a clean kill with the first barrel and wounded another with the second barrel. I then made a sneak on a bunch of geese feeding near where some men were plowing. By following the team I got within two hundred yards of them, and by lying flat down I got some weeds between me and the geese. I then crawled across the plowed ground up to within fifty yards of them, and when they raised I knocked down four.

I also broke my record again in the afternoon. I had noticed geese alighting a mile away, seemingly on the prairie, and I went over to investigate and found that the geese were going into a small slough for water. After they had all gone out to feed I concealed myself in the high grass near the water. I had probably been there two hours when I heard the geese coming. What a noise! Sounded like a big political meeting, and everybody shouting. Soon the geese were all around me, and such splashing as they alighted in the slough. I waited until they had all got in the water, and then crawled as close as the water would permit and raised up. Such flapping of wings and cackling! It was enough to raise the hair on a man's head. But I raised the Parker and poured two loads of No. 4 chilled shot into their ranks, feeling confident I would have all the geese I would ever want, but found that I had killed and crippled only eleven, and succeeded in getting all of them. But how so many shot could get through such a flock of geese and only knock down eleven I could not understand.

On October 22 I put my decoys out at 1 p.m. in a wheat stubble, where there were some honkers feeding. I had hardly got well settled in my pit (the wind was blowing a heavy gale, just an ideal day for goose shooting), when a flock of brants, or white geese, came in sight. On they came; circled, and came over the decoys. I raised and imagined what a neat double I would make. I pulled for the leader's neck and saw him double up in fine shape; then I selected another and fired, but he only flinched and I had only one goose. I broke my gun to insert fresh shells, still watching the birds, which, by this time, were several hundred yards away, when I saw one leaving the flock, and after a few flaps more it went to the ground. Out of the pit and over the stubble I went, and soon said to myself: "Well, I made a double, anyhow."

Soon the flight set in from the lake in earnest. A flock of honkers numbering several hundred were now heading for my decoys. They circled a few times and then came up in good shape and well together. I fired into the most compact part of the bunch, and killed six dead and wounded another that struck the ground a hundred yards away. I soon retrieved it and, gathering up my dead geese, went back to the pit again, and succeeded in bagging eleven more during the afternoon, making eight honkers and eleven white geese, or brants.

October 29 found me at Devil's Lake headed for home, after one of the most delightful outings I ever experienced.

Dayton, O.

GOOSE SHOOTING IN DAKOTA
By Nanit
1884

Editor's Note: *Nanit was the pen name of C. R. Tinan who wrote the chapter "The Wild Goose" in the book "Shooting on Upland, Marsh, and Stream" (1890) that was edited by William B. Leffingwell. In this article he was well qualified to write about goose hunting in those times.*

For every reader of *The American Field* that has shot a goose there are, undoubtedly, ten who have never had that pleasure. I opine then that nothing I can write for the columns of our pet paper will prove more interesting than something on wild goose shooting on the stubble fields of Dakota.

It was during the fore part of November last that the geese were here by the hundreds, and every hour I could spare from my office found me in the field. In a previous issue of this paper I have related how a friend and myself once brought in eighteen geese from an afternoon's shoot. If we had had a few of Danz's patent decoy geese at that time we would have shot more geese than would be thought possible by one not acquainted with the country. When I say that Danz's patent decoy geese are even more effective than it is claimed I but echo the sentiment of everyone who has used them. So indispensable are they to my outfit now that I would as soon think of going out without my gun as without them.

We, that is, a brother sportsman and myself, learned of a wheat stubble about five miles south that was said to be visited by a large number of geese every morning and night. We debated a long time whether to go on the trip in the morning or at night. As a rule the morning shooting is the best, but it is cold work, turning out of a nice warm bed an hour and a half before daylight on a raw November morning, and driving across a prairie in the face of a strong wind. However, we concluded to make the trip in the morning. Shells, guns, and a dozen decoys were in readiness, in fact it is a "cold day" when you don't find the guns and belongings of Nanit in shape for a hunt.

The next morning long before the light of day we were pounding on a livery stable door and demanding admittance. The man in charge was soon aroused, and as he swore softly to himself hooked up a horse for us and away we went. The air was full of frost, and by the way, a man who has not seen a frost in Dakota don't know the real meaning of the word, or all that it implies. It was so frosty and cold I took my time for the drive, thinking the geese would be later than common in their morning flight, as is usually the case on either an unusually cold, frosty or windy morning. This morning proved an exception to the rule, for we had but just arrived in the field and taken out our guns, shell boxes and decoys, when four flocks came in, it being at this time just daylight.

My friend at once drove off at a hurried pace to a neighboring straw stack to unhitch the horse, while I quickly dropped down in the stubble, thinking I could obtain a shot at one of the four flocks that all the time kept circling around and over the field. But as I had no cover and none was near at hand to make one, I waited in vain. The geese could see me, and I imagined I could hear them saying to one another:

"That's him!" "Look out!" "Look out!"

Of all the strange noises made by any game birds these black geese make the most peculiar. Novice has heard them and knows whereof I write. His article on Dakota goose shooting, that recently came out in this paper, was true to life, and describes the shooting and sport much better than I can do it. Come out and take a hunt with me, Novice, next year, and I will show you goose shooting that is sport, and no mistake. *Revenons a nos moutons.*

There was nothing to do but arise and go to work setting out the decoys; six one way and six another, as they were profiles. While I was busy at this I kept an eye on the geese, which, much to my surprise, did not leave, probably being loath to quit the field and hunt up another. I worked lively, and had just completed getting the decoys in position when my friend returned, and without waiting to secure sufficient cover for a blind, we dropped down and waited. We had no sooner done this when one of the flocks made direct for the decoys, right to the very spot where I had been at work not two minutes previous, and in plain sight of the geese. As they swung over the decoys we raised and poured four charges of No. 1 shot into their ranks. My friend missed with both barrels, while I did not do much better, but crippled one so badly it dropped down on the prairie about one hundred and fifty yards distant. We were unable to find it, however, a farmer found it the following day and had a nice dinner off of it, so he informed me.

Our shooting frightened the remaining flocks away, and we took time then to find a place where we could command the decoys and still be partly concealed. Taking the decoys up, we carried them further up the field to a rise of ground, near which place was a clump of tall grass. My friend occupied this natural blind, while I lay down on the prairie at the edge of the stubble. My corduroy suit being of the exact color of the dead prairie grass, a very little grass to pull over me, as I lay on my back, was all that was necessary. We thought our whole work would be for naught, for a full half-hour slipped by with no sign of a goose, and our thoughts began to drift back to the warm, cosy bed at home. A lake of perhaps five acres in extent lay to the west, about half a mile distant, and we could hear the geese over there talking at a great rate. My companion suggested his going over there and scaring them out, thinking I might get a shot at them. I knew that he was cold enough to freeze and wanted to move about and warm up, and told him to go ahead.

I did not care to go. I have hunted enough with decoys to know one never leaves them without wanting to kick himself for so doing. The game always comes when you are absent from them. I lay quiet, and waited while he went over to the lake. Sure enough, he found it full of geese, but, for reasons best known to themselves, the geese came not my way, but left for the west. It began to look dubious. It was 8 o'clock by this time—an hour after sunrise—and not a goose. My friend soon returned, and I proposed returning home. I was cold, and ready to cry quits. Not so my companion; he had got warmed up by his brisk tramp, and felt like remaining all day.

While we stood discussing the question whether to go or not I discovered two flocks about a mile distant coming our way. We made for cover like two prairie dogs, and as I lifted my head to watch their coming I could see another flock in the rear of the two first sighted coming in the same direction. On they came, rising and falling as each mound and depression was met on the prairie, and oh how unsuspicious they were when they came over the field and saw, as they thought, a dozen of their fellows busy with their morning meal, and oh how surprised they were when two objects arose under them and death and destruction into their company, three of them falling with a thump, thump, bump. We never stopped to pick them up, but slipped more shells into the guns and waited. The next flock came in directly over me before reaching the decoys, and as they afforded a fine shot, not being over twenty-five yards high, I dropped one with each barrel. They did not give my companion a shot, but flew directly across the field, and in turning again saw the decoy duck, but none of the human family as we were both well concealed. The geese evidently were completely deceived in the decoys, and looking so natural and life-like, probably reasoned that there was nothing to be alarmed about after all, for in less time than it takes to write it they were again over the decoys with set wings ready to alight when two more dropped to the report of my gun, and one fell to my fellow-sportsman as they swung over him, making five out of this flock.

This illustrates better than any words can do, the effectiveness of these decoys. I admit it does not seem possible that a flock of geese once shot at—birds that in cunning are only equaled by the wild turkey—would turn and again decoy. But such is a fact, as I have known them to do so many times. There was no time to pick up geese, for we heard others coming, and the sound of their noisy cackling could be heard in every direction. We became a little excited at this point and did some wild shooting, but out of as many flocks we knocked down five, one being only winged and fell in the midst of the decoys.

The killing of the thirteen geese could not have consumed over ten minutes of time. It was indeed what one might call a "hot corner." There were, probably, about fifteen flocks came into the field in that length of time. The winged goose afforded us much amusement. He would walk up to one of the decoys and talk to it in a language unintelligible to us, but we are of opinion that he swore at those decoys in the strongest goose language at his command. Still, he would not leave their company. Once or twice I walked over to the decoys when, at my approach, the goose would waddle off across the field, only to return to them when I again returned to my blind.

Our shooting was over, and after several vain attempts to find the first goose I brought down, we made preparations for home. How a black goose can conceal himself on a prairie with the grass not over four inches high, and of a yellow color, is more than I have ever been able to find out. I have learned this much, and that is— to hunt them up as soon as they fall, no matter if they seem to come down dead as a stone. I have lost more than one of them, thinking it would be easy work to find them in the short, dead prairie grass.

While we were picking up the decoys the winged goose remained among them, reasoning, undoubtedly, that if they were not alarmed he need not be, and it was only after the last decoy had disappeared from sight that he realized the truth of Pinafore (don't shoot), "things are seldom what they seem." I picked him up tenderly from across the field where he had waddled, after the decoys had gone, and stowed him away under the buggy seat, thinking I would keep him for a Thanksgiving dinner. Our dead geese made the springs touch bottom, but we arrived home in good shape. I fixed a place for the winged goose, and went over to the hotel for a cup of coffee. When I returned my goose was dead. He either died of a broken wing or broken heart. It is hard to tell which.

Kimball, Dak.

GOOSE SHOOTING IN NORTH DAKOTA
By H. A. C.
1892

<u>Editor's Note</u>: *The author of this article gave his address as Island Lake, N.D. I know of at least three lakes named Island; one is east of Jamestown, one north of Medina, and one near Rolette. I believe this locality was the one east of Jamestown since a hunter from Fargo was hunting with him and transportation to the other lakes would have been difficult at that early time.*

As I live in one of the best shooting districts in the West for geese, ducks, and crane—both white and sandhill—I shoot occasionally, as most sportsmen will probably acknowledge when I say that I buy powder by the twenty-five pound keg and have averaged a trifle less than two kegs per year since 1882, and that I have worn out two breech-loading shotguns—one Bonehill and one National Arms Co.—within the last few years.

As to the amount of game killed, I will say that Col. M__., of Fargo, and myself killed four hundred odd geese—did not count ducks and cranes, although I killed a crane weighing twenty-two pounds and which measured six feet three inches from tip of the bill to end of middle toe—in sixteen days.

On the morning of October 12, 1892, the Colonel and I were shooting about two miles east of the lake, and the geese, after leaving us, went to some stubblefield, we could not tell just where. Having surfeited themselves with grain, the geese began to return to the lake before we had time to gather up our decoys and get our team, so we had to drive home without locating them. Arriving at the house, which is on the banks of one of the best game lakes in the country, we loaded our shells and ate our goose dinner. Turning to the Colonel, I said:

"Well, Colonel, we're stumped for the afternoon. I know pretty well where the geese are feeding, but whether I can find the right stubblefield or not is a conundrum."

"Well," said the Colonel, "all we can do is to make a guess at it and locate them for morning."

Some readers may say, Why didn't they follow the first flock that left the lake and find where they went? But on fine days the birds leave the lake about four o'clock in the morning and keep up a steady stream until about six o'clock when the flight is over, and by the time you get your decoys out, two pits dug and team attended too, you have wasted so much time that you only get the end of the flight, which is very indifferent shooting, as the last birds arriving, expecting to find thousands there before them, and find only a small flock of about twenty-four decoys, either become suspicious, or, as I suppose, rather go with the crowd, and fly off to hunt them up, which generally is not hard for them to do, for probably some field within a mile or so will be covered with them. The dark ones are hard to see in the stubble, but there are usually white ones enough to make a field look as though it was covered with snow. You will do well if you get into more than one flock in four, no matter if you are a good caller. The writer, from patient practice and long experience, is adept at calling birds, whether Canada, Hutchin's, Laughing or Snow geese, white or sandhill cranes, or wild ducks and yet I know that it is far better to get fixed in the field before the geese begin arriving or leave them until the next flight, as they will not go back to the same field after being once disturbed.

On stormy days they feed in the stubble all day, just going to the lake for a drink and right back again. As some are coming from and others returning to the lake, it makes a steady flight of birds, and a person well located will have fine shooting all day. We drove about six miles east and came to a field where the birds had been feeding, and I said:

"Colonel, here is a field in the right direction; what do you say to trying it?"

"All right!" said he, "You attend to the team and I will put out the decoys."

We used one dozen Canada and one dozen Snow geese decoys. After driving the team behind some grain stacks and tying the horses to the wagon, I walked back to where the Colonel was. By this time he had the decoys all set. We did not have to dig pits, as there were wheatshocks in the field, and we were soon nicely settled in a couple of shocks ready for the slaughter. I had my Chesapeake dog, Bose, with me to retrieve birds not killed that would run off and hide in the grass. I was watching the west for the approach of the birds, when Bose commenced to growl, and looking up—well, if there wasn't a pretty sight for two sportsmen, dressed in colors from their hats down as much like stubble as possible, and hidden in wheat shocks to keep the geese from seeking them, to look upon! Right in the middle of our decoys and looking as though they had discovered some new kind of biped, genus unknown, and hesitating whether to run or stand their ground, were two women. How they got there I was for the moment too surprised to tell. Just then the Colonel took in the situation, and was as surprised as I was; but matters were becoming desperate, as the geese were coming. The first flock that came acted as if they wanted to alight, but not liking the addition to our decoys, went on. Just then the Colonel frightened the women half to death, for they did not seem to know that we were there, by addressing the elder one as follows:

"Madam, did you never see geese before? If you have we will be very much obliged if you will move on. If not, please satisfy your curiosity as soon as possible, for the geese will not alight as long as you are here."

They turned and left for a house half-a-mile away without a word, and that was the last we saw of them. We had poor shooting from that time on, as most of the geese passed over to a field east of us, we killing only seven. The Colonel consolingly remarked, however, that we would have our revenge on them in the morning.

I will say right here for the benefit of any fellow sportsmen that have never hunted geese, that they feed twice a day in the stubble in fine weather, going out a little after daylight—the flight lasting from one to two hours—and returning to the lake from nine to eleven, where they stay until about three o'clock in the afternoon, when the evening flight commences, some few flying as late as sundown. If you do not know where they are going, follow the flight until you find where they are feeding. Be careful not to disturb the geese. Let them leave of their own accord; then dig your pits, set out your decoys, and get some one that is part goose, like the writer, to call them in. Have everything ready before the return flight; for you will have your hands full. If you are not in the field they are bound for, although they may pass directly over your head, about one hundred yards up and look down at your decoys and answer your call, it is only an occasional flock that you can turn; but if in the field they are going to they will come in in splendid shape to your decoys.

Gathering up our game and decoys, we drove home, and finding supper awaiting us, we did ample justice to delicious broiled crane breast, served by the ladies in elegant shape, and embellished by some of the Colonel's inimitable stories, one of which I will here try to repeat:

He was one time in a town where they were holding revivals. Living in the town was a man named Mr. B__, who was a great wag, and having a cork leg like Mr. Wegt, and also an impediment in his speech, each added to the effect. Some one finding a jug of whiskey that had been hidden, and wanting to find to whom it belonged, had one of the preachers take it and say: "We have found this jug. Will the owner kindly come forward and get it." There was no response for some little time, when Mr. B__ arose and started with his hope-and-go-fetch-it gait for the jug. Picking it up, he looked it all over, and, not seeming to be able to tell from the outside, he pulled out the cork and smelled of it. Still he was not satisfied; and he tasted it. Then not being fully assured, he opened his mouth and let it go glug-glug down his throat until he had taken a good stiff pull. Then he concluded it would take another drink before he could be certain. By this time all were on tiptoe of expectation. He raised the jug once more, and let it go glug-glug-glug, until he had taken a tremendous long drink, and then he set it down and turned to the preacher and said:

"N-n-no, t-t-t aint mine. Mine's vinegar," and started for his seat.

That brought the house down, and it also ended the meeting, for every time a preacher went to speak some one would snicker, and then everybody would haw-haw right out in the meeting.

Returning to our former subject, perhaps the reader would like to know what load I use for goose shooting. I use a 12-gauge gun and load with 4 ½ drams of powder and 1 1/8 ounces of No. 2 shot in left barrel, and No. 4 shot in right barrel. The Colonel uses the same size shot, but as he shoots a 10-gauge gun, he uses 5 drams of powder and 1 1/4 ounces of shot. A great many hunters use BB's, but my experience is that two's and four's are best at twenty to fifty yards, although larger shot may be better at longer range if you hit the bird. Last Fall I stood under the bank of the lake as the geese were coming in from the east against a high west wind—consequently they were just skimming the ground, rising a little just as they reached the bank—and killed twenty-two in less than two hours with No. 6 shot.

As it was ten o'clock and we had a mile to drive the next morning and get fixed for shooting by six o'clock, we retired and slept well until the alarm went off, then we got up, drank a cup of hot coffee, ate a piece of toast to last us till after the morning shoot, hitched up and started a little after four o'clock, and were on the ground by five. I took the team over to an old claim shack and unhitched it, while the Colonel set out the decoys. A good many sportsmen scatter their decoys, placing them ten or twelve feet apart, but I always have the best luck to bunch them pretty well, as they can be seen farther. I place them to the windward of my blind, as the birds always come in against the wind. If they are coming with the wind they will fly past, circle and come up against it before alighting, and when they are hovering over the decoys with their legs hanging down, ready to light, they present a shot that is hard to miss, although it is sometimes just the same.

There are two things that a stranger to goose shooting has to learn. He may be a good quail, prairie chicken or duck shot, but he gets left on geese. At first he does not realize how fast the bird is flying; being so big it looks as if a mallard duck would get right away from it, but let a greenhead fly alongside of an old "honker," and you will find that they will go along together, and not bother the goose at all. Consequently, when a novice shoots at geese, if he covers the leader, he will probably down one about three feet behind. The other trouble is, he seems to be afraid to let them get too close, shooting sixty or seventy yards, thinking they are only thirty or forty yards away. As long as they are coming to me I let them come, knowing from experience that they will not get too close.

By the time we were ready to shoot it was broad daylight and so foggy that you could not see over a hundred yards. I said, "Colonel, we will have a fine shoot this morning, as this fog insures a long flight." "That is so," he said, "they won't all come out in a flock about ten miles long. Hark! I hear some now." They kept getting nearer, answering my call, until they suddenly loomed up in the fog like great white specters, they being snow geese. By this time they saw the decoys, and came straight to them, about fifteen feet high, with their red legs hanging down and their wings set ready to alight.

I covered one and pulled the trigger. It doubled up and came down on the broad of its back; I did the same with the other barrel and the Colonel followed my example. The next flock followed almost immediately. Taking a toll of three out of that, we were ready for the next. From this on the fun was continuous, not giving us time to gather up the dead birds until we had sixteen down, and then we had to hustle, as there were others coming.

The flight lasted until nine o'clock. When we gathered up our geese and decoys we found we had killed fifty-three birds, all the different species of geese in North Dakota contributing their share to our bag. As the morning's shoot was over, we started for home very well satisfied with the number of birds we had killed and the sport we had enjoyed.

Island Lake, N.D.

SPORTSMEN VS. CINCH SEEKERS
By S. D. Barnes
Fort Worth, Texas
1895

Editor's Note: This article contains thoughts that are just as relevant today as when published over 100 years ago. The essence of it is in the final sentence: "We must...depend more on skill and marksmanship...and discourage that sort of sportsmanship which measures the enjoyment of a day afield by figuring the gross weight of the game that is bagged."

If we wish to further the cause of game protection let us legislate market-shooting out of existence, shorten the open seasons, and give our heartiest cooperation to those who are willing to spend time and money in restocking our depleted fields, forests and streams. Further than this, let us remember that we are sportsmen and not meat-hunters, and, by reducing the caliber of our guns and the weight of our shot charges, give to what there is left of fur and feather a bare chance to escape extermination.

Recently, while on my way from San Antonio to Corpus Christi, I met and conversed with a person who proudly claimed the title of a true sportsman. If I should give his name it would be at once recognized by many of the readers of *The American Field*; consequently I refrain from adding to his present notoriety. He had come to Texas for quail and duck shooting, and confided to me his desire to "break the record" before he returned North. He showed me his gun—a brand new Parker with two sets of barrels—and he persisted that it was the most perfect and desirable arm ever built. It was a 10-gauge; and, with the cylinder barrels, he claimed that he had a "dead cinch" on every bird that dared shake a wing at forty yards rise; "a fly couldn't crawl through the pattern at that distance," said he.

"Thirty-inch circle?" I asked.

"Thirty nothin'! It's nearer six feet," said he.

And then I put the gun in its case once more and began to talk of deep water at Corpus, of the corn crop for 1895, and the value of the prickly pear as an ensilage plant. I had longed to meet a bona fide sportsman, but now that my wish had been satisfied I longed as earnestly to be freed of his presence.

In my mind an avowed pot-hunter may be a gentleman, but the sportsman who slaughters game with a cannon and yearns after "dead cinches" is too small potatoes to train in the same class. The majority of us have been game-hogs at some early period of life, and the writer of these lines presumes that he has done as much as the next man toward the extermination of game; but while the boy who flock-shoots on the ground with his first gun may plead ignorance as his excuse, what can we say in defense of an up-to-date sportsman who, after reading weekly accounts of the scarcity of game, will order a 10-gauge cylinder bore gun for quail shooting? I am not a crank on small calibers and light loads. I have hunted game with guns of all weights and gauges and have yet to see the time when three-fourths of an ounce of shot would cover as wide a circle as three ounces. My friend of the 10-gauge Parker was evidently a man of experience in the field, and our views coincided to a certain extent. As a game annihilator his gun approximated perfection, and had he been a professional market-shooter I most certainly would have commended his choice. But imagine the result if every true sportsman in our country should favor their gunmakers with duplicates of his order!

It is probable that I shall spend less time afield in the coming quarter century than I have spent in that which is past; but I have a brace of growing sons who have inherited the old man's fondness for the gun and ability as a marksman, and I am reasonably anxious that there shall be game for them to shoot as long as they may desire to hunt it. I hardly think that either of my boys will ever invest in a cannon, or have need to do so, for I am training them in a different school to that; but unless there should be a radical change before long in the sportsmanlike methods at present in vogue, the coming generation of gunners will find nothing left them in the way of game, barring field mice and English sparrows.

Granted a quick eye and a reasonable acquaintance with his gun, one should kill a single bird almost as readily with a 16 or 20 gauge as with a closely choked 12-gauge; and those who really hunt for the sport alone seldom feel inclined to shoot in the thick of a flock for the sake of observing results. The sportsmen of San Antonio, Tex., in the midst of the best all-around game range in America, have long since discarded the 10 and 12 gauges for guns of smaller bore, and the most successful shot among them all pins his faith to a little 24-gauge, shooting it side by side with all sorts of guns held by all sorts of men, and always keeping well to the front. If a duck is beyond reach of Critzer's 24-gauge there is little use of reaching for it with anything larger. As a flock gun it would not be a success; but then if it was a flock gun Critzer would not wish to own it. He is not that sort of a sportsman.

I have spent all my leisure time for more than twenty years in hunting. (I use the term hunting advisedly, for shooting, as practiced in the game preserves of European countries, has never been exactly suited to my fancy. I like to find and flush my own game without other assistance than that of a good dog, and the hunting has always been, to me, the best of the sport.) I have killed game in many different localities, and with almost every imaginable size and description of modern firearms, but the most enjoyable sport I have ever known was gained with the least expense of powder and lead. Some years ago I killed a Canada goose with three-fourths of an ounce of No. 8 shot from a 16-gauge gun, and, though a hundred men have told me it was a scratch, I never believed it such. I held ahead, and the center of the charge struck as I had intended it should, breaking the goose's neck. I could kill a quail at that distance four times out of five; why not a goose? I have killed a number of turkeys in the same way and I fail to see where the element of chance comes in, or how a 10-gauge gun could have killed cleaner or better. I prefer a rifle to a shotgun for all-around work, for it has a longer range, is more accurate, and makes fewer cripples. For deer shooting I use a .45-caliber; either a .45-60, .45-70 or .45-90. All riflemen have their fads, and mine is a fancy for straight shells. For turkeys and all smaller game my choice is a .22-caliber, and if there should be among your readers anyone who has been led by experience to a similar selection I trust he will aid me in striving to awaken an interest in the rimfire .22 as a hunting cartridge.

Not long since I saw it stated that the manufacture of 8-gauge guns had practically ceased because a need for them no longer existed. This is a mistake. In the history of the world there has never been a time when the record-seeking gunner needed an 8-gauge so badly as at the present. Public opinion is against their use, and it will be a happy day for the lovers of field sports when room is made on the shelf for guns of all calibers larger than sixteen. We have to do with a case where the exercise of self restraint is of the utmost importance. We cannot eat our cake and keep it too, and if we persist in hanging onto our big cylinder bores, and shooting with an eye to supplying our own larder and those of our friends, we might as well spare ourselves the trouble of educating our sons in the ethics of field sports. We must drop flock shooting, depend more on skill and marksmanship and less on "smothering" game with a handful of shot, and also discourage as best we may that sort of sportsmanship which measures the enjoyment of a day afield by figuring the gross weight of the game that is bagged.

THE SPORTSMAN AND THE FARMER
1904

Editor's Note: Remove the date and the contents of this editorial are just as relevant today as 100 years ago. A couple of quotes have an important message for those hunters who wish to find places to hunt. "There is no reason why city sportsmen and farmers should not be the best of friends, and in many instances where the man is a true sportsman and a gentleman, they are." "If sportsmen will treat the farmers as they themselves would like to be treated were they living on a farm, they will not have much difficulty in getting all the shooting they want, but if they will not do this they have no reason to complain if they are ordered off the land."

"City sportsmen are complaining," says an exchange, "that the farmers are barring them off their land; that nearly every farm in the county where the paper referred to is printed is decorated with signs warning hunters to keep off the premises," and that in a few years the sportsman who does not own land of his own or belong to a club that has a preserve will find little shooting except waterfowl, and they will have to be hunted on the river or other public waters.

This same journal argues that the farmer is justified in posting his land, stating that he is the owner of the land and everything that runs or flies over it, and that he is entitled to everything that the land raises or attracts. The editor also says that the farmer has been abused by sportsmen and that his live stock has been shot full of holes, consequently the farmer is justified in posting his lands.

That part of the statement which says that farmers have been abused and their stock injured by hunters, we do not question as true to a certain extent, but to the part which says the farmer is the owner of everything that runs or flies over his land or that which the land attracts, we take issue. The game law of nearly every state declares that the game in the state, whether on Farmer Brown's or Farmer Jones' land, is the property of the state, consequently the man who owns the land upon which the game has been reared has no more right to the game than any other citizen of the state, and if he takes it without violating the law and subjecting himself to prosecution, he must do so only as the law prescribes.

The farmer, beyond all question, has absolute jurisdiction over his own land, and the man who goes upon it without permission can be prosecuted under the trespass law; but he has no more legal right to the game which has been reared upon his land than any other resident of the state.

Editors of country papers and others who advance the idea that the game on a man's land belongs to him, and that all sportsmen are enemies of the farmer and care nothing for his fences, buildings and livestock, are doing more to create an estrangement between the farmers and sportsmen than all other people combined. There is no reason why city sportsmen and farmers should not be the best of friends, and in many instances where the man who hunts is a true sportsman and a gentleman, they are. The sportsman has no more right to enter upon a man's land and begin shooting, without first obtaining the owner's permission, than the farmer would have to enter the sportsman's home and help himself to a meal of victuals, and no gentleman sportsman will do it if he knows the farmer objects to shooting on his land.

In the majority of cases, when a sportsman approaches a farmer in a gentlemanly manner and asks the privilege of hunting over the farmer's possessions, the right is cheerfully granted, while if that same man was to go upon the land and begin shooting without permission, the chances are ten to one that he would be ordered to vacate at once, and no amount of argument would cause the farmer to change his mind; and the man who does not recognize the fact that a farmer has control over his own property does not deserve to be permitted to hunt anywhere except on government land.

Farmers as a rule are not selfish but they do want sportsmen to respect their rights, and in this they are perfectly justified. If after a sportsman has been given the privilege to hunt upon a farmer's land, and he meets with success, he will take the trouble to go back to the farmhouse before starting for home and leave a mess of game and a cigar or two—if the farmer smokes—he will be invited to come again and as often as he chooses; but if he leaves the place with a well-filled game bag and never as much as offers the farmer a bird or thanks him for the sport he has enjoyed, the probabilities are that he will not be invited back, and he should not be, for he has not shown that he appreciates the favor granted him by the farmer.

It sometimes happens that a farmer has two or three sons living at home who like to hunt, and he wishes to save the game on his place for them and their friends when they have finished the Fall work and have the time to hunt, and where this is the case, if the sons kill the game in a lawful manner and use it at home or give it to their friends, no one should take exception if the farmer does not grant a stranger permission to shoot over his premises.

If sportsmen will treat the farmers as they themselves would like to be treated were they living on a farm, they will not have much difficulty in getting all the shooting they want, but if they will not do this they have no reason to complain if they are ordered off the land. If, on going to a farmer and asking the privilege of shooting on his farm, he refuses you and begins to tongue-lash sportsmen generally, exchange as few words as possible with him and move on. It seldom ever pays to waste words with such men. They probably have a reason for their action, and whether it be good or bad, you will gain nothing by arguing the question with them. Often when such men see that they are not creating much displeasure by their action and that their course is actually losing them friends, they will experience "a change of heart" and the next time you meet them, they will invite you to come out and take a hunt on their place. It never pays a sportsman to antagonize the farmer; neither does it pay him to be uncivil. If one expects favors he must be a gentleman and considerate of the rights of others.

SPORT IN DAKOTA - NO. 1
1887

Editor's Note: This article, authored by "W.T.D.," is an account of a group of hunters who traveled by railroad from Buffalo, New York, to hunt in western Minnesota and in the Devils Lake region of Dakota Territory. In addition to some interesting accounts of their hunting experiences there are graphic descriptions of the countryside as it was at that time. For example, in No. 3 is the following statement: "The country lying between Dalton and Moorhead, Minn. is a vast plain, fenceless for miles, and without a tree to break the monotony of the scene except those found in the vicinity of lakes or seen along streams.....Prairie chickens, ducks and geese are present everywhere; on both sides of the track prairie chickens were seen rising out of the grass in large and small flocks, while ducks were almost constantly on the wing." Devils Lake in Dakota was at a high level in 1886, estimated to be seventy miles in length, and two steamboats made daily trips between Fort Totten and Devils Lake City, a distance of fourteen miles.

We are all here upon the vast plains of the great and glorious West where the sun sets upon the prairie at night and rises from it in the morning. Our party met in Buffalo, N.Y., at the time agreed upon, with the exception of one member who joined us at Cleveland, Ohio. We left Buffalo for Chicago by the Lake Shore railroad on Sunday morning, October 3, (probably 1886 HFD) at 6:35 a.m., occupying the Pullman "Santiago," a veritable little palace of itself, provided with all necessary conveniences and comforts. The interests of the public, as well as those of the Pullman Company, are well served and safe in the hands of such a man as Mr. Bennett their district superintendent. The Lake Shore is a great system, enterprising and liberal at every point, ably managed, and run upon the Jacksonian principle of "the greatest good to the greatest number." We are grateful to many officials of this road for personal courtesies to our party, among them Mr. J. A. Berch, general eastern and southern agent; C. B. Couch, Esq., general eastern superintendent; and Mr. J. L. Freeman, general baggage agent. These gentlemen are always alert to anticipate wants, and supply demands of travelers over their road.

Our heavily loaded train went sweeping through Ohio and into Illinois at the rate of about forty-five miles per hour. Along both sides of the track we caught bird's-eye views of lovely landscapes, magnificent farms, bewitching lakes, and stately groves; all aglow with golden colors fresh from the brush of Autumn, Nature's own inimitable artist.

Our car was to all intents and purposes converted into a cabin and camp-fire. We gathered about the little table of our stateroom, and, amid lemon juice and curling wreaths of fragrant smoke, unfolded many a tale of hair-breadth escape from the ferocious and maddened beasts of the jungle. We reproduced mental pictures of mornings on the marshes, in the years behind us; of evenings along the passes among mallards, canvas backs and "reds"; swapped fishing and other yarns too numerous to mention; discussed the live and dead political issues, and wondered whether Henry Ward Beecher would bring back his doctrine of evolution boxed up with dynamite or carry it along loose. Like the gallant soldier, "we fought our battles o'er and o'er," and I trust they were all fought before. After many sly glances from one to another conspicuously full of a certain phrenological inquisitiveness, we finally began to emerge from the initiation of acquaintanceship to find that we were friends, the majority being strangers but a day or two before. I made a mental picture of the party by the mellow lights of the sleeper and will give you just a peep at them.

The Baron, captain of the company, is a gentleman of sturdy build, "six foot one way and three foot t'other," and weighs an eighth of a ton. He can appreciate or perpetrate a joke with the keenest relish, and can always be depended upon at lunch. Judge weighs a few pounds less; is of easy ways and modest wants; the picture of innocence; but is frequently found closeted with Duke, the Baron's private secretary engaged in planning embarrassing situations for some one of the party, the execution of which he enjoys best at long range. Nap (from his resemblance to Napoleon) is also of aldermanic proportions, but not propensities. He is a pleasant companion and the soul of good humor, and therefore often made responsible for much that should be charged up to others. He has a big heart and the company would be incomplete without him. The Deacon is of "white cravat" pretensions; tall, slender and of clerical mien; a trifle dyspeptic in disposition; but never permits the gong to blow twice on that account. When found in mischief he simply poses as "injured innocence" and that settles it. Of course we are charitable enough to take it all back; he is a full unit in all our joys and sorrows. Duke is an irresponsible youth of strong convictions, quick impulses, unfailing digestion, and is withal the cashier of the party. He is perfectly orthodox in his views, and has a great fondness for music. No one who knows him can question his sincerity. On the subject of self we are all supposed to be more fluent than agreeable. Permit me to say that the writer stands next to Baron for avoirdupois and is "the pink of propriety always." If your readers prefer to doubt it, their judgment will be entitled to great respect.

Never in the history of picnics, excursions, or social reunions was a party of six more strongly drawn together by bonds of good fellowship. The will of one was the pleasure of all; every one was a leader and the rest followers. The best in the land was good enough for us, and we feasted on it every hour. In our cozy quarters we reverted again and again to a recital of personal adventures by land and sea, in storm and sun, until we were wrought up to the highest pitch of enthusiasm. We talked ourselves into ecstasies over game and gunning, and back into silence and meditation. The judge and deacon were professedly great duck shots, each one confident that he will down the first duck. Baron and Nap were unwilling to display their skill so cheaply; nothing would appease their thirst for gore save the dying struggles of a thoroughbred grizzly at their feet, and they prefer that he shall be the brute that has chased all other hunters out of the woods. Duke and I were to test metal on the slough, along the coulees and in the stubbles. What beautiful pictures were drawn of marvelous bags and magnificent shots, wonderful scores and victorious shooters to be; not a duck should be missed, nor a goose escape, nor a grizzly be left alive. Just think of it, ye punt gunners, nothing but a grim harvest of death and acres of graves all around us; the whole Territory of Dakota literally strewn with fur and feathers and irrigated with blood. What a fearful outlook for the wild animals of the West!

But Duke now announced that we were only ten miles from lunch, and "what a change came o'er the spirit of our dream." All faces were wreathed in smiles. The Deacon looked especially happy, for it must be known that his dyspeptics are the sort which will endure some discomfort rather than forego the joyous sensations following the demolition of a big dinner.

After a short run we brought up at the dining station where everything was bustle and business and only, "Twenty minutes for dinner!" But what a quantity of edibles were mowed away in those little minutes!

On finishing the repast our servant, a golden-haired daughter of Erin, gazing horror-stricken upon the general wreck of the bill-of-fare and upon the total absence of everything eatable, looking as though she had lost all her property by some calamity, cried out in great alarm:

"Howly mither, would yez look a-that! Faith, an' it's the clanest bit of a job that wuz ever dun at the counter. Nuthin' left but the foorniture and napkins, and only five o'them!"

Looking daggers at Duke and the Deacon, who had only two ribs of beef each besides three dozen fried oysters and a whole tripe, she yelled:

"Thim two had all the ribs o' the beef, and I'm blest if they ain't looking for the baste himself this minute!"

With some assistance from Nap and I, Baron and Judge got safely back to quarters while the train was moving, and we were soon trundling along at rapid speed toward the beautiful metropolis of the west. After a long rest from refreshments and thoroughly fumigating our improvised cabin with a delicious brand of the weed, we found that we were rapidly nearing the suburbs of Chicago, when "grips" and other portable luggage were hustled together to be transferred to the "Tremont" for the night. We were greatly fatigued from the long ride of the day previous and breakfasted late on Monday in consequence, with appetites at a fearful discount.

We left Chicago for Saint Paul about two o'clock p.m. on that splendid line, the C., M. & St. P. R. R., which is doing an immense passenger traffic, and which is so deservedly popular with business people as well as sportsmen and tourists. The ride through Wisconsin and into Minnesota was a delightful one and fully justified the reports given us by eastern friends of the beautiful section of country traversed by this road. We whiled away the hours with "Sieben oud" and other innocent and approved methods of a amusement, and now that the ragged edge of enthusiasm and expectancy were worn down, we began to get a more sober view of the possibilities ahead of us. Two of the party suggested that we should pursue the original plan of the trip as far as Saint Paul, leaving all shooting and other arrangements beyond there to be decided upon after conferring with friends in that city. This course was unanimously adopted, but was an unwise one and a mistake, as the sequel will prove.

   We were now leaving the miles behind us in a cloud of dust, forging ahead with the throttle valve wide open, and while our unconscious sleepers were in dreamland, we came flying into St. Paul about the time its early people were breakfasting. With all haste we drove into the hotel Ryan where we enjoyed a superb breakfast. This hotelry was by common consent voted one of the finest on the continent, and its manager, Mr. E. P. Emerson, a gentleman of culture as well as a model man of business. His sole ambition and aim seems to be the welfare of his guests, and he belongs to the precious few who appear to win their own happiness by forgetting it in ministering to others. We were visited at this establishment by Mr. W. E. Powell, general solicitor, and Mr. O. F. Clark, general passenger agent of the C., M. & St. P. R. R.; also by Mr. Jas. Eagan, general superintendent St. P., M. & M., who formerly occupied the same post with the Canadian Pacific. In company with, and at Mr. Powell's request, we visited Minneapolis and were amazed at the growth of that city, as well as the magnitude of her business interests. In St. Paul we also made the acquaintance of Mr. Fee, a painstaking and obliging general officer of the Northern Pacific road, and a gentleman of advanced views in railroad matters, representing a road known all over the world as one run upon broad gauge principles. In fact much of our enjoyment in the twin cities of Minnesota was due directly to the personal interest and hospitality of general officers connected with the great trunk lines centering in Saint Paul.

   After a consultation with friends and sportsmen of Saint Paul to learn if possible of the best shooting grounds beyond there, we went into a committee of the whole, and when the "pros" and "cons" were measured up it was decided that Dalton, Minn., should be the bloody scene of our first engagement with the ducks. We departed St. Paul, with many sincere regrets on the 8:30 a.m. train on the St. P., M. & M. R. R. Shortly after crossing the "Father of

Waters," we found ourselves in the land of lakes and lakelets, chain after chain of them passing by in swift review. The scenery along the road was a varied panorama of matchless beauty, that could furnish pictures for the painter, inspiration for the poet; and meditation for the philosopher. The weather was charming and the hunters happy. At St. Paul we had taken the precaution to telegraph to Dalton to have teams there to convey us to Ten Mile Lake, about three or four miles across the prairie from Dalton.

About one hundred miles out from St. Paul we saw a great many ducks, chiefly in small flocks; but they were over and all around us. Many lakes and sloughs were dotted with little bunches of them, and we began to have high hopes of grand sport. Nap thought six such able-bodied sinners should kill a car load a day. Judge elevated his Roman feature at such a small estimate, and the rest of the party joined him in his sneers. Prairie chickens were seen, sometimes in large numbers, sailing away from the track as the train dashed by. Scores of them could have been shot from the train, but the law forbid, and we respected that decree. A startled jackrabbit would occasionally leap from his grassy cover and strike a bee-line for the setting sun, fast as his graceful gait could take him. Snipes and quails, too, were on the wing. The managers of the St. P., M. R. R. may well publish the fact that their road runs through one of the great game sections; it is only a truth which any sportsman may verify by his own experience.

After an interesting ride of about 200 miles, we arrived at the little village of Dalton about 4 p.m. and found a "dead X" and a spring wagon waiting to convey us to Ten Mile Lake. The ride to the lake in that "dead X" was a painfully romantic experience. Away we went, rolling over the rough prairie, up little hills and down little hollows, into little ruts and over little rocks; "ka-chuckchuck; bump-chuck." "Ouch!" would often be the only word that could forcibly describe our discomfiture. Of course it was jolly fun at first, as such things always are; but after we had gone a mile or two the novelty of the situation wore out as well as the actors in it. Baron said he knew he had lost a pound per mile. Judge and Duke insisted that it was worse than ague and "rumaticks" together. Nap declared that he would rather go tobogganing down the Rockies on a hand car. The deacon was all "broke up," and the dogs took the prairie for it, while the wagon box was rapidly filling up with loaded shells from broken "grips." The writer thought it would be wise to temporarily abandon the shoot and put in at some health resort for general repairs. On nearing the lake we heard the continuous booming of guns like the roar of war. It was after 5 p.m. and flight shooting was at its height. Shooters from several different states had possession of the pass, and were wasting ammunition with surprising liberality upon "sky scrapers" of every variety, bagging about two out of a possible ten.

Our way to the hotel led directly across this pass and the temptation to do a little evening shooting seized me so irresistibly that I jumped the "X" with cartridge bag and gun case, containing a ten-gauge No. 12 Smith hammerless, one of the latest triumphs in gunmaking. Once fairly upon the ground, I felt of my bones to discover if they were all in place, limped around in a circle for a moment or two, and then looked about me for a stand. The desirable places were all taken; no blinds or places of concealment left, so I sat upon an accommodating log by the water's edge and awaited the approach of the "tribes of the air." They came and went in small numbers, but appeared to be nearer heaven than earth. But as twilight began to deepen into dusk, canvas-backs, red-heads and butter-balls ventured nearer until they were not more than 60 to 100 yards high. One of the gentlemen just above me left his stand for one a little further north, and I took possession of the rushes abandoned by him. We had but three retrievers with us, Nig, Jr., remaining with me. A little bunch of six red-heads came whizzing over me, about 60 yards high and with the wind. I held about four yards ahead of them with an experimental dose of No. 6, propelled by four drams of King's Quick Shot No. 2 and scored a pretty miss. Additional shots with the same results convinced me that a change of prescription might be more fatal, so I tried no. 5 shot and 4½ drams of the same powder. A single mallard now came down the pass, offering a fair broadside. Fire and smoke, belched froth from six guns, but on he came, cleaving the air with not a single feather ruffled. Impatient and a little excited, I rose from the rushes and delivered my right as he was straight overhead and what a beautiful miss; but, instantly recovering and leaning back-ward, I discharged my left, holding what I should guess to be six feet ahead, when he wilted, lost his bearings and plunging headlong into the lake behind me with that thud which, though death to the duck, is delight to the shooter. Nig retrieved him handsomely, being proud of the opportunity to do so. This was a long shot and much admired. One thought it was a full hundred yards, but I should say about ten less, although I record it with as much pride as if I believed it to be more. The flight of ducks over this and adjoining lakes was not so large as expected, but it would be a paradise for "dude" hunters as there were mud hens and gulls in abundance.

As it grew darker the ducks came within easy range and fell in rapid succession to guns all along the pass. Many pretty shots were made and many misses. I found on counting up that my bag consisted of two mallards, one canvas-back, two red-heads and three butter-balls—eight in all—and two lost in the grass. It was just encouraging enough to believe that fair bags might reasonably be expected on the morrow. Gathering up my fowls I trudged along toward the hotel to meet my companions. I laid them at their feet, expecting to be received with loud "hoorays"; lionized; envied; wrapped upon in the "stars and stripes," and carried on their shoulders; but what was my surprise when Nat opened up thus: "Where did you buy 'em?" With something in his eye besides a tear, the judge added: "Any more at same price?" Baron remarked: "Look kind o'stale; guess you got 'em cheap." While the Duke smoothed my feelings the wrong way by asking if I "sneaked up to somebody's game box, shot my gun off a time or two, and claimed all the ducks." Deacon, more outrageous still, like a great prelate orated on this wise: "You must account for those ducks being in your possession on more reasonable grounds than your shooting them; we couldn't entertain that proposition at all." Why I could have scalped every one of them. But we shall see later on; "it is a long lane that has no turn."

 Kingston, Pa.

SPORT IN DAKOTA - NO. 2
1887

The early and greater part of our first evening at Ten Mile Lake was spent in unpacking boxes, selecting shells and shooting paraphernalia, and making elaborate general preparations for giving the early morning ducks a roaring reception along the pass where I had been the previous night. That experience, though of an unpretentious character, aroused my friends to a certain degree of enthusiasm and they even indulged in a little quiet arithmetic somewhat after this fashion: "If one man can kill eight ducks in half an hour, how many can six men bag in twenty hours?" You will observe that the "eight-hour law" had no application in this case. Of course we remember it is said "figures don't lie," but sometimes it requires a little artful manipulation to make them tell the truth. But it was clear to my companions that even under the most unfavorable circumstances there would be opportunities to "buy 'em" if we failed to "shoot 'em," with chances for bagging them by the latter more reputable and sportsman-like method.

After all our arrangements and plans for the morning had been made, we adjourned by common consent to an accommodating bench on the north bank of the lake, just in front of the little hotel, to drink in long and refreshing draughts of the bracing air of Minnesota, and enjoy in the meantime, from this slightly elevated position the charming effects of moonlight on the lake.

Ten Mile Lake is a beautiful sheet of water, but somewhat exaggerated in size, unless indeed it be in circumference. The hotel, so named from some strange freak of fancy, is situated upon the north bank. It is a two-story frame house, neat in appearance and of modern design, commanding a broad view of the surrounding country. But, respecting the extravagant nature of its apologies so artistically interwoven with the absence of something more desirable, I have little to say. Let that feature be forgotten and nameless evermore. The lake is bordered on three sides by a rank, dark growth of rushes, grass, brush and receding timber, forming excellent cover for cautious grouse and other birds.

The scenery in the immediate vicinity of the lake is of a diversified character and in striking contrast with the long and monotonous reach of prairie which looks so bleak and brown beyond. We sought repose only when nature made her demands imperative, and left a call for "Five o'clock in the morning."

After a night of unbroken rest, breathing the pure air of heaven instead of the malarial poisons of the East we breakfasted with the lark and were soon in good shape to try conclusions with the ducks. Three of the party decided to break ranks and establish blinds upon the upper part of the same lake. Bless the innocents, they thought we failed to penetrate the object of their disloyalty, which was to intercept the ducks nearer their place of rising and thus get them within easy range. It was Deacon, Duke and Baron who deserted us, saying: "Good morning, gentlemen, we'll count feathers with you at noon."

They had a brisk walk of about a mile before them. Their departure left Judge, Nap and the writer to stumble along down hill through the little "neck o'woods" leading to the stands which we had already selected. The former section of our party was accompanied by Sport and Nig Jr., while we were happy in the possession of Nig Sr., and a fine native retriever, all of them of unexceptional parts and having their full share of animal intelligence. The morning was to be a lovely one, and the day bright and beautiful. It was neither too warm nor too cold, but tempered to a delightful average as to weather. The sky was cloudless, barring the shadowy haze of early morning, now fast dissolving before the oncoming of another sun. The air was tremulous and musical with the song of happy birds, and all nature seemed to be kneeling and lifting up her voice in some form of worship. I would not forget the peaceful calm of that morning, the thoughts it suggested, nor the feelings that were wrought in us as we silently threaded our way through the tangled brush. Upon entering the winding woodland path a little beyond, the lake came into view, the dreamy waters of which were now fretting into foam by the light winds which were sweeping over them. Emerging from the woods at the edge of the lake, what a vision broke upon us! Just look upon it; see the scores of thousands, ye deluded lovers of ducks, and wish that ye were there. The lake was a restless mass of life, covering more than a hundred acres. But, hold! You are as much deceived by the picture as we were by the reality. Said Nap in a whisper:

"Great Caesar, just look at 'em! Millions! Did mortal ever see the like before?"

"Yes," added Judge, "Millions!! - and mud hens every one."

With that cruel sentence he laid a withering hand upon the scene. The spell was gone, and we were obliged to feel thankful for the few butter-balls, red-heads and spoon-bills flying by. After taking a careful "lay o' the land," Nap and Judge selected stands in the rushes next the timber, confidently expecting all the ducks would come to them to be "gathered in." The writer went on to the old stand, doubting whether he could verify his share of the morning's figures. Only a little work was necessary to make the blind one of comfort as well as concealment, and in a very few moments ducks in twos, threes and fives could be seen upon the wing on all sides. But they were all local ducks and had been shot at until their knowledge of a gun's range was marvelous. In reality they were trained ducks and very few of them were in the habit of being killed or even wounded. Where one was shot at within seventy-five yards, ten were saluted at a greater distance! Large bags were out of the question; but the fusilade was not lessened on that account, neither was the ardor of the shooters dampened by it. Presently the words, "Mark! Mark!!," uttered sharply and in quick succession, reached me, and, looking diagonally along the pass, I saw five beautiful mallards sweeping in to Judge and Nap, who arose just in time to bring down one each. They were two pretty shots, and they turned the rest nicely out of range for me. I smiled and waited; but it was not long before I was surprised by a pair of canvas-backs, flying so low that I failed to mark them until they were almost directly over me. Quickly turning about, I sent one of them whizzing into the lake dead, and his mate is probably sunning himself in southern waters at this writing. Larger flocks of red-heads and butter-balls were flying now, and for a time shooting was fast and furious.

In war times the continuous booming of these three guns would have alarmed an army and sent its men pell mell to their guns. Stream after stream of fire belched upward and duck after duck was handsomely—missed! In fact, it was so agreeable to them that some returned a second time, just to get missed again, and they generally got it.

The steady "bang, bang, bang" on the upper pass indicated that a lively scrimmage was in progress there, and we naturally measured our companion's success, or lack of it, by our own. Nap even wanted to bet a "trade dollar against a hundred cents" that they were either killing mud hens or missing ducks. He found no takers. As to the counting up process, we hung our hopes high above defeat, and even felt eager for the time to arrive.

The local ducks around Ten Mile Lake cling with great tenacity to their course in the upper air, so high that they could hardly be disturbed by a cannon ball. They could defy us except in rare instances when they ventured near enough to make killing possible. We blazed away at them till about ten o'clock, when the flight ceased, stragglers only being on the wing. The morning's shoot was by no means satisfactory or successful, our bag containing fully fifty per cent more disappointments than ducks. We were rewarded by a total of less than sixty, including nearly every species, a few tantalizing dippers thrown in.

At eleven o'clock Baron and his party were seen wending their way toward lunch, with weary steps and long faces. They manifested no anxiety to hear our experience or relate their own; but we finally wrung from them the tardy confession that twenty ducks, three mud hens, a king-fisher and a muskrat was all they had to explain the emptiness of more than one hundred excellent Climax shells. Deacon observed with great soberness that, "Ten Mile Lake was a highly exaggerated place for anything except mud hens, and ducks on their way to heaven." Baron and Duke were now ready to try pastures new, and we all regretted having broken the original compact.

After a short consultation with all members present, it was determined to sample the afternoon fishing and enjoy the flight shooting in the evening. We dined at the hotel as usual, and enjoyed a little target practice at a loon far out on the lake for a noon spell. Although the bullets struck the water very near him, he still lives to tell how near. Three of the party—Deacon, Baron and Duke—roamed the prairie at their own sweet will. Nap decided to share the glory of their victory, but preferred to let them win it first. Judge and the writer rowed the lake to interview the fish. The best fishing grounds were pointed out to us by a youth employed at the hotel. They were said to be near the southeast shore of the lake and we lost no time in reaching them. The large fish included perch, pickerel, and Oswego bass. The smaller varieties are those common to most Western lakes. Bass are caught weighing up to seven or eight pounds, and pickerel are taken sometimes weighing from twelve to fifteen pounds. They are simply a larger type of the pike of Eastern waters. The sport of capturing these fish is too tame and commonplace to be called pleasure. They have no fighting qualities whatever, and even seem as happy out of water as in it. Judge caught several bass, but he cannot tell to this day whether to call it fishing or not. After witnessing the domestic nature of these pet fish, the writer preferred to be a disinterested spectator. The boating was delightful and a compensation in part of the almost intolerable fishing.

On returning to quarters, we met the rest of the party coming in tired and only moderately successful. They had crossed the upper lake in a boat and found that ducks were passing in small numbers at long intervals and as usually were investigating the mysterious regions of the clouds. They were soon ranged in line along the shore and concealed from view by the long rushes, and intended to surprise us later by a fine score; but the only surprise was reserved for them. They had killed but eighteen—a few canvas-backs, three or four mallards and the rest butter-balls and red-heads. Deacon remarked that such shooting was only a "ruinous blight of one's hopes," while a nod of assent "went round the room." We took advantage of the precious hour preceding darkness, when, upon all well regulated waters, it should be the flying time of mallards and other large ducks, and we were well prepared to receive them. The flight was fairly good and it was enjoyed by the entire party. Baron defended a blind on the road near the timber; Judge and Duke on the same pass below him; while Deacon, Nap and I were seated in the brush and grass a short distance apart, waiting anxiously for the old drakes to wake up and fly. They started out in singles at first, and were inclined to follow the pass occupied by Baron, who made some very handsome shots with his Smith gun, a few of the ducks being away up. He kept Nig Jr. busy searching in the grass for the dead and crippled ones. Judge and Duke were serenading those missed by Baron, but at each fire the ducks began to climb the air, which made killing them a very uncertain thing. Nap sighted a large flock coming directly toward him and watched them almost breathlessly as they swung off to the right and slowly came back in a circular course, making a low side shot. He scored one fine plump mallard with his first barrel and an unaccountable miss with the other. He felt only half as happy as if he had bagged two, and turned his gun over the over again to discover why it made a miss with the left. Just at this point Baron cried, "Mark! Mark!" and, looking up, I caught a glimpse of several canvas-backs as they went whirling by. Quickly turning, I sent a charge of No. 6 shot after them and instantly one began to lag behind as though he had forgotten something. He continued his downward flight for about a half mile and was reckoned among the irretrievable cripples; which, after a day or two of rest, would join his companions in their regular flights.

Nig Sr. was a grand retriever, owned by Conductor Hanly, of St. Paul, and kindly sent to us at Ten Mile Lake by him. He could be depended on to attend strictly to business without instructions or interference of any kind and Mr. Hanly received our thanks embellished with a few ducks for such voluntary kindness.

The rest of the evening shooting was on a par with that described, the whole number killed being less than forty ducks. Anything less than twenty-five ducks to each shooter per day was considered but a loss of precious time and a waste of good ammunition.

The hours of the evening were employed chiefly in collecting and arranging our shooting traps for transportation by the early morning "dead X" express to Dalton, and we looked forward to that inevitable event with a feeling akin to grief. But there seemed to be no way of escape except in the lake, or at the wrong end of a gun, either of which would be a too fatal alternative.

When the hour came for mounting the "dead X" there were no passengers. Their courage was unequal to the occasion. With a suggestive shrug, Baron announced that his people "were looking for him instead of an obituary." Nap and Duke thought "if the dogs couldn't stand it, they wouldn't try." With convincing emphasis Deacon said: "Why it is simply monstrous to expect gentlemen to endure such an indignity! It is too compromising for anything." The matter was finally settled amicably by two of the party taking the prairie for it, thus making it possible for the rest of the party to go on springs. Just one "dead X" experience across a rough prairie will be sufficient to give any man a lively appreciation of something more comfortable. The walk to Dalton was both breezy and healthful, highly appreciated by Judge and the writer, who carried their guns and bagged some game on the way over.

A very large percentage of the settlers of Northwestern Minnesota are Norwegians, Germans and Finlanders. They are an industrious, law-abiding and happy people. They fled from the curses enforced by the aristocracies of their respective governments, to find an asylum here in the "land of the free," where they can toil on unmolested in the pursuit of happiness, and win a home where "all men are created free and equal." They have been ground down so long by the iron hand of foreign injustice that the freedom they are permitted to enjoy in this country is almost like an escape from death. They are slow to avail themselves of the advantages of our educational systems, inasmuch as their first and greatest need on reaching our shores is the erection of a home. The wants of these people are few; their habits are simple and inexpensive. Their propensity for saving is universal. In most instances their only capital is trained muscles, rugged health, a big determination, and from five to ten children; and they thank God that they can rear the latter where some day they will be recognized as men and women, instead of being regarded as the chattels or slaves of mercenary rulers, or the half-paid servants of royalty. They are already beginning to reap golden harvests upon the prairies, and hoarding it in their coffers until in the near future this element may become an important factor in the affairs of the Northwest.

Kingston, Pa.

SPORT IN DAKOTA - NO. 3
1887

Some of our own people who now occupy cozy homes in Northwestern Minnesota give glowing accounts of past experience and future prospects. They look back to the East with a sigh, and their long residence there simply as a sad recollection that lies wrapped up now among the rest of their sorrows. We all pity ourselves because we did not go West a hundred years ago. And—but at this stage of my digression Baron and the rest of my companions were seen at a distance making for the station at high speed. If our train had been on time they would not. Judge and the writer took time by the forelock, starting at least an hour in advance of them and reaching the station with a full half hour to spare. Only a few minutes passed before the train came thundering in, and we were soon flying down grade on the way to Devils Lake, in what ought to be the state of Dakota.

The country lying between Dalton and Moorhead, Minn., is a vast plain, fenceless for miles, and without a tree to break the monotony of the scene except those found in the vicinity of lakes or seen along streams. For farming purposes the thousands of fertile and unoccupied acres traversed by the St. P., M. & M. R. R. are probably not surpassed anywhere, and that company can be relied upon to redeem their pledges and carry out their contracts with individuals in every case. Lands can be secured from them and fine locations without number. The only reason that our Eastern farmers fail to investigate this matter is due to their ignorance of its advantages in the way of climate, fertility of soil, excellent markets, liberal prices paid for farm products, etc. The St. P., M. & M. R. R. runs through a fine game section of the Northwest. Prairie chickens, ducks and geese are present everywhere; on both sides of the track prairie chickens were seen rising out of the grass in large and small flocks; while ducks were almost constantly upon the wing. As we neared Moorhead the country became more rolling and broken, and widened out almost incredibly. Immense straw and hay stacks arrested the eye of the visitor, as they lifted their dark forms in the distance, and he unconsciously compares them to the sentinel ships of the ocean, or, thinks of them as veritable ships themselves.

Moorhead lies in the valley of the Red River of the North and is 220 miles from Winnipeg, capital of the province of Manitoba, in the British Dominion. It is 250 miles from St. Paul. The Red River is the dividing line between Minnesota and Dakota. Fargo, Dak., is just across the river from Moorhead, and has a population of 8,000. Moorhead has a population of 5,000. Both these towns have fine hotels, elegant residences, large business blocks, extensive factories, and wide streets lighted by the electric system known as the Van der Poehle. Two private steamboat lines are in successful operation upon the Red River, making Moorhead and Fargo places of considerable importance, being at the head of navigation. The activity in business circles here is a feature which was frequently commented upon by our party, and it became more marked in view of the general dullness of the East. Business is done upon business principles; while the people of the East are studying what to do, the West is doing it. While we are discussing the feasibility of plans, counting the cost of projects and improvements, the West and Northwest are making them, reaping the harvest, and counting the cost in their balance sheets at the end of the year, frequently entering on the right side of profit and loss account the Dutchman's "von per cent."

The beautiful and almost boundless prairie beyond Moorhead will doubtless prove to be a revelation to any one who has never seen it. It is of a gently rolling nature and extends far beyond the range of human vision, away out apparently to the sky itself. The Dakotan's toast expressed it better than any words of mine can do, when he said, at the London banquet, "It is bounded on the north by the Aurora Borealis, on the south by the eternal equinoxes, on the east by the rascality of political circles, and on the west by the day of judgment." He was right, only his eastern boundary would appear a trifle narrow. "Hoist up the flag and long may she wave," over the West and Northwest, if nowhere else.

> "Breathes there a man with soul so dead,
> Who never to himself hath said
> This is our own our glorious West?"

If there breathes such a man he ought to go to church and ask the Lord to forgive him. The indescribable character of the ravishing sights in the beautiful wonderlands of the far Northwest makes it a difficult task indeed for any writer to portray to his own satisfaction in words that which required the master brush of Nature to paint. Words become poverty stricken in the vain attempt, and—but I am in the wrong channel again. Shooting was the chief topic of conversation on the way to Devils Lake, and we were exceedingly anxious to get hold of fresh and reliable shooting notes from that section. In fact, we were talking the matter over when Mr. S. B. Bennet, of Devils Lake City, made himself known to us as a sportsman of that place. Mr. Bennet was found to be a man of versatile talents, a master of mimicry, and a jolly good fellow. He informed us that our objective point was a good country for game and that we might reasonably expect to find good shooting within a few miles of the town. Our hopes were again rosy with promise. Ducks and geese were represented as being there in fair numbers. But, as ducks were to be our principal beverage, we were more directly interested in reports concerning them.

A conspicuous feature of the trip—one that shall remain green after the rest have been forgotten—was the midnight ride through half a hundred miles of howling prairie fire. The sky was painted red by it. The air was full of it. The great prairie was one hissing, roaring sea of flame. The bonfires and campaigns of a century would be as a candle to the awful impressiveness and grandeur of the scene. The flames assumed fantastic shapes on every side of us. They were coiling like serpents; zig-zag, like lightning; in straight lines; hollow and solid squares; sometimes semicircular; leaping upward; sweeping onward; swaying to and fro upon the wind; now halting for fresh fuel; then rushing madly on again with a fury resistless and unrelenting as fate itself. The finest effect produced by these fires, and the grandest display I ever witnessed was when a mammoth straw stack began to totter and fall. It was a solid mass of flame and the wind lifted it into the air in bunches, resembling gorgeous chariots of fire dropping sparks and stars in their course. In some places the occupants of little homes were seen manfully fighting the flames with buckets and wet blankets to protect their property from the threatening fires. But we plunged along through flame and smoke till we reached a stream intersecting the track which checked the fires and we were again encompassed by the darkness of that memorable red night.

Nap was one of the most enthusiastic and hopeful shooters of our party; he was excitable and anxious to distinguish himself on the lake or along the passes, and he had wrought himself up to a great pitch of expectancy in regard to the sport of the days to follow. He had taken his berth and was soon oblivious to his surroundings; but no wonder that in his visions countless flocks of ducks went sweeping by. They were coming in, going out, flying over, and making straight at him. Self-defense was a necessity. He would pick up a shell (or go through the motions), put it in his gun, take deliberate aim and pull as naturally as though actually shooting. Then with a smile he would inquire:

"Say, Deacon, didn't you see 'em tumble?"

With the stealthy tread of an Indian, Judge and Duke were creeping up to Nap's berth. One of them pulled the curtain aside, while the other put a duck call to his ear and blew a startling "Quack! quack! quack!" The sleeper, all in a perspiration, raised upright in bed and excitedly called, "Mark! mark!!!" Intently watching the flight till it came in range, he suddenly grasped his boot (a beautiful ten gauge) and raising it to his shoulder, heel up, he blazed away. Dreadful havoc was the result of that shot, for he was heard to call:

"Here, Nig; here, Nig; fetch 'em all in, old boy. Take care, sir; don't you muss a feather!"

Of course he killed the whole flock. This was too much for his tormentors, who burst into such peals of laughter that he suddenly came to his senses. He took in the whole situation, however, and, with a sleepy look inquired with a well assumed indifference:

"Say, Judge, how far is it to Devils Lake City?"

As this episode is somewhat damaging to Nap's reputation for level headedness, I promised at the point of his old hunting knife never to mention it, and I propose to keep that promise if I break every other.

It was not long until Devils Lake City began to loom up in the distance. After many days we were really pulling in at last. We engaged quarters at Hotel Benham, named after Col. Benham, the present proprietor. Here we received letters from Eastern friends and from "the girls we left behind us," saying what a great relief our absence proved to be; how they could wake up in the morning without having to hunt somebody's boot, and breakfast at eleven instead of eight, and no big man about to kick the dog, denounce the cat, and make things tropical in general. Then, the late Fall shapes! "Too lovely," "Great improvement over last season." "A perfect beauty for only twenty-five dollars and a half, and they would throw off the half!" But, oh! If they would only keep on the half and throw off the rest. They even hinted that they would do everything in their power to help us off earlier another Fall, so we might stay longer—just because we enjoyed it so. We just envied them!

Devils Lake City was named after the lake near the town. Although only four years old, it has nearly one thousand inhabitants and people are pouring in instead of moving out. It is well located, the streets running slightly up grade from the depot toward the center of town and sloping back from there toward the lake. Buildings are large and substantial. Business is well represented in point of extent as well as variety, and the people are doubtless there to stay. Two churches, two newspapers, two good hotels, several banks, a handsome Presbyterian church in Gothic style of stone, and a fine school building are among the prominent features of the place. The water is alkali in character hence not friendly in its effect upon the "tenderfoot," but no great inconvenience was experienced by us on this account. Duke was the only one affected by it, and he was only sick during one night. There was a disposition in one or two of our number to go from the city far out upon the prairie and establish camp as headquarters for operations during our stay; but wiser councils prevailed, in view of the fact that excellent shooting grounds could be reached within an easy and pleasant drive from the hotel, without having to spend so much time in transferring our large outfit from one point to another.

The dogs were in splendid spirits, and exceedingly impatient here to pursue their favorite sport of retrieving. The life-giving air of that glorious country seemed to have an unhappy effect upon Nap's pointer. He began to expand with the prairies, and took delight in doing as little as he pleased, or, a good deal of what he was not wanted to do. Prompt application of raw-hide proved a good punishment and he was obedient to commands and perfectly respectful thereafter.

We made Hotel Benham our headquarters for several days, and had teams at the door at an early hour every morning to carry us to various shooting grounds recommended by the sportsmen of the city. Ducks, brants, and snipes of different kinds could be seen at any hour of the day, flying across the head of the lake, not more than a hundred rods from our hotel. In fact, it was a good pass for the morning and evening flights, as the fowls were on the lake during the day, and on the wing morning and evening passing to and from different waters. It was not unusual to see very large flocks of ducks near town, some of them containing hundreds and flying low enough to make bagging easy. A place called, "Spaulding's pass," or the "Mauvaise Couleè" (meaning bad grain stream), distant from Devils Lake City from eighteen to twenty miles, was said to furnish fine sport, and we prepared for a pilgrimage to that paradise, starting at five o'clock a.m. the following day. But guide and driver failed to be on hand. Still we were not to be thwarted thus and determined to try it alone, after getting safe landmarks and correct bearings. Baron and Nap said it would be "an accomplishment to boast of should we go to the coulee without assistance." Judge and Deacon "Knew we could do it." Nap said. "It requires a big head to suggest it." But we were ready and the horses eager to start, so we mounted the long spring wagon, drawn by a pair of dashing bays, put Judge in charge of the reins, and made him master of ceremonies for the day. As Judge drew up the reins to start, Col. Uline, a new friend, came to us with an additional word of caution respecting the best course, saying:

"Now, gentlemen, you first cross the railroad at the lake, and keep on for about a mile, when you will re-cross it. Don't leave the main road till you cross it the third time; then bear off northeast, and keep that direction till you reach the Mauvaise Couleè. With my best wishes for your pleasure and success, gentlemen, I bid you good morning."

"Many thanks, Colonel," replied Baron; "your directions are clear, and we expect to get there by daylight."

"If we don't, we'll get somewhere else," added Duke.

But time was passing, and we struck out boldly, confident of reaching the coulee without adventure or mishap of any kind. We were soon spinning over the plain, crossing the railroad, re-crossing it, and repeating the operation for the third time, as had been directed by the pleasant Colonel. So far we knew that no mistake had occurred. There seemed to be one well beaten trail and the rest were simply auxiliary. The distance from Devils Lake City was not more than four or five miles, and we had not doubled it before serious doubts were expressed about things in general. By some stroke of *leger de main,* the railroad was now on the wrong side of us, and—but I will tell you in my next something of the sensation of being lost in "God's country," upon a prairie about one hundred miles one way and three hundred the other.

Kingston, Pa.

SPORT IN DAKOTA - NO. 4
1887

The directions of Colonel Uline were strictly observed, and at the start it was not believed that anything in the way of insurmountable difficulties would be likely to be encountered. Leaving all evil predictions behind, we went spinning over the prairie after a spirited team, enjoying the crisp, clear morning with the mercury about fifty degrees above zero, never even dreaming of the amusing little complications to be unraveled later in the day. Indeed we were not more than six or seven miles out from the city when several braves among us began to express doubts about everything in general. For instance, the railroad got on the other side of us without our crossing it. Of course it must have been accomplished by trickery, *leger de main,* or diabolism of some kind. Then, too, the sun proved fickle and erratic in its course. We had been accustomed to see it rise in the east, but now it was majestically rising out of the south. All creeks and sloughs ran up hill—something they were seldom known to do even in Dakota. Three or four trails ran parallel to the one we were on. Three or four more made away to the right. Five or six others led off to the left. We knew what was left, but which was right? Our best compasses registered falsehoods every time. All signs were simply treacherous and misleading. Even the main trail, so clear and well defined at first, was now beginning to be provokingly indistinct. At last it just ran into the grass and stayed there.

"What shall we call it, anyway?" said Duke.

"Guess we're left," coolly replied Baron.

"Great Caesar, Deacon, how does it strike you?" said Nap.

"Well, gentlemen," said he, "I regard it as a very serious deviation from a desirable course."

Deacon was right, and Judge was laughing over the apparent lack of confidence in himself as guide, coachman, and director-general. But he cracked his rawhide and away we dashed over rough plowed ground, and everything else that our wheels could climb. He was making a beeline for a trail visible about a mile distant. The ride was an amusing repetition of the "dead X" experience upon a small scale, and Deacon feared we would all go to eternal smash under Judge's driving, which he mildly denounced as "reckless cowboy horsemanship." On nearing the new-found trail, it was discovered to be only the private "right of way" belonging to some settler, and by no means a solution of the problem before us. We stopped for consultation. The horses enjoyed it and the dogs were having a happy time roaming the plain in quest of prairie chickens. It was finally determined to make for the nearest sod shanty for directions. It looked but a few minutes drive, but turned out to be fully five miles off. We arrived, however, without need for repairs, and Baron dismounted for information. Repeated and vigorous knocking at the front and only door brought forth a muscular giantess of the Northland, who seemed startled and annoyed at seeing such a "heap o' folks." She stared at us in blank amazement, trying to divine the object of our mission, then bestowed a loving look upon Baron, put half of her apron in her mouth, folded her arms, and was ready for the interview. With a most winning smile, the gallant Baron inquired:

"Can you tell us, my good woman, the best way to the Mauvaise Couleé?"

To make it short, he got this terse and witty answer:

"Maucoo unga punga yarok!"

That settled it. Baron looked grateful; the picture of happiness. Nap whispered.

"I tole you so."

Judge lighted the latter third of a cheap cheroot for the fourth time, swung his number thirteens over the dash board, and lustily

called for Baron, saying:
"Come on; I can go there now with my eyes shut."
But Deacon capped the climax with:
"Well, gentlemen, I should expect to be far more successful in reaching the coulee with my eyes closed than open."
This speech brought down spire, shingles and all, and Baron joined us again in the attempt to get through by the "unga punga" route. Being clear as mud to us now, we renewed our search for the coulee with a happy feeling of increased confusion. Judge put the bud to the pacers (in Devils Lake parlance) and we were soon bounding over the plain, into badger holes, over tufts of buffalo grass, and Dakota hills (eighteen by twenty-four inches; actual measure), through little sloughs, and around big ones, across broken sod and stubbles, until in ascending a gentle grade, we were suddenly confronted by a nameless lake, approaching at about its center. "Misfortunes never come single," but in squads, thought we. But, becoming accustomed to the train of difficulties, it was now a favorite beverage with Judge, who suddenly wheeled to the left and circumnavigated the new obstacle in fine style. On we rode, apparently in full view of all creation, but—lost! The deepest solitude of some dark old forest, surrounded by the weird and solemn voices of the night, could not have intensified our sensation of loneliness. We thought of the cheering comforts of Eastern firesides, and longed to be—on the right road to the coulee! But where were we? Out upon the boundless acres of Dakota, where, at the close of day, we could only wrap ourselves up in the mantle of night, without even a barb wire fence for a mattress, or a hill bigger than a bologna for a pillow.

"Look!" suddenly exclaimed Nap, excitedly pointing toward a moving object in the distance. The party instinctively rose to their feet, inquiring, "What is it?"

"It's a live grizzly!" shouted Duke.

"No it isn't; it's a big cinnamon," said Baron.

But Deacon declared it was "unwise to undertake the solution of so difficult a question at such a distance; it's coming straight for us," he added in some alarm.

"Ha, Ha!" laughed Nap, making the true discovery. "It's a man; a big man; a live man!" And he was right.

"Hello!"

No answer.

"Hello, neighbor!"

Mute as the stars. But on coming within reasonable hailing distance he was found to be a man; a master of the situation, as well as of the most vigorous and forcible English. He put us on our way singing "pity the sorrows of a poor old man" and other suggestive and pathetic anthems.

Under favorable winds we were due at the coulee about 8:30 a.m.; but now, with all the unfriendly fates of the Northwest arrayed against us, it was high noon and several miles yet to go. We halted long enough to refresh the inner man with lemon juice and lunch, fed the dogs and horses, and started on again. About a half hour later we suddenly beheld the coulee nestled cozily in a depression of the prairie, looking placid and serene as though it had never been lost at all. Congratulations were the order of the hour. Every man was enthusiastic in his admiration of the picture before us. About two hundred yards west of the dark stream we came into the half broken trail that entered the rushes leading to the ferry, and were soon standing by the flat boat tied by the bank waiting for Captain Piper to pole us across. He came; a rugged specimen of Franco-German lineage, dwarfed in stature, but willing and helpful in more ways than one. A short distance on the other side we found three trees which served the double purpose of hitching posts and a shady shelter for the horses. While unpacking we could see nearly every kind of waterfowl crossing the passes, but before we selected shooting positions we made a hasty tour of the Mauvaise Couleé. It is a long, dark, sluggish and irregular stream, three feet wide here, fifty yards there and about a fourth of a mile beyond. Both shores are fringed with tall grass; hazel and other brush characteristic of the country. Throughout its entire length it is dotted with grassy islands and clumpy bogs, furnishing excellent hiding for the gorgeous mallard and timid canvas-back. They were there, too, picking their feathers, bathing, and playing hide and seek with the sunbeams that were quivering in the grass. The Mauvaise Couleè country is a veritable feeding and breeding ground for them. One would think that, as Nature has fashioned everything to their needs and uses, it may have been the birthplace of the species.

Judge stood at the point of brush which runs out a short distance into the stream. Nap and Duke selected places just below the ferry, leaving Deacon, Baron and the undersigned upon the opposite shore, planted well in among the rushes, and about one hundred yards apart. We were ready for the ducks, and the dogs were waiting for us to give them something to retrieve. There are nine different varieties of snipes in the Devils Lake region and they go almost wholly in flocks ranging from any number up to several hundred. One flock, flying the gauntlet over Baron, lost a round dozen of their number. He had Nig Jr. bring them out with great pomp and ceremony. "First blood," he shouted, and that proved to be the signal for a general engagement with the winged tribes of the couleé. It was kept up for nearly an hour. Ducks were everywhere, darting into the stream and rising from it. Nap and Duke made several fine shots below the ferry, some of the noblest ducks of Dakota folding their wings at the report of their guns. Soon the startling call, "Mark!" was heard, and, looking quickly along the edge of the woods, I saw five handsome mallards heading toward me. Rising at the supreme moment, I had the pleasure of dropping the leader, and the regret of crippling one of his mates which sailed on for half a mile and dropped into the grass, lost. Here Deacon called to Baron, excitedly, thus:

"Hello, Baron, I fancy I see the greatest flock of ducks that ever darkened a continent!"

"Where?" asked Baron, with a doubtful eye.

"Can't you see that long, dark line out yonder?"

"Why, yes," he replied, "and it's a good indication of a thunderstorm, too."

"But don't you discern a greater distinctness now? Very soon their forms will be seen, and first thing you know you will be shooting at that same thunderstorm, and gathering up ducks as the result."

The dark line came swinging on, swaying from right to left, narrowing up and widening out until Deacon's prophecy came true. They were ducks, and such a flock! There must have been more than a thousand in line. They came over us utterly unaware of the half dozen death-traps in the rushes, and were knocked out in handsome style. Judge bagged two, Baron two, the writer three, and the rest one each.

Flight shooting was all that was anticipated, and even surpassed the best accounts given us respecting it. Single ducks were constantly whizzing past, and we began to prefer that class of shooting as being better for practice. Flocks therefore received no further attention. A beautiful mallard drake was seen some distance in front, coming straight down stream, turning his head to one side and the other, keeping one eye on the watch for lurking foes. "Mark!" said Judge. On he came, gracefully rounding the back edge of the little woods in the rear of Baron, and suddenly wheeling in among the guns. "Bang! Bang!," and two more from Judge and Baron failed to arrest him. The writer sent some No. 6 too far behind him; but Deacon fortunately brought him whirling down into the stream. He instantly recovered, however, "trimmed ship," and began to paddle away, evidently expecting a serenade of more thunder, and Deacon's second was necessary as a finishing stroke. Realizing that he had one of the gorgeous kings of the coulee before him, it certainly added a full cubic foot to his stature, and he shouted in great triumph, "*Veni, vidi, vici.*" That duck was too precious a treasure in Deacon's eyes to allow any dog to retrieve him, so he proudly undertook it himself. He had gone but a few paces in the direction of the duck, when to his horror, he found himself planted in the middle of one of the most treacherous alkali beds, perfectly at its mercy, and evidently on his way down to the Celestial Empire. He was powerless to extricate himself, and called lustily for Baron to assist him. Baron accordingly approached Deacon very cautiously, saying:

"Well, Deacon, you've made a pretty mess of it, haven't you?"

"I hope not," he replied, "but I incline strongly to the belief that it may ultimately make a mess of me unless relief comes quickly.

After making a mat of rushes for a footing, Baron began tugging and pulling at Deacon until great drops of sweat poured down his face. He tried it again and again, but failed as often. Then he clasped him under the arms and with a "Now, Deacon, yo-heave," he pulled till the buttons flew. "Once more; all together; now, yo-heave!" But Deacon was anchored like the rock of ages. Baron, with a feeling of desperation, seized him for the last time saying, "Up you come, Deacon; all together, now; yo-heave!!" By this final herculean effort Deacon was so forcibly torn from his moorings that he nearly lost his boots, and both he and Baron fell violently backward. He sat like a weary child in Baron's lap, while Baron sat about two feet in the mud looking every inch a hero. Of course Deacon was inexpressibly happy over his timely rescue, and shuddered till his great frame shook as he looked back to the deadly spot which was so nearly the scene of his demise. His first question was, "Where's my duck?" The second, "Where's my gun?" But fortunately he had left it in plain sight, sticking muzzle end down in the mud. What a picture of a tenderfoot abroad, and how it would have stirred the soul of Puck!

With the approaching twilight came a greater number of canvas-backs and mallards than we had seen at all, and they were flying low, as a rule. They just poured in from every conceivable quarter; into the water with a swish; out of it with a splash. The air became vibrant with the motion of their wings. It was a spirited scene, enlivened by the flame and roar of guns, and rendered even more impressive by the somber character of our surroundings. Nap and Duke were having fine sport below the ferry, frequently dropping the nice, plump singles as they passed their way, and only the best birds were fired at. The evening shoot was splendid—glorious, and we abandoned it long before the flight ceased because we had enough and were not ambitious to become notorious as game butchers. But I must not neglect to describe the most beautiful shooting scene of the trip which was laid here.

Duke left his stand at the ferry to come in. Judge and Baron started toward the ferry, and, reaching it, stopped a few minutes with Nap for a little visit. A minute or two later three beautiful mallard drakes were marked by them, coming directly over. The three shooters were instantly in line ready to receive them. On they came; up went three guns; "bang! bang! Bang!;" down went three ducks headlong into the stream. Baron took the leader, Nap the next, and Judge captured the third and last. These gentlemen are probably relating that experience while I am writing it.

The evening round-up showed a total bag of sixty-three snipes and nearly a hundred ducks to six guns for less than three hours shooting. Double the number could have been taken, but these were sufficient to pass around among Eastern friends, who were beginning to be clamorous for some evidence of our success. The honors of the shoot were divided between Judge and Baron. I never thought favorably of a hammerless gun for field use, doubting whether its delicate parts would stand the strain of heavy charges in a hot corner; but my experience with the Smith hammerless gave me unbounded confidence in its strength, as well as its fine shooting qualities. Up to this time I had fired about a thousand shells, without a single misfire, misfortune or disappointment, hence I became greatly attached to the gun for general purposes. Accidental discharges are out of the question if ordinary care be observed. The hammerless hereafter will be my field gun, loading four drams of King's Quick Shot powder No. 2 in Climax shells for general shooting.

Night was now upon us with all its ghostly forms. We gathered up the game, drove to the "shack" of Captain Piper, who took charge of our horses and dogs and promised us the best the "shack" afforded for the night. The hostess gladdened our hearts with the assertion that they had "lots of ole pork and sour bread." "Just what we have longed for every since we landed, haven't we, Judge?" said Nap. While the pork was "fryin'," the "taters bilin'," and the coffee "steamin'," we could not resist borrowing a glimpse of the internal arrangement. A little red bedstead stood in on corner, two-thirds of a cook stove in another, a heap of fuel in the third, and a yellow dog in the fourth. The walls were hung with fancy grass frames trimmed with prairie chicken feathers, and exaggerated illustrations without number. A table of rough boards, two two-legged chairs—one without a back—a long bench, a broken lantern, two pounds of tobacco—well; that settles it. The meal was splendid, and thoroughly appreciated. After a short talk and a long smoke, Baron and Deacon were elected to occupy the bed. We hired the host to bring us a load of straw and then give us sole possession, himself and wife going to her parents for the night. We spread out the straw and blanketed it in true camp "meetin'," fashion; then turned in to sleep, "perchance to dream." The shack was eight by ten feet on the ground, sided with pine boards running lengthwise. We could see all the stars but one through the roof, and everything else through the cracks in the sides. Many a king would have sold his crown for half the happiness that reigned in that shack. We were off for Devils Lake City in the morning, reaching it safely.

Kingston, Pa.

SPORT IN DAKOTA - NO. 5
1887

Devils Lake is roughly estimated to be seventy miles in length, and it is said to be a body of salt water. Two steamboats make daily trips between Fort Totten and Devils Lake City, a distance of fourteen miles. In addition to these a government tug was used in early Spring to transport military and other supplies from the city to the fort, but in some mysterious way it was burned one night to the water's edge. The fire was no doubt of incendiary origin and conceived of "malice aforethought," but the guilty one escaped the punishment which he so richly merited.

A portion of our Sabbath at Devils Lake City was delightfully spent in making a somewhat extended tour of the lake on the steamer Minnie. The captain proved to be a very genial and well-informed man, and entertained us quite agreeably. We passed several pleasant and instructive hours inspecting the fort, examining the many curious features of the Indian mission school, and exploring the old log buildings of the Northwestern Fur Company, now occupied by major Peck and family as the military post, or "mazopia tipi" in the Sioux language. These old buildings are about one hundred feet in length, nearly square, and perhaps eight feet high, with an open court in the center which was used as a place for storing furs and other Indian merchandise. It is a quaint old curiosity for visitors who take an interest in the commercial means and methods used and practiced by fur traders among the Indians in earlier years. Fort Totten is a handsome and substantial piece of masonry, built of gray stone. It covers several acres of ground and is situated upon a hill (so-called) on the north bank of the lake, commanding an excellent view of the lake itself as well as its chief points of interest. At the present time the Seventh cavalry and Fifth infantry are stationed there.

The Indian mission school is a two-story Gothic frame building, admirably adapted to school purposes, and furnished with the most improved Eastern conveniences and comforts. The school is under the general supervision of the Indian Bureau at Washington, but is subject to the local directorship of Major Cransby of the Fort, a very excellent and efficient officer, whose well-known solicitude for the welfare of the little warriors only renders him doubly competent to act as their guardian. The school is taught, with one exception, I believe, by sisters of the Roman persuasion, who are doubtless doing a noble and unselfish educational work—a labor of love. The discipline of the school seems unexcelled, but the denominational character of it may be right or wrong. Whether it is right to enforce a religious preference when there has been no opportunity to express a choice is, probably, debatable ground. The school numbers forty-seven girls and twenty-nine boys, ranging in age from four to ten years; after ten they are promoted to a higher grade located at another point in the Fort. But what sad little faces. To look at them you would think some common sorrow had become interwoven with their lives. You see it in their eyes, note it in their actions, hear it in their voices; it appears to pursue them like an evil dream. Perhaps they realize that they are the last of their line, and that they will soon have to be numbered among the extinct tribes of the Northwest. Sisters Page and Klepin, who were made responsible for our entertainment, gave us an interesting exhibition of their musical ability by requiring two little maidens to sing for us the touching song, "Sister Emma." Their ages were about four and seven, and, though not particularly impressed with the sweetness of their voices, yet the sad character of the composition was so completely in harmony with the dismal drift of their little lives, and the sentiment of the song seemed so plainly to express heartache in the singers that we were deeply stirred by the performance. If the melancholy of the scene was but an artful exhibition calculated to arouse our sympathy and remind us of the unhappy condition of this people; or if it was honestly intended to illustrate the fact that under systematic instruction they are capable of pale-face acquirements, in either view of the case that part of the entertainment must be admitted to have been an unqualified success.

Fort Totten is on the Sioux reservation. This immense Indian farm covers over two hundred thousand acres of the very flower and heart of Dakota. There are about eleven hundred Indians, all Sioux, within its boundaries now. One chief of the hereditary line, Wanata, swells among his people and is a handsome though decrepit representative of his race. These people live mainly in huts furnished with furs, blankets, pipes, papooses, beadwork, feathers, etc. They wear "white men's" clothes for the most part, but some of them refuse even now to abandon their gaudy feathers and trappings. The men hunt and loaf about generally, while the squaws and children do the work and make articles of beads. There are, however, some industrious ones among them; which is attested by the fact that they harvested, during the past season, more than 40,000 bushels of wheat.

Minnewaukan is the Indian name for Devils Lake, and is so noted on all the older maps. The definition of this musical name is "spirit water." The Sioux adhere to a faith which admits of a deity and a devil. They named the lake in honor of the devil, to conciliate him so he would be rendered harmless to them. They worship the devil most because from him they have most to fear. Their superstitions are deep seated as the marrow in their bones. They fully believe that the floor or bed of Devils Lake is carpeted with howling fiends comprising the departed spirits of the worst scoundrels of all nations; that they are in league with satan himself, and that they are watching from their watery caves for poor Lo to appear upon the lake, when they will gobble him in. Hence it is that never has a "buck" been seen gaily paddling his birch canoe upon the beautiful lake.

The Fort Totten side of Devils Lake is fairly well timbered with oak, ash and elm, and a certain species of cottonwood. There are some rocks along its shore weighing several tons each. They are a conglomerate similar to those found among the coal formations of my native state. In fact the surface indications of coal are quite as promising as any in Pennsylvania, and there is little doubt in my mind that a rich deposit of coal will yet be discovered within rifle shot of Devils Lake City.

The remainder of the day of our return from the Mauvaise Couleé was quietly spent arranging little strings of game for friends in the East. We shipped them by the afternoon train through the American Express Co., one of the most prompt and obliging monopolies of that country. It is only just to say that sportsmen may safely intrust their game to them and rely upon speedy shipment and the most careful handling; all the officers are gentlemen, and some of them are sportsmen of the first water, hence they must be manly men.

Duck shooting all over the Devils Lake country was all that any reasonable sportsman could expect. But, as we were soon to have a "goose chase" we promised to give them no further cause for alarm. Exciting reports of brant and goose shooting upon the Lacota stubbles now determined our next stopping place. Baron, Deacon and Duke, however, had been persuaded to interview the same game at Thomas, about twenty-five miles further west, on the St. P., M. & M. R. R. After numerous fraternal "shakes" with the good people of Devils Lake City, our now divided party boarded trains in opposite directions, Nap, Judge and the writer heading toward Lacota, twenty-five miles east of Devils Lake City. We slowed upon to the station about noon. The platform was literally covered with brants, geese and ducks, grouse and jack-rabbits, awaiting shipment by sportsmen who bagged them. We were informed by the station agent that there seemed to be no limit to brant and goose shooting; that they were so abundant that there was little choice as to grounds. We found mine host Standish prepared to receive us at the Palace hotel, and we did full justice to the excellent dinner provided. The hotel is made bright, cozy and homelike by the affable and intelligent host, and his pleasant wife, and our stay was rendered one of the pleasant memories of the trip West. Lacota is a town on the St. P., M. & M. road, in Nelson County, and is a substantial and thriving place. Three years ago it was virgin prairie; now there is a population of more than four hundred, and gives good promise of a healthy future growth. Two fine churches and a grade school adorn the town in addition to several stores, banks, and elevators, one of these due to the private enterprise of a Mr. Hovey, a genial, warm-hearted and prosperous grain dealer.

On the afternoon of our arrival here we were fortunate enough to secure the services of "Alexander" as guide in our shooting excursions. He is unquestionably one of the best brant shooters and one of the most intelligent guides of Dakota. We put him fully in charge of all shooting arrangements, and promised a cheerful obedience to his directions. About two o'clock he called for us at the Palace with a splendid team of black horses, and a driver of his own selection. We were soon out of sight of Lacota, going in the direction of the goose grounds. We seldom saw a trail, or any resemblance of one. The prairie was covered as far as we could see with tall standing grass, countless knolls, from knee-high away up to six or eight feet above a level. Sloughs were simply too numerous and aggravating to mention. They were always where we did not want them. We would have sold them all at a great sacrifice. In fact, we would have disposed of several to any one who would have taken them out of our way. Goose pits had been dug all over the prairie, a distance of a few hundred yards apart. They were generally about three feet wide, six feet deep, and seven or eight feet in length, intended to conceal comfortably two or three shooters.

Our attention was directed to a novel sight in the distance. Looking away to the right we beheld what at first seemed to be a huge snow bank, lying against the sun side of a long knoll; it looked like nothing else and strongly reminded one of a bleak Wintry day. The writer unconsciously committed the blunder of inquiring, "if snow banks were common in Dakota in October," and received the reply that "all such snow banks could be found to be alive." A few minutes sharp driving gave us a satisfactory explanation of the guide's answer. The snow bank proved to be simply a solid mass of live brants, with a generous inter-sprinkling of brown geese. They appeared to cover every available square yard of a twenty-acre stubble, and numbered no doubt well up among the thousands. This was admitted to be the finest game picture of the trip. We were yet fully five hundred yards from the flock, but could see them craning their necks, and moving about among themselves. Driving a little to the right of them was intended as a ruse to disarm their suspicion, but it was noticed that they were greatly excited and confused. Presently, as though by magic every one of that great flock faced us in a steady and inquisitive stare. That was the supreme moment, Alexander turning to Nap, said, "Get right out into that bunch of grass, lie flat, and keep your gun out of sight; don't rise till you hear them above you."

Seeing a convenient pit to the left, he gave me the same instruction, taking Judge a little further on, when he was dropped out in a rank growth of buffalo grass. By this time the brants were wild with fear, and commotion. They were terribly in earnest about something and were chattering like a crowd of Hungarians full of beer. Some wanted to fly, even started, but came back because their companions were still undecided. They were evidently all waiting for the signal of a leader and anxious for it to be given. Alexander now gave his driver these directions: "Go south; put your horses on a dead run, and come in on them from the rear." Disobediently "peeking" out of my pit, I shall never forget the picture of that flying team. The horses seemed to be in the air, only touching the ground occasionally because it was in their way, and leaving but a cloud of dust to mark their course. Guide and driver had all they could do to hold fast to the wagon, while the seats were "playing taps" in the wagon box. On, on they flew like maniacs, rounding the knoll at terrific speed, until they were out of sight. Away went the brants, slowly winging their way upward, file after file at first, then an acre or more at once. Then came the frantic team, dashing up the knoll in their rear, guide cracking the whip, and the driver shouting to the horses: "Git there Nellie!! Ged-ep Sam!!!" Thus they came tearing over the knoll and down among the frightened and tardy brants. The driver, with all the breath he could muster now checked the team with along and lusty, "Whoa!!" They stopped almost with the suddenness of a bucking broncho, with heads down, foaming and panting, when Alexander rose to his feet, gun in hand, and sent eight of the belated ones of that flock into the dust. His shooting was grand. The entire flock now began to fly over us, and what a magnificent sight! Fluttering and bewildered thousands came screaming over us with their thin slow wings gleaming in the sunlight like nothing we ever saw before. The medley of sound was deafening. They were scared out of their wits. They went swinging to right and left, and circling back; in some cases the same birds coming over us two or three times before taking final leave. It was "bang"—"bang" from every shooter, and the birds frequently came whirling down in the grass.

    A full hour must have passed before the flock got out of sight. Judge bagged six, Nap five, and the writer six making twenty-five birds from one flock. Brants could often be seen in large numbers at long distances, either picking over the stubbles or sunning themselves on the knolls; but as it was the easiest thing in the world to shoot all we wanted, we found more pleasure in occasional than in constant shooting, and lying in the grass waited for them to come to us instead of chasing after them. Of course I promised to say nothing about the Judge's "goose chase" and I will not; but, there surely can be no harm in writing it. His experience comes so fully within the old familiar meaning of the term that I am sure it will be appreciated. He crippled a single goose that sailed on some distance and came down on his right. Dropping his gun, he made for it in graceful three-minute style, losing his hat, and almost losing his reputation for cool-headedness. It was an exciting race—a close contest but Judge was rapidly gaining on the goose, and finally when reaching out to pick it up, he stumbled and went headlong into the grass. The goose only a few paces beyond stopped, looked around as if wanting to help Judge out of his trouble; but, just then he raised his head out of the grass and with some emphasis addressed the goose thus:

"If I had a gun I believe I'd shoot you!"

That was too much for the goose, so he sprang into the air, and—well, Judge has been looking for that goose ever since. He retrieved his hat and gun, but, the goose "Oh, where was he?"

Counting up the total bag for that afternoon, we found forty-one brants, two dozen snipes of various kinds, and two jack rabbits. It goes without saying that we were delighted with brant shooting, and it was determined by unanimous consent that we would spend the forenoon of the following day, at least, in the same pursuit and not far from the same locality.

Kingston, Pa.

SPORT IN DAKOTA - NO. 6
1887

One must become accustomed to some of the atmospheric eccentricities of the Northwest before he will appreciate them at their par value. Let me explain: The remarkably successful afternoon among the brants of the Lacota stubbles, described in a former letter, was warm, bright and still. The mercury registered as high as seventy degrees above zero. Coats of any description were burdensome. The remark was frequently heard that it was "Too warm for comfort." But, during the night an old "nor'wester" came down without any "advance agent," making the windows rattle, shaking the foundations, screaming around the corners, and howling through the streets, like a demon let loose for a frolic. The next morning was keen and cutting, cold enough for the most hardy Esquimaux. This was a satisfactory demonstration of the"law of extremes," and a somewhat unusual one for October. But Alexander and his turn-out were at the Palace promptly at seven, and all were soon aboard for another goose chase.

Only a short distance from town, it was noticed that the air contained millions of frost needles and the wind drove them into our faces in a pitiless way. Judge wore a heavy ulster, but complained of the cold. The writer rented a dogskin overcoat, and was just a little too comfortable, in a general way. Nap, however, to his sorrow and utter discomfort, depended upon a light-weight overcoat, and he stammered and shivered, and shuddered and shook till he could not tell the truth about anything. Yet as this day was to be both the continuation and conclusion of our goose shooting we were not to be thwarted by any common obstacle. The violent winds made the birds exceedingly wild and shooting difficult, but we succeeded in surprising several fine flocks, and bagged eighteen of their number before they took their final departure. We revisited the scene of the preceding day's sport and secured several brants there, Judge and Nap doing most of the shooting while the writer lay in the grass nursing neuralgia. Brants by the thousand were seen at points far distant, but the cutting wind becoming more and more intolerable we turned in before noon, satisfied with moderate returns for our courage in facing a Dakota zephyr. It takes heroes to do it; but we had really bagged all the game we wanted—about fifty brants—and we counted that experience among our rarest jewels. The brants of Dakota are very fine specimens of the species. They are colorless, except their wings, which are a light shade of brown, and their weight will approximate about nine pounds as an average. They form a dainty dish for any table. They have a rich game flavor, not fishy and greasy like the duck, and usually tender.

I want to say a word here about the Climax shells, made by the United States Cartridge Co. Out of three thousand fired, though a remarkable statement, it is true, not a single misfire or disappointment occurred. Surely that speaks volumes for them.

We became a good deal interested in "sod shanty" life in the vicinity of Lacota. People dwell in them for different reasons. A few are here from refined circles in the East, in search of health only, enjoying the broad acres of pastoral life; but, as in other places, the many are of foreign birth, making permanent homes, living in the happy consciousness of being able to breathe the unpolluted air of Dakota without having to pay royalty for the privilege to some titled superior. Those innocent souls think that America measures just thirteen inches to the foot. Some nameless rhymester of the plains, inspired by his solitude, has given us a pretty picture of his inner life in the following parody on "The Little Old Log Cabin in the Lane." He christened it

"The Little Old Sod Shanty on the Claim."

"I am looking rather seedy now while holding down my claim,
And my victuals are not always served the best,
And the mice play slyly round me, as I lay me down to sleep,
In my little old sod shanty on the claim.
Yet I rather like the novelty of living in this way,
Though my bill of fare is always rather tame;
But I'm happy as a clam on this land of Uncle Sam;
In my little old sod shanty on the claim.

Chorus:
The hinges are of leather and the windows have no glass,
While the roof it lets the howling blizzard in;
And I hear the hungry coyote as he sneaks up thro' the grass,
Round my little old sod shanty on the claim.

But when I left my eastern home so happy and so gay,
To try to win my way to wealth and fame,
I little thought that I'd come down to burning twisted hay,
In my little old sod shanty on the claim.

My clothes are plastered o'er with dough; I'm looking like a fright,
And everything is scattered round the room;
And I fear if P. T. Barnum's man should get his eye on me,
He would take me from my little cabin home.

Oh, I wish that some kind hearted Miss would pity on me take
And extricate me from the mess I'm in.
The angel—how I'd bless her, if thus her home she'd make,
In my little old sod shanty on the claim.
And when we'd made our fortunes on these prairies of the West,

Just as happy as two bed-bugs we'd remain;
And we'd forget our trials and our troubles as we'd rest
In our little old sod shanty on the claim.

And if Heaven should smile upon us with now and then an heir,
To cheer our hearts with honest pride to flame,
O, then we'd be content for the years that we had spent,
In our little old sod shanty on the claim.
Then when time enough had lapsed and those precious little brats,
To man and honest womanhood had grown,
It won't seem half so lonely when around us we shall look
And see other old sod shanties on the claim."

 I sincerely trust he may find that willing "angel" and yet become surrounded by a "baker's dozen" of the little responsibilities which he seems to long for.

 We were to meet Baron and his friends at the train next morning, on the trip homeward, and naturally enough felt some curiosity to learn how our success would compare with theirs. We had artistically arranged our brants and other game in long rows upon the platform, and in the most attractive style, so they might see it at its best. We even spread every bird out as far as he would spread and—well it had the desired effect. When the train came in three intensely anxious faces peered out of the baggage car door, and in eager haste inquired:

 "Is that your game, gentlemen?"

 "Well, yes," replied Judge, adding "and we are directly responsible for the death of every bird."

 Nap asked Duke what they could "show for the time squandered at Thomas'?"

 "Only a hundred ducks and nothing better," he replied.

 We gave them graphic accounts of our grand experience, and

detailed the skillful shots, and everything else calculated to fire them with envy and disappointment, till they all looked weary and sad.

I have shot nearly every game bird of America, but for downright fun and a royal meal give me the white brant of Dakota as the equal of the best. We were obliged to decline, with sincere regret, many invitations to shoot at various points, among the number one from Mr. W. H.S. Brady, of Hillsboro, Dak. This young gentleman has been most successful in grain growing upon a large scale and is really one of the rising young grain kings of that country. He started with nothing and it turned out to be good capital, and he had all that he needed of it.

It was my intention at first to entirely omit the cowboy chapter, reserving it for a camp-fire tale, but as it would leave the sketch of the trip incomplete, I decided later to include it. I prefer to suppress the name of the town where this incident occurred because the place might be supposed to be the stamping ground of such characters when in fact it is not so.

One evening, immediately after tea, the writer feeling tired and thirsty repaired to the saloon for a soda (plain soda, unembellished). After drinking it and lighting a fresh cigar, I started toward an unoccupied table for a newspaper, when the front door opened, letting in a jaunty and elastic specimen of the genus cowboy. Lightly tripping across the floor he kept saying:

"I live in Dakota, I do, and I'm on the shoot."

He would cock his "Dakota gun"—a .45 caliber three pound Merwin & Hulbert, twelve-inch barrel, send it whirling upward and catch it by the stock as it came down. He slammed his gun down upon the bar, exclaiming:

"Rum or blood, sonny!"

The dispenser of fire-water promptly handed out the "rum." Addressing the hotel man again:

"Your treat, wasn't it, bub?"

"Yes," replied the bartender, knowing well the character of his customer. Approaching me, he yelled:

"Hello, mister, have some bug juice?"

Not answering to that name, he inquired of the man at the bar:

"Say, bub, what ye got there in them corduroys, any way, is it alive?"

But, before he could answer, the gun slinger was facing me with:

"Say, ole corduroys, have some pizen?"

I answered:

"Were you speaking to me, sir?"

"Well, yes, I s'pose I was; are you goin' to gulp some 'red eye' with me?"

"No, thank you, I have no occasion for it."

Stepping back a pace or two, he brought forth his twelve inch persuader, twirled it about his finger, put it to his mouth, spit in the barrel, cocked it, presented it full in my face, and in a mocking tone inquired:

"Will you drink with me, quick?"

"Why, certainly, if you are in a hurry, I'll accommodate you."

"What'll you have?"

"I'll take some Apollinaris water."

"That's too light for this climate; take it raw?"

"I prefer it light; am not used to anything with a club in it."

"Well take your 'polonay' water then."

We accordingly drank it down like old friends. Noticing the muddy condition of my long boots, he said:

"Say, mister, your boots look like the deuce; get on that stool and have 'em shined. Say, coon (addressing the colored bootblack), what'll you charge to shine them boots?"

I demurred again, but the "Dakota gun" settled my scruples a second time.

"Charge just one moon, boss; purty big job, them," answered the coon.

"All right, coon, here's your moon [a silver dollar], and you shine 'em clear to the top."

It was an artistic job and the knight of the brush did not make more than twenty-five cents on the dollar at it either.

At this juncture Nap entered the saloon and I felt that was where "the fun would come in." Looking at Nap, he inquired of me:

"Who's that—does it belong to your gang, too?"

"That's Nap," I replied, "he's one of our party, and a royal fellow."

"Hello, Nap! Screamed the king of the ranch.

No answer.

"Hello, Nap! Come here and liquor up."

But, Nap, indignant at such a liberal abuse of his *nom de plume,* only gave him a withering look.

"I tell you to come here and down some Old Crow," sternly commanded the knight of the trigger, as he playfully made a survey of Nap's countenance through the sights of his little cannon.

The request was so forcibly put that Nap could not consistently refuse, especially when he realized that the slightest pressure of that trigger might send him to "the happy hunting grounds." Vainly trying to get out of the line of fire, he executed more gymnastics, high jumps and funny business generally than a clown in three rings. He answered our cattle fiend thus:

"Why—yes—yes, of course—certainly I will drink any—What'll you —say, don't point it at me; it might go off—what'll you have to drink?"

"See here, didn't I tell you to guzzle with me?"

"Yes—you—you did, and I'm going to do it, too."

"Well, spit it out quick!"

"Spit out what?" queried Nap in dead earnest.

Ha! Ha! Who could help it; I could suppress my feelings no longer. It was "either bark or bust." When it was made plain to Nap that he was to make choice of irrigants, he named lemonade, which fortunately was not objected to. They drank it in silence, but Nap kept a sharp eye on that Dakota gun, shaking his head as though there was something repulsive about it. He submitted with becoming grace to the shine operation, but, as fully fifty per cent more material was necessary to cover the superficial area of his boots, the job cost the cow fellow a full "moon and half." It was done in artistic taste, however; even the straps glistening like ebony. About this time Judge started in at the side door to find what had become of us; but putting this and that together, he surmised the actual situation and retreated in great confusion. Up the outside stairs he went, tumbling into the window at the landing and darting off through the friendly darkness of the hall. He cleared just four steps at each bound. Our mutual tormentor was right on his heels, reaching for the window as Judge was picking himself up on the other side of it. This little episode gave Nap and me the key of escape. We stood in the front door until the one at the side began to open, when we instantly sought safety by the upstairs route, leaving our dare-devil cowboy acquaintance in undisputed possession of the drug department of the hotel. We were informed next morning that he made the night hideous with his diabolism, and spent about a hundred "moons" to do it; that he was one of the worst "Wild Bills" of the Northwest. I wish you could only see him on his native heath, when he is full of rum up to the neck; he can make more music than a German band, a fog horn, and a steam piano, all in full blast.

After a day in Minneapolis, and a night in Chicago, our trip Eastward was uninterrupted by delays. We returned to Buffalo by the Great Rock Island and Michigan Central roads. They are splendid systems, offering among other attractions, sure connections, fast time, frequent trains, elegant coaches, and courteous officials, while the scenery en route is unsurpassed. It will be interesting too, for sportsmen to know that there are no charges on these roads for dogs, game, etc. A recapitulation made it plain that our trip was a blessing to the whole party in a physical sense, a most important feature, besides affording that relaxation from business cares so sadly needed to rouse tired energies, and rekindle the ambition for renewed struggle in the battle of life.

The vastness of Dakota and its advantages can never be fully known from a description of them simply. They must be seen in the flesh to be understood in the soul. Even then it will seem more like the memory of a pleasant dream than anything real and tangible— like the whispering of the wind in rustic woodlands or a gorgeous sunset; we feel it, we know it, it thrills us with emotion, but who can describe it? Boundless in extent, rich in resources, a fertile soil and glorious climate. No wonder Horace Greely said, "Go west, young man, go west." Surely it has proved a boon to many a man who went there in pursuit of "health, wealth, and happiness" and finding all of them in an incredibly short time.

We found ourselves in Buffalo about four o'clock a.m. where we disbanded again to become citizens of the United States in "store clothes" instead of corduroys. In conclusion, the members of our party desire to offer sincere thanks for all the courtesies received, and also for the many pleasures planned for our entertainment by the warm-hearted ones of the great Northwest. "May they live forever and die happy at the e'end o' that." Thus ends an unpretending sketch of a memorable shooting trip to Dakota.

Kingston, Pa.

In the Marsh Over Decoys

DUCK AND GOOSE SHOOTING AT LAKE THOMPSON
By Greenhead
1898

To the sportsman who, for a brief period each year, plies his chosen pursuit either for the mere physical benefit derived therefrom, or with the deeper attachment conceived in the early years and nurtured through the grave school of life, the Western Middle States offer a vast field of recreation and instruction. Away out on the rolling prairies of South Dakota, with the Western Horizon ablaze in the full glory of an Indian Summer sunset, with the silent night on every side creeping on apace, one may there easily discover the mystic thread of contentment. Away back in the long ago Lake Thompson was a much larger body of water than at the present time. Now, nearly a mile of crisp, short grass rustles between the original and the present rush-grown shore. From the crest of a little bluff, studded with glistening hardheads, a really beautiful view is presented. Far out on the flats a herd of cattle are grazing contentedly, while in the foreground a pair of jack-rabbits are frisking about in fancied seclusion. Back of the hill, to the eastward, stretches a mile or more of neglected cornfield, and over this tangled expanse a brand of lusty prairie chickens are directing their flight with the last glinting rays of the sun flashing on their bronzed plumage. Away to the westward, where the plover's piping note sounds faintly, the silent lake of to-day spreads out for five or six miles to the southward. The little 16-gauge Parker for once lies mute upon the short brown grass, though the jacksnipe's derisive call echoes and reechoes, and the waterfowl on their way to Lake

Whitewood for the night stream overhead uninterruptedly so low that the ring of their sharp pinions sounds with startling distinctness ere they vanish in the gloom to the eastward where the big, round yellow moon is shyly peeping into view. Another annual fortnight is nearly exhausted, and with the diminution of the remaining hours, my spirits, hitherto buoyant, became correspondingly depressed, still, intermingled with my varied emotions, rise visions that only the hunter who has visited the famous Lake Thompson region can entirely appreciate. The pathetic is encountered in close company with the ludicrous, the instructive with the divertive, and thus the mental diary of each day's incidents turns before me like some huge and mysterious panorama of the past. From the day of our unlooked-for arrival at the hospitable door of our stranger host, not an hour passed but was fraught with something of more than ordinary interest.

Our party numbered five persons; our destination was Lake Preston Station on the line of the Chicago, Milwaukee & St. Paul Railway, which town was reached after a ride of nineteen hours from the Cream City. The date of our arrival was October 6, 1897, and here we had secured conveyances for transporting ourselves and outfits to Lake Thompson, five miles distant. Out of the town wound our little caravan, Big Pete, the red-whiskered Norske, bringing up the rear with a lumber wagon rigged with hay rack for carrying our boats, which, fortunately for us, we had brought from home, for neither love nor money will avail in securing suitable boats in that country. Even the village dogs forgot to bark as we passed from their midst, and the flannel-shirted groceryman paused in the act of thrusting a corncob in the neck of a brown molasses jug, to square himself and devote the space of along minute to a critical survey of the party and equipment. Whatever his observations were the intervening distance rendered them unintelligible, and presently we were in the country, with our road winding around the edge of a slough of several acres in extent. The field glass was unlimbered, and, to satisfy the cravings of curiosity, the grassy surface was eagerly scanned just to see if a few welcome forms could not be discovered beyond the bunches of mudhens gorging themselves out in the middle of the slough. We had no trouble in locating a bunch of teals over against the further shore, and, cracking the rawhide over the ponies' ears; we rattled on across the prairie. Hundreds of ashy-coated gulls were wheeling and careening over our heads and off across the rolling expanse on either side where the freshly turned sod showed rich and black, a vast army of these restless scavengers had assembled. After a time, the glimmer of water was discovered off to the right and, feeling intuitively that this was the lake we were looking for, the horses' heads were turned in that direction. Only two houses appeared against the Western sky, the first obviously too small to shelter our little party, the other a rather hopeless prospect as its owner was clearly engaged in extensive alterations and improvements. Emboldened, however, by the friendly overtures of a couple of well-fed dogs, we entered a yard filled with wagons and farming implements and boldly tackled the proprietor, an apple-faced descendant of some hardy Norseman, whose gray eyes rested on us inquiringly and unsuspicious of our intent. A few introductory questions on our part as to the settlers residing near the shore of the lake further to the south, the lake itself, and the supply of birds, and, the ice being broken, we speedily found our new acquaintance to be a man of more than ordinary intelligence and thrift for a South Dakota farmer. A farmer for more than thirty years within the confines of the state of Iowa, in his fiftieth year, the beautiful tract of land had been disposed of and with wife and nine children a new home was sought upon the Dakota prairies where the proceeds of his sale enabled him to purchase three times as much land as he had owned heretofore. Entering into life, where we found him six months later, he had already done much to improve his place and had set an example of thrift for his less industrious neighbors.

Already a fine well, one hundred and seventy feet in depth, above which a steel windmill noiselessly spun, a new, well-painted barn, and other evidences of improvement were visible. By a unanimous vote taken while en route from the station, the lawyer had been elected to act as spokesman, and presently he inquired if accommodations for board and lodging could not be secured for a short time. To modest demurs and objections we interposed vociferous protests, until finally Lewis, one of the numerous progeny, was dispatched into the house to interview his mother on the subject of boarders. His prompt reappearance from that lady's domain suggested to us that a not overly favorable report was coming, which was immediately verified by Lewis:

"Naw, she don't want 'em."

"Well, the old lady's got her hands pretty full now, so I guess you fellers 'll have to jog along a ways further," ventured our acquaintance. "They's 'leven of us now with the two carpenters, and thrashers is coming next week," he went on, apologetically, and it was early apparent it was going against the grain to deny us the hospitality of his small roof.

Noting this, the scribe descended from his perch and made his way around to the back of the dwelling house, where he entered an open door and confronted the important personage referred to, busy, indeed, in the midst of her duties. A fire was snapping in the stove upon which several iron kettles were steaming vigorously. From one I detected the savory odor of a huge beef stew; from another the appetizing smell of cabbage. Great brown potatoes peeped invitingly from the oven doors ajar, and a big coffee pot puffed fragrance to sniffing nostrils. Though no lawyer, I made an eloquent appeal right then and there with that coffee pot all the time tantalizing me with the possibilities of a point blank refusal, but the jury, to my surprise, and without leaving the room, rendered a satisfactory verdict and our troubles for the time being were over.

"Well, well," remarked our host upon learning the result of the interview, and I more than half suspect he was secretly pleased with the outcome, "you fellers 'll have to sleep in the barn 'long with the boys."

But this announcement only served to increase the enthusiasm of the crowd, which straightway proceeded to hoist the duffle to the hay loft in the new barn, where an empty oat bin was assigned to us to serve as a dressing room. Upon the hay our blankets were soon spread for the night, and with a tight roof overhead what more could a reasonable mortal demand on a hunting trip, while the recollection of that first meal in a Dakota farmhouse still remains with me. When it was all over and we had strolled out into the open air, the silence which ensued was better proof of the excellence of the fare than words could possibly have been. "Better than pot-luck in camp, with dishes to wash afterward," was the unanimous expression later on.

Three-quarters of a mile down through the farmer's pasture land to the westward, upon the shore of the lake, lay our three boats in readiness for the morning shoot. The cartridge bags had been filled, guns oiled, and rubber boots gotten out. Outside pipes were glowing and experiences were being recounted. Presently as it grew shadowy, great flocks of teals began skimming across the fields to the eastward, and inquiry disclosed the fact that they were on their regular scheduled flight to Whitewood Lake for the night, from which body of water they return with the break of day. At 9 o'clock we climbed the ladder leading to the dormitory where a row of sleeping forms were found in the hay. The boys had preceded us. The jeweler and the lawyer had agreed to share each other's blankets; the railroad man and the lumberman suddenly discovered an affinity in each other, and thus it transpired that the scribe found himself an outcast, something to be avoided, but straightway consoled himself with the thought that a time would come later on when he could square accounts and join as loudly as any in the uproar that greeted the appearance of the railroad man clad in a pale blue nightgown. From the dusty recesses of the oat bin he emerged with an air of superiority that provoked convulsions of merriment from his associates. Shades of Diana, had it come to this, that a mighty Nimrod of the nineteenth century includes a nightshirt in his list of necessities when packing his "turkey" for a trip to the "wild and woolly?" The lantern's dim light threw uncertain shadows against the cobwebbed rafters, flickered and went out, plunging the place in total darkness. The smell of the hay had a soporific effect upon me, and even a musical plung, such as usually attends the drawing of a tight-fitting cork, followed by mysterious gurgles here and there in the darkness of the mow failed to check immediate slipping into dreamland. Talk about your hemlock boughs furnishing a delectable couch whereon to court sweet Morpheus! "twould be a difficult matter to induce our party to believe that anything could excel Andrew's hay mow for contributing to soul-clogging oblivion.

With the faintest perceptible indication of approaching dawn, further efforts at sleep were rendered futile by the vigorous crowing of a white rooster perched amid his admiring followers in a lean-to adjoining the barn, and as there was no partition between the two buildings, chanticleer's rollicking salute to the morning came floating up to us with startling clearness. With unvarying precision each day's approach was heralded by the white rooster's solo. Following this would sound the heavy tread of Andrew's feet, and then his voice would roar out a summons for the boys to roll out and start about the morning chores. Then the flinty ears of corn would go rattling into the horses' feed boxes, and a vigorous craunching would ensue. Above, five recumbent forms, as many little frosty puffs following each breath, gave evidence of the morning chill. Presently, from somewhere out toward the house, came a lusty bellow:

"Hey, pile out, you fellers; breakfast is ready." Like magic the covers were flung one side, the long boots pulled on, and four dusky forms slid down the companionway. The fifth was left behind to illustrate the fallacy of wearing a nightshirt while on a duck hunt in the Dakotas.

The eastern sky was beginning to flame gloriously under old Sol's benign influence. In the kitchen, a roaring cob fire added comfort to an appetizing meal, and when the party emerged from the house, every member of it was thoroughly warmed through and ready for the initial shoot.

Down the lane toward the lake we straggled in Indian file, followed by the lusty good wishes of our genial host. Around us the sun was making merry with the frost crystals that clung tenaciously to the tall fireweeds that adorned either side of our path. Larks with odd, unfamiliar bits of disjointed song scuttled into the shelter of the long grass. Arriving suddenly within sight of the boat landing we were startled by a rush and roar of wings, and out from the shore, where they had been quietly sitting, started a large flock of teals and pintails. Simultaneously with their flight another and larger flock further down the shore took wings. Wheeling and circling, loath to depart, for the space of five minutes the air was full of birds, many of which returned and alighted within twenty rods of us as we made our way down to the shore. As we had but three boats and the work of the first trip was more to ascertain the general character of the lake than to do any great amount of shooting, the railroad man and I walked south, down the shore through the canes and tall, dry, wild sunflower stalks, while the remainder of our party started out with the boats, taking various directions south and southwest. Half a mile down the shore Harry and I espied an attractive looking point jutting a hundred yards or so out into the lake, and we lost no time in making our way to it. Out on the extreme point we hastily gathered together sufficient dry material with which to put up a small blind, behind which we ensconced ourselves with a canvas decoys out (which, by the use of my rubber boots, I was able to place in position), tossing upon the waves thirty-five yards distant. The three boats were by this time far down the lake, and the mighty roar of great bodies of birds came more and more frequently as the boats progressed further and further southward. The nodding decoys beckoned in a flock of five greenwings, but their incoming flight unfortunately kept them in range of their canvas counterparts until they dropped lightly among the stools. It took them but a moment to discover the deception, and they sprang hastily upward, bent on making a speedy retreat. The sixteen's tiny loads of nitro cracked sharply, and the black powder smoke from Harry's twelve obscured all for a moment, but when that lifted three birds were seen among the decoys, their tiny blue feet beating a tattoo upon the water. Down the lake we could faintly hear the nitro pelting at intervals, telling plainly that the boys were among the flocks which could be seen rising in dark clouds against the Southern sky. Up the channel came a flock of dark birds on heavy wing, and yet their approach was more rapid than a first glance would indicate. Three hundred yards distant they passed our stand, a beautiful flock of more than a hundred brant. "Vainly the fowler's eye might mark thy distant flight to do thee wrong," quoted Harry, but this burst of poetry met with a restraining check, for approaching birds claimed our attention, and cripples had to be shot over and retrieved. The latter proved no difficult feat, as the water in no place exceeded two feet in depth and the bottom, when reached, was formed of hard clay. Between the shots at ducks we were given frequent chances at yellowlegs, golden plovers and numerous other waders that were constantly passing over the point on their short flights to different feeding grounds. Later the wind freshened up to such an extent that sitting on the exposed point was no longer a pleasure, so we decided to return to the land place, carrying with us a very satisfactory string of birds as the result of our first experience among the feathered game.

An hour later the boats had returned, and interesting to us were the experiences of their occupants. The jeweler had found a large bay filled with scattered clumps of bulrushes, where the birds fairly swarmed, seeming determined not to leave their chosen feeding ground. In an hour he had exhausted his shells, and for the space of another hour he had exulted in the full satisfaction of witnessing the greatest flight of wildfowl he had ever seen. The lumberman had discovered what appeared to be a second large lake far to the southward, and joined to the one I have already introduced, by a shallow expanse of water thickly grown up to rushes, over which a great horde of birds were constantly passing. He, too, had a variety of birds scattered over the bottom of his boat, and the attorney tied him as to numbers. That afternoon, as the shadows grew long, upon the north side of Andrew's barn hung a beautiful display of birds. Upon the south side of a long hay rick, five animated figures had spent a couple of the afternoon hours stripping off the feathers from two dozen fine, fat teals and pintails, for our host's wife had promised us birds for supper provided we would manage the picking. As the sun crept lower and lower in the West, the picking done, we walked down toward the lake in our shoes, with guns upon our shoulders, to while away the time till the supper bell should sound. Crouching in the short barley grass upon the water's edge, we received the flocks that passed overhead in leaving the lake on their regular evening flight to Whitewood Lake, and in this diversion it was fairly dark before we realized the fact. Back to the house with ravenous appetites in readiness for the excellent repast we found smoking upon the table. The birds were pronounced delicious by all, and right here it will be proper to say that fatter or finer flavored ducks than those found on Lake Thompson during our stay would be hard to find.

One morning a cloudy sky and fresh southwest wind betokened a favorable day for shooting among the scattered clumps of bulrushes, so C-(the lumberman) and I took the "Get There" and headed in that direction. H. H-(the jeweler) followed close in our wake, and our prediction regarding the birds was more than realized, for upon our arrival the bay was found to be swarming with birds. With my waders pulled up I found it quite an easy matter to walk over the entire bay, dodging from clump to clump as approaching birds were sighted. Finally C- and I located in a couple of thick growing bogs some eighty yards apart, while H. H- pushed further back into the bay. For the space of an hour shots came with charming frequency, making it oftentimes a difficult matter to keep the dead retrieved, as the fresh breeze drifted dead and cripples rapidly away. A big fat redhead presented a faultless incoming shot and plunged straight at me in his fall as the little 16-gauge cracked. Without taking time to reload I fired the remaining shell into a bunch of teals that whipped momentarily into view from behind a mass of rushes. I could not tell what execution had been done for some minutes, as other shots demanded my attention. But later on while out on a retrieving expedition I found a pair a greenwings close together in the edge of the rushes. A pair of pintails came in over my head from behind, and before I had discovered the location of those whistling pinions, the twain had reached a point midway between C- and myself. Our two shots sounded as one, and his bird pitched dead, while mine, with a tattered wing flapping wildly in the air, and badly body shot besides, fell ten rods distant behind one of the little bogs. C- immediately pushed out after the bird, while I remained in my blind to watch the flight. A blundering spoonbill flew into a charge of sixes from the sixteen and tumbled in a heap almost at my feet. I had barely time to thrust in a shell and pour both barrels into a flock of widgeons overhead, bringing down two dead, then I turned to pick up my spoonbill; but lo! Though only a few seconds had elapsed since I marked him not six feet from me, he had disappeared as effectually as though the earth had opened and swallowed him and any amount of search failed in its purpose. I heard a rapid fusilade out in the lake, and in the midst of it saw a long line of geese heading in toward the rushes. Someone had evidently routed them from the open water of the lake. One, two, three flocks of ducks went whirring past me, but I was intent on getting a shot into the ranks of the oncoming geese and allowed them to pass on unmolested. Fifty, forty, thirty rods they lessen the distance, and I was beginning to feel good and certain of a shot, but as I clinched the chilly barrels the more tightly, a swerve in the course of the flock took the birds to one side of my position. But though they avoided me they failed to escape C- and his 12-gauge. I had forgotten him for the time being, but as my eyes followed the flock I saw a dark figure rise out of the rushes, a pair of barrels were leveled, and with the nitro's crack a great body was convulsed in mid air; the wings refused to properly perform their functions, the neck was distended and curved to one side, the red legs hung down, and as I watched, the second barrel barked and a total collapse and heavy fall followed. C- exultingly swung his prize aloft and whooped lustily in his exuberance of spirits. I swung my hat in the air for a moment and dropped to receive approaching ducks. Half an hour later H. H- rejoined us with a 7x 9 smile adorning his usually sedate features. Three great dark birds rested heavily on top of a goodly number of ducks in his little craft. Feeling well satisfied with the results of the morning's shoot, we started for the landing.

One day the wind blew terrifically, and Andrew's two carpenters quit work, declaring it was too rough a day to shingle, and struck out for home. We had just returned from the lake, having found that the gale was making the lake an extremely uncomfortable place to remain, and, to our host's delight and approval, we fell upon those veranda roofs, and in a couple of hours had them well shingled and tinned and ready for a rainstorm. For this service we rose several degrees in the estimation of our host, whose horses and wagons were thenceforth ours to command.

Day after day the wary honkers managed to evade the little sixteen's blandishments, until I was well nigh discouraged, for nearly all of the party had scored, some of them repeatedly. But my day was coming, though at that time the fact was unbeknown to me.

One morning C- and I, in the boat, rowed leisurely south two or three miles and finally lodged, through sheer laziness, in a bulrush bog out near the line of open water. The surface of the lake was nearly calm and the birds were moving, but sluggishly, and at intervals. Perhaps not more than half a dozen mixed ducks lay in the bottom of the boat where we were stretched in the full enjoyment of the surroundings. The warm sun poured down upon us and we were beginning to feel drowsy, when all of a sudden there floated down to us a distant reverberating boom. "Twas but a single report, but rank black powder was clearly responsible for the Fourth of July immensity of sound. We looked at each other and grinned, then turned our eyes southward to where the sound came from. A miniature storm cloud was floating off from the shore of the lake, but our eyes quickly discerned a vast flight of birds moving northward in our direction. Little rows of shells were laid out on the boat's bottom in readiness for the arrival of the winged hosts. Presently the first of the mass passed over and we allowed them to go by unharmed. Behind them, as far as the eye could see, nothing but ducks, ducks, ducks appeared in the distance. From the space of fully ten minutes the scene beggared description. Never in the course of my life have I seen such countless hordes of ducks of every description and variety. We were fairly in the center of the flight, and for several minutes, strange as it may seem, remained perfectly quiet in the boat, transfixed with interest at a sight so unusual. Then the guns cracked as rapidly as shells could be thrust into the smoking chambers. The barrels grew warmer and warmer, till presently by mutual consent we suddenly ceased our execution, for eighty rods distant a gang of geese were bearing down upon us. Cartridges loaded with two's replaced the finer shot and we crouched lower in the bottom of the boat. There were seven of the great, dark fellows, and their course, if unchanged, would bring them squarely over our stand. On, on, the broad wings bore them swiftly. Now and then a hoarse note clanged out on the still air.

Pintails, teals, widgeons, mallards and gadwalls were still darting over our heads, the rush of their wings constantly ringing in our ears. The great birds were nearly directly over us and entirely oblivious of our proximity, when we rose to fire. One old fellow, seeming a perfect mountain floating along slightly apart from his fellows, particularly attracted my attention, and holding well ahead, I pressed the right hand trigger. A well marked stagger was noticeable as the big twos lodged amidships; but onward he pressed to join his comrades. Sliding the barrels a trifle father ahead, the left barrel cracked, and through the transparent vapor I beheld the little gun's first goose plunging downward, an inextricable jumble of wings, legs and neck. I heard the sound of impious language behind, and glancing over my shoulder found my elder brother standing on tiptoe in an endeavor to mark the fall of a second big bird which was sailing off across the rushes with fixed wings and legs hanging, barely clearing the tops of the tall growth. Through the calm air came to us distinctly and bell-like the notes of approaching geese, and down into the bottom of the boat we sank after hastily marking the spot where our cripples had disappeared from view. A flock of eight or ten birds was coming down upon us, though slightly to one side. As they presented a raking shot to C- he rose and poured both barrels of the 12-gauge into their ranks, while I hesitated a moment, as the distance appeared a trifle too great for the little gun. Following the double report, there was a confused mass of forms before me, out of which a single bird presently emerged, evidently in distress, for the great body was twisted and skewed and barely held suspended in midair by the rapidly fanning wings. At this target I took two deliberate chances with the little Parker at sixty-five yards, and had the satisfaction of feeling that both loads had found a lodging place, for after a sinking flight of forty rods the game struck the water never to rise again. A comrade, either also wounded, or through sympathy, alighted upon the water with the wounded one. We lost no time in pushing forth from the canes and starting in pursuit of the pair. C- manipulating the oars, while from my seat in the stern of the boat I directed the course. We were within sixty yards of the pair when one took wing, breasting toward us slightly. He had not flown twenty feet before the heavy shot caught him full, and down he thrashed, churning the water into foam with those powerful wing strokes. The other bird had turned over upon the water and was stone dead by the time we slipped alongside and gathered him in. Over among the rushes we later on stumbled across the bird first struck by C-, and although a fine flight was still in progress, we headed for the landing, C- at the oars, the scribe in the stern with both guns, and nearly covered up with birds of all descriptions.

With many an interruption in our progress, to slip now and then into some small bog to await the arrival of a flock of teals coming down the lake, or running a few rods out of the way to chase a cripple, we finally reached the landing and, after a heavy tramp up through the meadow managed to deposit our loads at the barn. That night many a hardworking Norske picked ducks after the sun went down, and odd enough it seemed to us, that these delvers in the soil should go without game during the royal Autumn season when an abundance of it could so easily be secured. Yet very few of these toilers ever taste game unless it is given them by the tourist hunter.

One warm afternoon, when all the boats were out to various parts of the lake, I decided to take a tramp to the southward, and with the little gun tucked under my arm, a couple of dozen fine shot shells in my shooting coat pockets, and a pair of Buck's waterproof, laced hunting boots, light and long, upon my feet, I sallied forth to conquer new fields. After traversing a mile of marsh I passed a point marking the southern limit of our explorations. Pushing leisurely on half a mile farther I paused to polish the dimmed lenses of my glasses, and while thus engaged a pair of snipes seized this as an opportunity to depart, and once in the air stood not upon the order of their going. A few feet in advance of the spot where I had paused to rest I found the damp earth well punctured with fresh borings, and I forthwith prepared for immediate action. Doubtless all of us have at some time or other found ourselves in hidden snipe grounds that seemed almost intended by the Creator as a retreat for the birds and a place where they might enjoy immunity from the predatory hunter. Two such places have I discovered in the course of my wanderings—one, hundreds of miles to the northward, where the lofty pine towers upward and limbless for one hundred and fifty feet or more, where a silent stream ran its course uncomplainingly through a forest of mighty trees. Down this river I guided my tiny boat one balmy afternoon in October, glorying in the shower of gayly-hued leaves that drifted down upon me as I passed by the hardwood ridges that now and then varied the wild and rugged scene. Presently there came a rift in the timber and a bayou, long and apparently devoid of life, stretched out before me upon the right shore. A long, tall, blasted pine stood like a petrified sentinel upon the brink of the river as though to challenge the intruder who might venture to wander, uninvited, into this secluded spot. A hawk, hitherto unseen, left the white pine and soared aloft uttering weird, uncanny screams. Other signs of life became apparent. A blue heron drifted off down the channel from a chosen frogging stand on the river bank. His great bill was sullenly buried in his gray frill of feathers and far behind trailed a pair of long, ungainly legs that seemed a useless appendage during these voyages by wing. With the hoarse "quock" and disturbance of this nocturnal fisherman, a startled note disclosed the whereabouts of a snipe. Off across the bayou he rushed. A shadow? No, two birds followed closely in the wake of the first. Presently they pitched among the short grass of the slough, and, nothing daunted by the spectral aspect of the scene, I left the little boat drawn up on the bank and started toward the spot where the trio were lurking. No sooner did I set foot in the bed of the bayou than I discovered two important things: First, that the walking was rendered very difficult by the sticky mud forming the bottom, and second, that thousands of birds had taken possession of the slough. To the right, to the left, before and behind me they rose in singles, in pairs and in squads. Only for a moment did I hesitate, then the tall pines echoed and reechoed loudly and long from my fusilade. For the space of an hour my barrels never cooled, though my shell bag at the end of that time hung limp under my right arm and the pockets of my shooting coat refused to receive more. Then I dragged my heavy boots over to the river bank and freed them from their clinging loads and, launching the little craft, I drifted on into the forest again, feeling certain that behind me lay the finest bit of snipe ground I should visit in many a long day, and in this belief I was correct. Now, after the lapse of many years, I once more trod a veritable snipe paradise, this time, instead of a bayou hemmed in on all sides by giant forest trees, a boundless expanse of sunken land covered in spots of shallow pools of water stretched to the southward for miles and miles. An abundance of cover, varying in height from the short, wiry prairie grass to the tall, rank, green bulrushes, afforded fine shelter for the birds, and everywhere indications existed that during the nesting season this had been one of the favored haunts of the duck, for their nests were found in nearly every large clump of rushes, and frequently eggs were seen lying exposed upon the mud flats. In one secluded corner thirteen eggs were discovered scattered about what had evidently been a nest early in the season. My scanty supply of shells rapidly dwindled down until it was actually harrowing to see fresh birds jump up at every turn. The afternoon was muggy and warm, and at last I paused with the little gun open in my hands and the last pair of shells smoking in mud at my feet, and mopped my perspiring forehead. Out by yonder tall green mass of bulrushes lay one dead bird, and a second one is, "jack-like," off to the right twenty-five yards or more making ineffectual attempts to fly. Even my fours had been expended at the fleeting sprites of the ooze, and, sadly retrieving my last pair, I struck out for the farmhouse through the mellow later afternoon sunlight.

Now and then a jack-rabbit, apparently with the full knowledge that I was headed for home without a single cartridge left, cantered out boldly into view and accompanied me a short distance on my way. Out on the lake, now a mile to the westward, the setting sun was bathing the calm surface with a great wave of golden light. Listening intently I could faintly hear the sound of distance shots somewhere in that mellow glow, telling that the boys were in the midst of the evening flight. The bluffs were reached, marking what was once upon a time the shore of Lake Thompson. Mammoth hardheads sparkled in the sun as I passed among them to the summit of the bluff and turned for a last fond survey of the lake where a most perfect outing had been spent. Dropping on the short brown grass I lamented the oversight of Nature in her failure to endow me with an artist's gifted hand that I might portray that scene in colors. Upon memory alone—that at best treacherous retainer—must I rely to furnish through the years to come the salient features of that endless, changeable and beautiful panorama.

In conclusion, should the good ship of fortune land any of the readers of this account upon the shores of Lake Thompson next season, may they find the birds as numerous as did we in the Autumn of 1897, and may they display prudence and humanity in their behavior toward our migratory friends, the wildfowl.

Milwaukee, Wis.

AMONG THE DUCKS IN SOUTH DAKOTA
By Greenhead
1902

Up in the baggage car of the Pioneer Limited on the Milwaukee Road, was one particular lot of duffle over which great care had been bestowed in the packing and which was soon destined to play an important part on a shooting expedition to Day County, South Dakota. Back in one of the luxurious sleepers, the owners of the baggage were wrapped in blissful, though sleep-infested, slumbers, in which vast flights of wildfowl were momentarily engaging their attention. There had been more than the usual amount of difficulties besetting the final preparations for this expedition and even at the eleventh hour there was a strong likelihood that all of the members of the party could not leave at the same time.

When the sun rose on the morning of October 18, however, it found our party dressed and up forward in the buffet car enjoying the beauties of an ideal Indian Summer morning. We were racing alongside the Father of Waters and the river banks afforded us much material for interesting discussion. On the opposite side of the track the foliage, gloriously decorated by the frosts, presented a kaleidoscopic variety of tints rendered more delightful by the flood of golden light from the rising sun. Maples, basswoods, birches, oaks, poplars and elms, all alike yielded their tributes to the season as the early morning breeze found its way through their branches. Beside the murky waters of the river were fishermen's huts and the nets used during the hours of darkness were hanging on stout stakes to dry in the sun. Men in caps and high waders were smoking their short-stemmed pipes, and the white smoke curling from the short lengths of stovepipe protruding from the roofs of the tiny cabins told of breakfasts being prepared within. Toddling children were everywhere in evidence, telling plainly that these rude houses were the permanent homes of these nocturnal squatter fishermen. Here and there long lines of cordwood extended for great distances along the banks ready for shipment by water. Small islands, sloughs and bayous were numerous, and often from the latter, as we dashed alongside them, there would mount hastily upward a flock of waterfowl. The dusky porter was summoned and shortly thereafter upon a tiny stand before us there rested a crisp brown roll; a pat of golden butter and a cup of rich, fragrant coffee, to tide us over until the Twin Cities were reached, where we were to breakfast at our leisure, owing to the fact than an hour would elapse before the train for the Dakotas was due to leave. Wabasha, Red Wing and Hastings were left behind and soon the smoke of Minnesota's metropolis was noticeable, and half an hour after we pulled into the station on time and in the very best of spirits. Half way up the stairway leading to the dining-room we met the third member of our little party, per agreement, and over our breakfast we congratulated each other upon the happy terminations of our troubles effecting a start together. During his brief business stay in St. Paul, the attorney had gained much useful information concerning the shooting grounds and the general opinion was that we had timed our expedition most propitiously, as a large northern flight of ducks had just reached the Dakotas and water was reported at an excellent stage in the lakes and sloughs.

    The morning meal disposed of, we busied ourselves making sure that every trunk and box was safely on board our train, after which, with gun cases snugly packed under our double seat, we gave ourselves up to pleasurable anticipations. What more satisfying condition can prevail than finally, after many trials and tribulations, to at last surmount all barriers and with a complete outfit safely on board the train which will land you on the shooting ground, you look ahead to the coming outing with unalloyed satisfaction? Throughout the clear, mid Indian Summer day we rumbled westward, now through vast fields of yellow stubble, attesting to the immense crop which had been harvested earlier in the season, now through cornfields stretching over the rolling country as far on either side as the eye could reach. Lusty strong-winged prairie chickens now and then shot up into the air from the stubble or corn and sailed away with set pinions. Occasionally some slough gladdened our eyes with its quota of ducks. It was near night when we reached our destination and, with hands full of grips and gun cases, we stepped off at Waubay, strangers in a strange land, yet full of confidence and anticipation. In the course of our ride westward, we had made the acquaintance of some sportsmen on the train from whom we obtained considerable valuable information respecting the country surrounding the town, as well as the desirable points to visit during our stay. After registering at the hotel, we started out on a short tour of investigation, calling at the judge's office, but finding the door locked and His Honor absent. Upon inquiry, we learned that it was somewhat difficult to procure the services of this gentleman during the months of September and October, owing to his long list of pressing engagements, and, knowing him to be a diligent shooter, our opinions of him went up several degrees even before we had made his acquaintance, which we were so fortunate as to accomplish a day or two later.

After the evening meal we strolled downtown and engaged a team and wagon, with driver, to make a tour through the various localities to which we had been recommended, intimating that it was our wish to start in the morning at as early an hour as possible. One night on the hard mattresses at the hotel convinced us that a change of lodgings would have to be effected as soon as we could locate something more desirable. An hour after the appointed hour for starting, our conveyance drew up at the door and we were soon thereafter clattering beyond the limits of the town, over the dirt roads of the open country. Six miles soon lay between us and the city, during which time many flocks of strong-winged chickens were started whose education since the end of the closed season had widened most amazingly, judging from the manner in which they flushed forty or fifty rods in advance of the rig. Out of these flocks were were now and then able to scratch down a straggler, which deferred taking wing with its more timorous comrades and remained under the cover of the friendly grass until the near approach of the team startled it from its hiding place, when, with a rush of wings, it would burst into sudden flight, calling for snap shooting from the wagon seat. At the end of half an hour our driver informed us that over the knoll to the westward lay an arm of Waubay Lake, where there were usually numbers of ducks congregated. This proved to be true, for as we drew to a standstill on the crest of the hillock a fine sight was presented to our gaze. A strong breeze was blowing from the southwest and as we reached the crest of the hill, we first saw nothing but the rolling waves away out across the lake proper. A few yards further and the secluded bay was disclosed to our view, and it was literally blackened with feeding and preening ducks which had sought shelter from the rolling seas in this narrow arm where the high banks afforded excellent shelter from the strong wind. This bay was probably fifty rods in width and ran northward perhaps three-quarters of a mile before joining the main body of the lake. Great rafts of teal extended down the muddy shores much further than the naked eye could discern their brown little bodies. Spoonies were busily and greedily feeding in the shallows; widgeon and pintail stretched their long slender necks to the fullest extent to determine whether or not our operations were likely to cause them any inconvenience; great fat redheads, and even one band of canvasbacks, were sleeping contentedly in the sun. Long and wistfully we gazed at the concourse of waterfowl, in doubt as to whether it would be advisable to try conclusions with them even though boats and decoys were at the town, but finally our better judgment prevailed and we decided to await the coming of morning, when, with a full and complete outfit we would commence operations systematically. Well satisfied with the introductory, we drove on a mile or more, then found ourselves on a narrow roadway insufficiently wide to permit of two teams passing each other. On the right lay another wide arm of Waubay Lake over which many small detachments of birds were flying. On the left, across a stretch of alkali ground, lay a small body of water the shores of which were white with the salty deposit. To the eastward, on beyond the lake last named, lay a series of depressions in the prairie which our driver informed us finally led to other bodies of water. Over the narrow road small detachments of ducks were passing and repassing and here we decided to pass an hour flight shooting. The writer was the first to leave the rig, then the lumberman, and lastly the attorney, whom the driver deposited close to the end of the narrow road and where some scrubby growth afforded fairly good cover. The cover was very scanty in my locality and lively work was called for on my part whenever approaching birds rendered it necessary for me to sprint to the opposite side of the embankment and there lie close to the earth and fireweeds. With long-range shells the Parker now and then collected toll from the flocks which passed overhead just out of reasonable gunshot. My companions were rather better located and were scoring a bird every few minutes. Accordingly, after a short stay behind the embankment, I joined them and together we shot for an hour or longer, then signaled the rig and drove on, completing a circuit of Waubay Lake, which we found to be a considerably larger body of water than we had anticipated. A little later we drove through the Indian reservation, dotted with tiny huts here and there, taking the place of the olden time wigwam or tepee. Continuing on our drive, we reached the shores of Enemy Swim Lake, a body of water of considerable depth in places and with more or less timber standing upon its banks. Here we did not alight, but skirted the shores for some distance, seeing many flocks of birds banked up out in the open water. It being close to the noon hour, there was little or no natural flight taking place, only a few strays at intervals coming in over the trees and at once joining the great flocks far from shore. A short stop was made in order to dispose of our basket of lunch, then we continued our drive toward home, passing close to the shores of Blue Dog Lake, the south end of which extends down into the country immediately adjoining the town of Waubay. This lake is quite a favored feeding ground for canvasback ducks and we could see considerable numbers of this noble bird tossing on the crest of the waves which were running high as we drove by.

The afternoon was by this time declining and at the suggestion of our driver we decided to try a slough close to town, for some twilight shooting. Arriving at this point we alighted and made our way on foot through the canes to the shores of the slough and found it indeed an excellent shooting ground. No birds were moving, but with the confidence born of long experience we arranged ourselves at advantageous points and contentedly awaited the dusk which was not long in settling. "Mark east!" was the first warning call, and simultaneously three corduroy caps disappeared from view as a wavering line of birds circled over the upper end of the slough and presently headed down the narrow channel. Once, twice, thrice they circled over the open water, then, suddenly towering, made a circle inland, which, fortunately for us, brought their big brown bodies nearly over our line of guns. A fusillade ripped apertures in the evening stillness, and the welcome thud, thud, thud of heavy rice-fattened birds gladdened the hunters' ears. Then followed a hasty dash through the tall canes for the purpose of retrieving the fallen birds, owing to the difficulty of finding them once the eye has been shifted from the identical spot where they crashed from view. They proved to be gadwalls, in fine condition. "Mark south!" and we had barely time to duck from sight before the channel was assailed by a considerable flight of the same variety of birds and they darted excitedly hither and thither, looking for a desirable place to alight. Following them closely, others appeared, and from then on until the darkness rendered shooting unprofitable the place was fairly alive with ducks, and when we reached the wagon on high ground we found we had gathered in a handsome bunch of ducks—gadwalls, mallards, pintails and widgeons.

Half an hour later we were sitting at the hotel table, our feet encased in slippers, discussing the merits of a tolerable meal. Later on, over a cigar, we decided to adopt the plan formulated in the morning, viz., to make an early start and shoot in the sheltered bay discovered that forenoon on Waubay Lake. Accordingly, the liveryman was impressed with the fact that we must have a rig at 5 o'clock in the morning and we saw that the boats were properly loaded into the rig before we returned to the hotel. Later that night, happening to drop into a little drug store to make a few purchases, I met a young man whose acquaintance we were destined to make later on and whose peculiarities will more than likely be referred to subsequently in this narrative. He was engaged in rolling a cigarette and a single glance was sufficient to detect that the youth had been maintaining a spirited engagement with the common enemy, Sir Tanglefoot. His age was doubtful; it might have been eighteen, and again it might have been twenty-four. He had a brown, leathery skin and beard of two weeks' growth. Upon his head, set jauntily, reposed a much-soiled flannel-lined shooting cap. A ragged sweater collar became up close to his swarthy neck and a tangle of black hair straggled down from under his headgear. A well worn and weather-beaten shooting coat covered his back and a pair of large hip boots encased his feet. His utterances were incoherent, but the druggist assured me that Billie would be all right in the morning and a trustworthy guide to employ. We decided, however, to employ the liveryman the following morning and give the guide his inning later in the week. On our return to the hotel we noticed a light in the Judge's office and straightway lost no time in presenting ourselves before him. We found him to be of the right material, and in the course of our conversation we were given much information of great value to shooters in a strange locality. That evening we were given the name of an elderly couple with whom we might perhaps make arrangements to board during our sojourn, and straightway we presented ourselves at that domicile where we found the lady one of those kind old souls who are never weary of providing the comforts of home to all those who are so fortunate as to secure accommodations at that fireside. Before many hours elapsed we were transferred bag and baggage, had our rooms placed to rights and were delighted with the change.

Before daylight next morning we were on our drive to the lake, the two-wheeled boat cart tracking behind the wagon drawn by a good team of horses. The morning was chilly and our greatcoats were a source of comfort during the drive, which ended just as the gray dawn was rendering objects faintly distinguishable. Before we had risen from our cramped positions in the rig and set foot upon the grassy shore, the air was full of startled piping, quacking birds, disturbed in the midst of their morning meal. On the way our plans has been formed, and, without losing a minute's time, I slid the Mullin's steel ducker into the water and rowed rapidly for the opposite shore. Half a mile from where we alighted a sharp point jutted out into the lake and here I had determined to make my first stop. The 16-gauge lay unloaded in the bottom of the boat and no effort was made to do any shooting as the ducks passed and repassed me during the trip across the bay. I did regret not having slipped shells into the little barrels on one occasion, when a flock of seven great canvasbacks fanned lazily past the boat not thirty yards distant, but with redoubled efforts the steel boat was soon grating on the bottom of the lake close to the point, and five minutes later the decoys were in position and the boat under cover in the barley grass lying in long rifts down the beach. I was barely under cover on the end of the point when a flock of widgeons offered a hasty shot as they raced past, going with the wind. A heavy male whirled downward and was split down the breast in striking the ground, so fat was the bird. Flock after flock passed up into the bay, usually following the center of the channel on their way in and passing south far outside of the graceful Elliston's, although now and then a straggler came in over the stools with wings stiffly set to receive the contents of the little salmon-colored shells which quickly began to dot the ground at my feet. Several large boulders had been rolled together out on the end of the point, and here I established my battery and commenced to accumulate a handsome assortment of birds. At regular intervals there came floating up to me the faint rattle of nitro from the blind at the foot of the slough and I knew my partners were likewise enjoying good sport. Overhead the sun shone brightly and a bracing breeze came rollicking down across the long stretch of shallow water. At the close of the flight, which continued until about 3 o'clock, our combined bag was laid upon the grassy bank and was found to number about forty birds, all in fine condition.

On the drive back to town a short stop was made at the slough three miles from the limits where, notwithstanding the fact that two or three other shooters were there in advance of us, we spent a pleasant hour twilight shooting on gadwalls. The lights were shining brightly in the cheerful dining-room at our boarding house as we alighted, and a grateful coal fire shed its warmth pleasantly, rendering doubly enjoyable the delicious supper of roasted wild duck to which we drew up our chairs after our first day's sport far from the Cream City and its routine duties. This important event having been properly discussed, the guns and cartridge boxes had to be overhauled and put in shape after which our plans for the following day had to be made. These consisted of a drive of twenty-four miles from Waubay to Dry Lake, where a succession of shallow sloughs extend for several miles over the lowlands and where, we were informed, good shooting was to be expected. After a refreshing night's rest on good, old-fashioned beds, and an excellent breakfast of broiled teal, we drove out of town, the cart and our two boats trundling along behind the wagon over the smooth dirt roads of the prairie. As on the day previous, "Billie" was our driver, and his yarns and laconic expressions tended to beguile the time consumed on the trip, which was concluded when the ranch of Mr. King was reached an hour before sunset. Here shelter for ourselves and team was procured and directly there arose a commotion among the barnyard fowls which we well knew would result in a supper of chicken at the King table. While the evening meal was being prepared our boats were hauled down to the lake shore for use in the morning, for we were disposed to try conclusions with the ducks on that lake early in the morning and visit Dry Lake later in the day. It is easy to feel at peace with the world when you are lying at full length with a couple of good comrades on the dry prairie grass on a bluff overlooking a shallow little body of water with flag-grown points and shores; with the rays of the setting sun falling in a flood of golden light upon waters fairly teeming with noisy, restless wildfowl; when the October evening air has just enough of frost in it to silence the insect life and make you involuntarily pull your sweater collar a couple of inches higher. As we lay there, each busy with his thoughts and absorbing the grandeur of the picture, a roaring band of strong-winged prairie chickens passed over our heads, followed by another and still another, and what was strange, no one entertained the least degree of regret that the guns were half a mile away. Truly we are a peculiar contradiction. Now keenly absorbed and intently anxious for yonder flock of circling birds to come within reach of the steel barrels so tightly clenched in the hands that death and consternation may be wrought amidst the feathered band, and at another time there is an unwillingness to disturb the perfect repose and serenity of a living picture by so much as a word or gesture. As darkness came on apace, two great owls appeared and flapped aimlessly over our heads, snapping their beaks noisily, apparently anxious to ascertain what queer objects had invaded their territory. The air grew sharper and presently the flight was at its height and the quacking birds were pouring in over the lake from all points of the compass. On the eastern horizon the yellow moon peeped up over a vast cornfield and by its mellow light we made our way back to King's house, to our supper of barnyard fowls, unanimously of the opinion that October is a good month in which to be alive and upon the incomparable South Dakota prairies.

A great gray bank of fog enveloped the lake when we reached its shores the following morning, and through it the whistle of wings sounded continuously, although the birds themselves were invisible in the gloom. Little trouble was experienced, however, in finding our way, and, leaving my companions snugly ensconced upon a point of canes at the east end of the lake, I rowed swiftly in the opposite direction. At the end of half an hour cover was gained and the Elliston decoys were bobbing upon the water. Overhead and on either side birds were darting in full flight like a swarm of angry bees. Presently, as if by magic, the fog lifted its mantle and drifted across the lowlands and the bombardment commenced. A long line of pintails presented the first shot and three of their number fluttered among the stools a moment later. As the sharp reports waked rattling echoes along the low shores, the entire lake and banks seemed to spring into life and the air was literally swarming with excited, quacking birds. In the midst of the excitement a vast army of chickens in full flight from corn to stubblefield passed overhead and before the last had sped beyond the reach of the chilled sixes, three gray bodies were lying upon the shallow waters. Another roaring of wings and another great body of ducks took wing from somewhere in my vicinity, filling the air with their calls. Five, seven, ten of the sixteens' salmon cases were lying at my feet before the flight had passed on and about my little boat were numerous lifeless birds, well marked, to be retrieved when the flight abated. For fully an hour and a half this sport continued, then, the weather being calm and mild and few birds dropping into the lake, we counted our bag and found it to be comprised of thirty-four ducks, five chickens, and a brant, surely a gratifying morning's work.

In the later afternoon, we once more repaired to the lake, and when the flight was over we had gathered in a goodly number of birds of great variety, including several fat mallards, of which we had shot but few thus far. As the moon was rising we loaded our boats upon the wagon which "Billie" had brought down to the shore and drove to the ranch house, where we partook of a duck supper, after which the boats were hauled over to Dry Lake, for use the following morning. For half an hour we feasted ears and eyes alike upon the glories of that evening entertainment as we stood waist deep in the long saw-grass and listened to the rushing wings above and about us, and, by the light of the moon, which threw long lanes of yellow light across the calm waters, saw countless thousands of feeding and preening waterfowl.

Long before daylight King's boys were feeding their horses preparatory to making an early onslaught on the stubblefields with the gang ploughs, and considerably before sunrise we were afloat on Dry Lake and pushing eastward, intent upon reaching some likely spot where a flight could be located and good cover secured. Here we met our first approach of a disappointment, for, being strangers on a lake of goodly size, and of many intricate channels, we were considerably handicapped. Moreover, the morning was breathless and the birds, though in great numbers, worked unsatisfactorily. On this trip, however, we discovered some excellent territory and are of the opinion that under more favorable circumstances this place would prove to be a very desirable one for headquarters for a two week's excursion into the game country. We sincerely hope to spend more time at this lake on our next visit, and with a good stage of water, shall anticipate finding an abundant supply of birds. There are more mallards here than on many of the larger and more open water lakes of Day County, and for them the writer entertains a high regard. Our birds were carefully drawn, cooled, and packed away, and with dinner disposed of and a last look taken at King's Lake, which had afforded us such pleasant entertainment, we bade adieu to the King family, leaving them the richer by a few round silver coins. We landed at Waubay that evening about 7 o'clock, and were glad to be once more at our hospitable boarding place with its air of comfort and good cheer. "Billie" received his orders to call for us with the team at 4 o'clock the following morning and acknowledged the same between puffs at his cigarette.

A gale of wind rattling the windows of our room under the roof awakened us at an early hour, and, knowing the day promised to be a favorable one for shooting, we made haste to dress and eat breakfast. We were on our way before it was fairly light, and decided to once more visit our shooting ground on Lake Waubay. Birds were abundant and excellent sport was enjoyed throughout the day, culminating when the lumberman brought down two Canada geese from a passing flock. A number of prairie chickens were also gathered in as they passed by the blinds. The close of the day's entertainment took place in the twilight on the slough near town, where we retrieved fourteen fine birds in a few minutes. After supper, we had an extensive task drawing birds, and the family cat waxed fat and friendly on the results achieved by lantern light. On the following morning we took breakfast with the family and later on were deposited on the bank of Blue Dog Lake, two miles from town. From there we paddled over to the island, and prepared to do some open water shooting, placing all of the decoys in one large flock, but as the birds secured were principally sawbills and butterballs, owing to the fact that few canvasbacks used the south side of the island channel as a flyway, we soon wearied of the sport of shooting trash ducks and an exploring trip resulted in the locating of an extensive slough inside of the fringe of tall canes which surrounded the island. Pushing through the dense growth we found ourselves in a favored midday retreat of the birds of which several hundreds were in evidence. Outside the waves were running high and the whitecaps sparkled thickly. In this slough we remained until 3 o'clock and only left when upward of fifty birds had been secured. These consisted principally of teal and redheads. From Blue Dog Lake one can push through a narrow channel, cross the highway and then find himself in a long narrow bayou, which, if followed for a couple of miles, will take him to the identical slough upon which we usually secured our evening shooting.

Out next experience was on Enemy Swim Lake distant from Waubay about nine miles. A high wind was blowing throughout the day, and while it was favorable weather for shooting, it rendered much exploring a difficult matter. This is a lake noted for its canvasback and redhead grounds, and while our total bag at night was less than two dozen, it was made up of these two varieties and many a shooter who has fired his last shot at dusk and returned home with a comparatively small string of these noble birds will readily understand that we felt that our time had been anything but poorly spent. Had we discovered where the birds were working earlier in the day we would have brought in more than double this number. The writer left the blind in pursuit of a crippled canvasback, taking with him in the boat only a scanty supply of shells. The chase occupied more time than was anticipated and when the capture was effected, the Mullins ducker was three-quarters of a mile from the blind. It was at this juncture that redheads were observed flying along parallel with the shore on the west side of the channel. As an experiment, three or four canvasback decoys were tossed out and the boat drawn into the tall cover to await further developments. Within an hour seven redheads were lying in the bottom of the boat and not a loaded shell remained. As the hour was late all thought of returning to the blind for a fresh supply of cartridges was dismissed. The writer is of the opinion that if a party would locate its camp on the shores of Enemy Swim Lake and there operate on redheads and canvasbacks, taking the trouble to thoroughly study the lake and its possibilities, excellent results would be obtained. There are other bodies of water conveniently located within driving distance of the lake, where other varieties of ducks abound, to say nothing of the great quantities of prairie chickens which are found everywhere on the stubblefields.

South of Waubay, Bitter Lake presents its long stretches of open water and numerous sloughs for great possibilities in the line of making excellent scores on ducks and geese. More of the latter frequent this lake than other smaller bodies of water, and with suitable weather, several Canada's may reasonably be secured in a day's shooting. Although we passed the lake several times on our drives, we did not once visit its shores, notwithstanding the fact that we heard it very favorably referred to.

All in all, our shooting expedition was eminently successful, and even now while nature's favors are everywhere in abundant evidence and the flowers, foliage and gardens are alike things of beauty, my thoughts are turning involuntarily to the brown Dakota prairies and the October days to come, and fond hopes are cherished that when these pleasant Summer days are gone and the frosts have wrought their miraculous work, when the landscape is ablaze with its kaleidoscopic coloring, the hunting kits and their possessors may be once more steaming westward over the Milwaukee road to the happy hunting grounds of South Dakota.

DUCKING IN DAKOTA
By Greenhead
1904

To secure most excellent sport shooting wildfowl, in addition to having the expedition rendered thoroughly enjoyable from the moment home is left behind until one has safety returned, it is simply necessary to secure transportation to Sisseton, S.D., over the Chicago, Milwaukee & St. Paul Railroad, and leave on the Pioneer Limited, pulling out of the Cream City about 9 o'clock in the evening. The train service is unequaled and it is a never-ending source of delight with the writer to rise early after a luxurious night's rest and work up forward to the buffet car, which, at this early hour, is practically or wholly deserted, and, stretched at ease in a comfortable armchair, enjoy through the broad windows the changing scenery which greets the eye as the long train, filled with sleeping humanity, sweeps northward beside the mighty Mississippi, faithfully following close to the water's edge in long, sinuous curves the stream's erratic course. Now so near the dark water rushes the train that from one's window a pebble could be tossed into the depths below, and again where only flitting glimpses of the river are afforded through its timbered banks. Here and there shallow lagoons stretch back some distance from the shores, and sometimes over, sometimes around these bodies of water the locomotive speeds, the chime whistle raising musical echoes through the woodlands. Elm, poplar, maple and birch are harmoniously intermingled and their foliage has yielded to the subtle touch of Jack Frost's merciless fingers, and where a few short weeks earlier all was green, the rich Autumn tints now flash resplendent in the rays of the early morning sun. And the picture is not lacking completion through the absence of the animate, for often from the sheltered banks of sloughs where they know so well their favorite tidbits are to be found are mallard and teal ducks, which rise in feigned alarm as we rush by, only to circle through the timber and soon return to their grubbing. For years I have undergone privation and discomfort indescribable that some distant and unfrequented shooting ground might be discovered, but now I am well content to confine my yearly excursions to points which are reached in pleasant journeying. I have visited a number of points in South Dakota in the past ten years, but none of them has appealed to me more strongly than the country adjacent to Sisseton, which is reached after a short ride westward from St. Paul, over the Milwaukee & St. Paul Railroad.

Our party of three members on this excursion will doubtless require no introduction to the *American Field*'s readers, as the lawyer and the lumberman have figured conspicuously in previous descriptive articles. Boats and decoys had preceded us over the road some two weeks earlier, going by freight, and advices from Sisseton prior to our departure from home apprized us of their safe arrival; therefore the amount of baggage accompanying us was inconsiderable as the train on the Hastings and Dakota division drew us away from the Twin Cities. A game of cards started early in the day soon languished for lack of interest and, like truants from school, we eagerly scanned the fleeting landscape for signs of game. Occasionally small lakes and bodies of water contained a sprinkling of wildfowl, which took flight as our train rattled past, and not infrequently prairie chickens swept on set pinions across the brown stubblefields. Our noonday meal was eaten at a little, new, unpainted wayside lunchroom, and after a brief stop we sped on our way.

Sisseton was reached before dusk and we were soon lodged for the night in a little hotel, not far from the station, to which we were directed by Dr. J. W. Carleton, with whom we had corresponded, but had never before met. The evening was spent at the hospitable doctor's office in that most interesting manner so familiar to hunters, planning a campaign, and when we retired that night it had been decided that as a party of local hunters, whose report on a certain district they were to visit was much desired, had not returned, we would spend the following day on a slough a short distance from the town, leaving at an early hour in the morning. The hotel proprietor assured us that his cook could not be prevailed upon to get breakfast as early as we intended leaving, but a brief interview with that damsel, upon whose spinster head full forty Dakota Summer suns had fallen, disproved the hotel man's assertion; therefore, amply fortified, we left the town behind us and when the sun rose that morning we were several miles distant and in the act of embarking upon a slough of good proportions and apparently well inhabited with ducks, of which many flocks were in evidence. Our party now included Dr. Carleton, Nels Nelson, a ranchman, and Maurice Schindler, a hardware dealer, in addition to ourselves. Few boats or decoys are employed by the local hunters throughout this section, the great majority of them drawing on a pair of Mackinaw wading pants and, thus equipped, making their way through the hard-bottomed sloughs, jumping the ducks and shooting as they travel.

We spent a pleasant day on the slough, returning to town late in the afternoon with a good showing of birds, including sprigs, gadwalls, redheads, teals, spoonbills and widgeons, and immediately instituted inquiry regarding the party whose return was being anxiously awaited. As there had been no word received from them up to the hour when we retired that night, a trip to Drywood Lake was planned for the following day, and before the first streaks of light were visible we were on our way to the lake, seven miles distant, in force, two of Nelson's brothers having joined our party for the day. Before arriving at the lake our course carried us through a grove of second-growth timber, down to a sharp point. As we entered the grove our appearance was greeted by a chorus of shrill barks and yelps from a pack of Indian dogs and our wagons passed within a few feet of a cluster of wigwams, from the openings in which were thrust begrimed Injun faces, surmounted by masses of tangled black hair. Arriving at the end of the point, our steaming horses were unharnessed and cared for close to the water's edge, and as our Mullins' "Get There" duckers (the only boat that will stand the rough treatment given on a trip of this character) were dropped noisily into the thin ice which had formed under the shelter of the overhanging underbrush, there arose a babel of duck talk and a roar of wings from the great flock of birds which had been feeding undisturbed in the little lake close at hand. Shells were dropped into the frosty gun-barrels and six pairs of alert eyes were intently fixed upon the circling birds, which, seeing nothing to alarm them, were apparently anxious to return to their feeding. The lawyer, the lumberman and the scribe, however, were too intent on getting out into the great windrows of fallen cane and flag, with decoys in position for the returning birds, to devote any time to the circling ducks, and lost no time in packing their belongings into their boats and pushing off for their chosen stands, while those who were unable to wade the deeper waters of the lake betook themselves to the grassy stretches further to the west. The attorney paddled his boat to the eastern shore and was soon placing his decoys. The lumberman and the writer, having but one boat between them, chose a station at the west end of the little pond where the ducks had been feeding, and only a short distance from the wagons. Two dozen Elliston decoys were soon in position and the metal boat cozily driven between two solid bogs in excellent cover. There was practically no delay before the engagement opened, for, while we were busy adjusting the plunder in the bottom of the boat, a large flock of sprigs came sailing in over the top of the timber, but from behind us, and consequently unobserved. They must have passed very close to our heads in their abrupt descent, for their wings, almost in our very ears, were the first intimation we had of their proximity. As it was, we might have taken a hasty snapshot, but we did not do so, preferring to allow them an opportunity to circle. This they were not destined to accomplish, for their course brought them within reach of the attorney, who promptly dropped a pair close to his boat. Then, almost before the snappy reports had ceased to rattle through the timber, a fool spoonie came blundering in over the trees and, wagging his head inquiringly, fairly delivered himself in person as a sacrifice at Diana's altar by guilelessly fluttering up over the decoys and making himself unnecessarily large by extending both wings and legs. The lumberman might almost as easily have gathered in the bird with the chosen implement of his profession, the cant hook, had one been within reach, but as the 12-gauge Parker happened to be ready, he used it with such deadly effect that the light of day for poor *Spatula clypeata* was extinguished without a struggle. The scribe eyed his elder brother severely for a moment, then softly murmured, "Murder in the first degree," while a little tuft of brown feathers was carried away on the breeze in the direction of the lawyer. But they weren't all such easy ones by any means, and more than once, after crouching low in the bottom of the steel boat until the whistling pinions had borne the gray and brown forms within reach of the tapering barrels so tightly gripped in the hunters' hands, the acute angle at which the birds came darting down was misjudged and the chilled sixes were sent speeding on a scoreless errand. Many of the flocks coming in over the lake in this manner, we soon learned to know, would not swing to decoys, so whenever the bunches came within reach they were met with a vigorous reception. Meanwhile our friend was often heard from, and his boat was frequently poled out from the cover to retrieve the birds. The distant and frequent boom, boom of black powder in the west, whence the remainder of our party had moved, kept us posted alike as to their whereabouts and their success, and so the morning swiftly passed until noontime, when, by agreement, all were to meet at the landing for dinner. Our two boats were accordingly drawn up on the shore and the work of dressing birds for dinner commenced before the waders returned to camp, each bearing his goodly bundle of ducks.

That was certainly a snug little shooting spot, that corner in Drywood Lake, and the memory of it, together with the delicious dinner of savory duck stew, will be a pleasant recollection for many years to come. Fate has ordained that the members of that little party shall never again assemble this side of the "Happy Hunting Grounds," for at least one true sportsman will be missing. During our sojourn at Sisseton he endeared himself to us in many ways, and when we again visit those shooting grounds, which I hope will be at no very distant date, we shall miss the welcoming grasp of that loyal hand, and as we gather around the campfire after the day is over I know the circle will be sadly incomplete without that cheerful face and welcome voice. The particulars of the tragic event which caused his death will be given further on in this article.

Flock after flock of birds streamed in over the timber throughout the meal, for which, I distinctly recall that seventeen small ducks were dressed. We devoured them to the last morsel and threw their bones to the dogs, and the afternoon was well along before those appetites were fully satisfied. Our execution on the water was comparatively light when we resumed operations, as we were to leave for town by 4 o'clock, and the evening flight was just commencing when we saw the horses were being harnessed and we were obliged to push ashore, load our plunder, and bid farewell to the little lake which had furnished us with so enjoyable a morning's sport.

Town was reached shortly before dark, and there we found the party whose return we had been awaiting, and listened to their report eagerly. They had found an abundance of ducks wherever they had stopped, and after a discussion of the various lakes a campaign for the next two weeks was mapped out and the evening spent loading wagons with boats, bedding, decoys, tents, supplies, etc., that all might be in readiness for an early morning start. This was accomplished, and before the sun had thrust his inquiring gaze over the hills and down into the town, we were on our way westward—two strong wagons and six men. We spent the first night at a large ranch, which we reached after dark and where excellent accommodations were found. About 10 o'clock the following day, when the ranch was many miles behind us, our eyes caught the glimmer of water off to the left, and we were told that Dry Lake lay in that direction and that excellent shooting was often secured there. Our destination being Clear Lake, however, we pressed on, skirting one end of the lake an hour later, where many circling mallards were observed across the bay, where bogs and cover extend for a long distance back across the flats. The territory looked good to me and I should have enjoyed camping there for a day's shooting, but the redoubtable Nels, who was our captain, asserted that a long drive lay between us and Clear Lake, and as he was none too familiar with the trail, he did not want to lose any time, so we only paused at the crest of the butte and swept the field glasses over the lake and made note of our impressions for future use. This lake, under favorable conditions, would, I feel confident, afford excellent sport for a small party and there are first-class shores for camping and landings, both of which are important considerations. Fit drinking water is rarely close at hand and should be secured at some ranch where there is a good well and kept in five-gallon tin cans, or, better still, a good clean barrel. While I have taken chances and occasionally used the water of these prairie lakes and sloughs without unpleasant consequences, the practice is unsafe and should not be followed. Over the brown hills we rattled, following a dim trail which in places, was hardly a trail at all, Captain Nels ever in the lead, with his fine team of horses. It was close to 4 o'clock p.m. when a shout from the advance rig announced that the lake was in sight, and presently we were skirting its high shores, endeavoring to find a depression through which we might drive and descend to the lake level. At length Nels announced his intention of driving down the bluff immediately before us, and, setting the brakes of his wagon, we watched him, with many misgivings, disappear over the edge with his cargo, but his excellent horsemanship landed him safely at the bottom and the second rig eventually joined the first, and soon the tired horses, freed from harness and collars, were enjoying a roll in the clean, dry sand.

Clear Lake in bygone days must have covered a much larger area than at the present time, for the waters which now bear the name break on the sands several hundred feet from the abrupt and bluffy shores.

As we were unloading our effects preparatory to setting up our tent for the night, the tall figure of an Indian appeared on the crest of the hill directly above us, and was visible for a minute, then disappeared and was seen no more. Wildfowl were circling over the bars and the musical gabble of geese sounded across the water. In half an hour camp was established and all sallied out to secure enough birds for supper. None of the party had ever before visited the lake, consequently few birds were brought in that evening, although none came back to camp entirely empty-handed. The writer selected a point just across the bay from where the camp was located and, throwing out a few decoys, squatted in the brown grass and awaited developments, which came quickly in the shape of five teals, which number was reduced to three when the 16-gauge had taken toll. Then the guns began popping in different directions and a big yellowleg came trailing past within easy range, sounding his mellow note, and the prospect of a dainty repast resolved itself into a dead certainty. Lower dropped the sun and the wind, and, in apparent sympathy with the day orb, subsided with him, and presently the lake lay calm and motionless, reflecting the distant purple hills and the ragged gold and crimson clouds suspended above the western horizon. Then the crimson tints paled to still more delicate hues, and while thus wrapped in admiration, with the Parker lying harmlessly across my knees, a little bunch of teals scuttled before me and inside the decoys and were out of harm's way before my surprise at their audacity was succeeded by the rapid movement incident to getting the sixteen to my face, but the chilled sixes only made an ineffectual effort to overtake the nimble fugitives, and finally wound up by making foolish little dabs here and there on the water and wiggled down and nestled in the bottom of the lake, where the celery was growing for the big canvas-backs, which we learned how to capture a day or two later. Then, when the shades were gathering closer about the point and I was just about deciding to push out and gather up my fleet of Elliston's, I caught a glimpse of a dozen or more dusky bodies swiftly boring through space, and I flashed the walnut stock to my cheek and almost before the whiplike reports went rattling across the placid expanse of water, one, two, three fat redheads plunged down on the sand close by. Then I relieved the Parker of the salmon-colored shells, closed the empty barrels with a snap, gathered in the result of my last hasty shots, and when the decoys had been recovered, paddled leisurely across the lake, with the clouds in the west constantly paling and changing color before my eyes, the many voices of the night sounding in my ears, peace and contentment reigning high up under my sweater and another sensation lower down, which required the presence of a fat teal, in addition to my plover, to dissipate, when seated before our blazing fire. Dear, old, gray-bearded doctor! I can see him now, dignified and grave, as becomes one who has ministered to the aches and pains of the afflicted for thirty-five years or longer, as he sat at supper that evening, with the cheerful firelight playing over his kindly face, his tin plate balanced on his knees, gravely engaged in the dissection of a fat teal. I can almost hear his voice as he paused in the midst of his meal and, looking around the circle, said slowly and with marked emphasis: "Gentlemen, what do you think of these Dakota teals, anyway?" My reply, while not audible, was nevertheless intelligible, for I immediately speared another section of the fowl referred to and promptly transferred the same to my plate. Later on the blankets were spread over the hay beds, guns were oiled, horses watered and fed, and then we crept under the canvas for the night. For a time I was dimly conscious of the team munching its provender close to the tent, then came oblivion. Next, Nels' lively Norwegian voice was announcing what was liable to happen to people who did not get up in time for breakfast. I could hear the doctor and Nels in conversation outside, and the former was saying, " Now, Nels, let's have some nice breakfast bacon and some of that nice home-made bread and creamery butter." When I finally looked outside, Maurice, whose voice was seldom raised, but who was always in the front ranks with a helping hand, was bending over the skillet. There was a smell of sizzling meat and the big coffee boiler was blubbering and throwing off brown fragrance. As I write, the scene all comes back to me once more and if aught else is required to refresh my memory, here lies my bundle of photographs, taken on the spot, and in them I see the same old faces, rendered familiar from daily contact on this October outing.

The morning was sharp and keen and the big collar on the sweater imparted a grateful warmth around the wearer's neck, but a steaming cup of fragrant coffee, poured by Maurice, startled the creepy feeling and a plate of hot bacon and eggs dispersed it altogether and, with shell-boxes replenished, we sallied forth for a tour of investigation. There was no scurrying away for fear some stranger might get the only good stand on the lake, for our own were the only guns heard on this goodly strip of water. About 9 o'clock my steel ducker was creeping slowly along the eastern shore, while its occupant was scanning the calm water for an elusive ripple, when my attention was drawn to a fine flock of canvas-backs, which, flying low, crossed a sandy bar and disappeared from view. Prompted by curiosity, the sharp nose of the steel boat was turned shoreward and the owner of the 16-gauge ascended a stony bank and found himself gazing out over a tiny sheltered lake upon which was gathered a goodly company of large ducks, principally redheads and canvas-backs. Camp was some distance away and temptation to commence operations upon the birds proving too strong, the boat was dragged across the narrow neck of land and launched upon the smooth water, where a few strokes of the thin spruce paddle drove the craft nearly midway to the center of the lake. Then those canvas-backs evinced their displeasure at my invasion by getting up noisily in scattered ranks and, making one awkward circle of the pond, showed their utter lack of sound judgment by blundering directly over my head and so low down that their great bodies and black feet could have been almost touched with a good, long bamboo fishing rod. Ye gods, what a temptation to shoot! But the paddle was kept deliberately at work while probably 1,000 canvas-backs and redheads streamed over, filling the air with the clamor of their hoarse calls and powerful wing strokes. But the experience of early years had not been effectually driven from mind by later years of close office application, and not until the decoys had been placed in position and the opposite shore gained was the 16-gauge brought into requisition, and then only to lie idly on my lap for the space of an hour and a half, during which time not a blessed shot presented itself.

 The usual process of figuring had been gone through with and calculation made as to just about how many of these magnificent birds could have been pulled down out of that flight, not making allowances for any misses either, for how could anyone slobber such great targets up about twenty yards above a fool head. These calculations completed and attention directed to the operations of a muskrat diligently at work on his Winter domicile, I was figuring how long a time would elapse before that particular house-building contract would be finished, when a sharp hiss from set wings near at hand warned me to remain immovable. They swept in from behind—big lusty fellows—and for some unaccountable reason had no eyes for that motionless figure squatted in the short brown grass. They were probably bent on joining their brethren on the water and were not looking for trouble. Those glossy counterparts on the lake, however, were only born a few weeks before, down in Elliston's workshop at Bureau, Ill., and the flock in the air ought to have realized that fact. They didn't seem to care about going through the formalities of a preliminary swing or two, but as quickly as a rapid flight could be checked, wheeled gracefully and started back. Meanwhile there had been ample time for the figure in the short grass to flatten itself until it looked as though a big touring car had run over it a few times, and the sixteen's barrels ought at the present time to show some effects from the gripping they received that day. Like a trained body those heavy forms swung mechanically nearer and nearer, in perfect order. The flat object on the shore in the short grass had a cramp in its neck now, induced by protracted and judicious "rubbering," and a frightful knotty sensation was momentarily increasing in one leg, down in the veal district. Would those ducks never reach the decoys? They were swiftly moving, too, and would consciousness be retained until they did? The question was answered affirmatively an instant later, and none too soon, for there are times when even a big flock of canvas-backs approaching will pale into insignificance. There was one critical moment when the tortured figure essayed and almost, but not quite, failed to gain a sitting posture in time to clap the barrels in line with a pair of gorgeous males. Then the sharp crack of the nitro seemed to dispel the nightmare and the second barrel pulled down an auburn-headed old rascal, fanning the air with both wings desperately; and then, while three pairs of black feet fanned the shallow water in diminishing struggles, the figure performed a rapid stunt, tearing off an inoffensive rubber boot to administer to the aching calf. When this had been accomplished the three royal birds were retrieved and laid in a row on the sand. Ah! Me, but they were beauties! Stroke the glossy heads and smooth down the rumpled plumage of the snowy backs. Note the powerful black bills, so useful in the quest for celery; likewise note the broad black-webbed feet, equally essential for those submarine operations, and say whether or not you have feasted the eyes on nobler game. A distant tinkle roused me from my entertainment and my eyes swept half way around the little lake before I discovered the cause—a lone bird which had swept in over the stony bar and started on a tour of inspection of the feeding grounds. Doubtless this specimen was a scout dispatched by the main body of birds in the big lake for the purpose of determining whether or not the feeding grounds were clear of obstacles, and the figure in the short grass was once more flattened and the sixteen's barrels advanced by degrees until they rested between a pair of rubber-booted feet, where they remained motionless. Cautiously the canvas-back, a big male, fanned on in his circuit, ever out of gunshot from the shore and ever watchful for danger. His long neck was turned this way and that, and presently, when some two hundred yards distant, he spied the Elliston's. They must have looked good to him, for he made a little cut across the open, instead of following the shores of a small bay, and passed the decoys, though well out of harm's way. On he went, and I had almost reached the conclusion that he would leave the lake and join the main flock to make his report, when he suddenly slackened his flight, and, making a graceful swing, bore down toward the stools again. The figure in the grass was invisible as the big bird approached, and for a moment it seemed as if the duck was determined to come in without hesitation, but when within thirty yards of the decoys there was a pause, and with a graceful sweep the game fanned lakeward once more. Again and again the performance was repeated until my patience was nearly exhausted. I had almost reached the conclusion that at the next swing I would take a chance at the bird, but the very next circuit was widened so that the big body was brought almost over the stools, and the sixteen sounded spitefully once. There was a resounding splash on the water, and before the walnut stock had been lowered from my shoulder I caught a glimpse of a flattened form and sturdy black bill creeping away beyond the decoys. Rising to my feet, that the scattering pellets might not perforate the Ellistons, I drew the second trigger like a flash, and with the impact of the leaden messengers upon the smooth surface of the lake, I saw through the thin, transparent vapor a struggling form, which soon lay motionless. Scarcely a desirable decoy, I thought, so the steel boat was requisitioned and the game was retrieved, and once more the brown grass opened and closed as the hunter sought its shelter. Twice more the sixteen was brought into service, and now the sand at my feet was ruddy and three more of the black-snouted gentry had joined their comrades upon the sand. Then a tiny boat was launched from the opposite shore, and before its occupant had taken many strokes I became aware that the lumberman was on his way across to join me. My throat had been parched for the last two hours and I earnestly entertained the hope that he had come direct from camp and had brought food and drink for me which proved the case, and I gladly retired with the lunch and can of warm coffee to a little clump of brush and the brown grass received his figure instead of my own. The brown paper parcel was found to contain two roasted teals and a liberal supply of bread and butter, which were devoured to the last morsel with a relish seldom experienced at home. With the coming of the lumberman, however, the spell appeared to have been broken, for no more birds sought the seclusion of the little cover, and after the lapse of an hour, we gathered up our spoils and headed for camp.

DUCKING IN DAKOTA (CONCLUSION)
By Greenhead
1904

Thus the days were checked off the calendar and our first week was drawing to a close. Then a caller appeared in camp and his tales of the birds to be seen throughout the hill country adjacent to Fort Sisseton awakened within us a desire to visit that wonderful district. There was a council held beside the campfire that evening, and before the sun was an hour high the following morning there was nothing to be seen at the foot of the bluff, where the tent had been, but a few tin cans, cartridge boxes and a mound of hay which had served for our beds, while away out on the brown hills to the westward two teams were trotting briskly in the direction of the fort, twenty miles away. We should have reached our destination shortly after the noon hour but for various and frequent interruptions, when the guns were dragged out from under the seats at some particularly inviting slough filled with birds. The teams would be driven around the edge, depositing here and there one of our number, until the pond had been encircled; then, when all was in readiness, a shot would put the ducks in motion and the guns would grow warm to the touch, while the dogs were kept busy retrieving game. This sport usually lasted only a very few minutes, for the birds soon left for other ponds, with which the country seems to be well supplied. As our course wound westward over the rugged country we drove for miles across hills and through swales, blackened and barren of growth, where the fires had swept within the past few weeks, and then, while Nels' team was far in advance, we heard the shout which we knew indicated that the fort was in view. Around a rise of land, and the cluster of buildings, perhaps two miles distant, was plainly seen in the midst of a grove of cottonwoods. Bunches of cattle and quantities of sheep dotted the landscape. Civilization was once more at hand. Across a little bridge which spanned a run we rumbled, and five minutes later we were among the buildings, arranged in the form of a square, all facing toward the center, where the parade ground of old, consisting of a square of perhaps two acres of land, is now grown high with weeds. Not a sign of life was anywhere visible as we drove around the plaza. The barns and sheds were tenantless, the doors were falling from their hinges, and the stone walls in places were crumbling. Windows were either entirely gone or rattling in their frames, with here and there a solitary pane of glass. The sun was nearly down and a raw wind swept mournfully across the plaza; a bit of tin water-spout, rusted and battered, hung against a brick wall and creaked dolefully as the draft of air swung it to and fro. A hen scuttled into the tall fireweeds, followed by a half-grown brood of little chickens, and we knew that somewhere, midst this accumulation of decaying pioneer landmarks, human life would be found. Then a bird dog suddenly rushed out, barking furiously, and the bent figure of a man rose from a little potato patch and stood leaning on his hoe as we drew nearer. In five minutes we had effected arrangements for our stay with our newly made acquaintance and learned from him the location of the principal sloughs, or ponds, where the best shooting might be expected. We decided to remove our belongings to one of the solid brick buildings, of which there were several, in preference to setting up the tent, and presently half of our number were taking possession of the officers' quarters, preparing hay beds on the floors and setting up a rusty iron stove which Mr. Beaman, foreman at the fort, kindly loaned us, while the rest of the company drove the teams down to the water and unloaded the boats in readiness for the morrow. The evening was spent in adjusting our comfortable quarters for a considerable stay, and a bountiful supper of ducks, chickens and grouse was keenly relished after our long trip.

The lumberman and the writer were delegated to spend the next forenoon together one of the sloughs, where, with the Mullin's boat, we were expected to keep the birds moving. Daylight had scarcely made its appearance before we were making our way laboriously through the tall canes on the east shore, dragging the steel boat to the water's edge. Finally, however, we were through with the worst of the traveling and emerged at a point where the boat could be launched. There were a number of little bogs, some hardly the size of the skiff, others twenty yards in diameter, out half a gunshot from shore, and in two of these we stationed ourselves, for the birds were already on the move in numbers, and almost before we were ready the engagement opened. The surroundings were admirable, for the slough was narrow, and shots were secured at almost everything which passed north and south. How long the body of water was we were at that time unable to estimate, owing to a sharp point one hundred yards south of our stands which obstructed the view of what might lie beyond. The ducks were nearly all of the larger varieties and as they passed and repassed the bogs flew low and decoyed perfectly. I heard a hoarse word of warning from the lumberman and dropped into the tall cover as three canvas-backs veered from their course through the center of the channel and sailed in between us. Through some unaccountable blunder we both pulled on the same bird, a big male, but our next two shots brought down the remaining pair, one of which was crippled and eventually lost although there was apparently no cover or drift stuff into which it could crawl. All three birds were plainly visible for the space of a couple of minutes after striking the water and were pronounced dead, and our attention was directed to the flight around us, but when the work of retrieving was commenced one of the canvas-backs was missing. About 9 o'clock the clouds which had been gathering all the morning precipitated a gentle rain. We should have discontinued operations then and there and started for the fort, but as we were eager to investigate the possibilities of the slough, the lumberman started for the north end and the writer paddled the steel boat down to and around the point. The wind was increasing and the rain was steadily falling in a dismal drizzle, which soon penetrated my canvas shooting jacket. Thinking to gain some shelter on the west shore, I headed across the slough, putting up great quantities of ducks on the way. The west shore I found to be ideal for shooting purposes, there being many little islets out in the bays, and on and around these the birds went up, flock after flock. Reaching the extreme west shore I tossed out half a dozen decoys where a large flock of gadwalls had been sitting and drew the boat up into the friendly shelter of the canes, where I prepared to await the end of the storm as comfortably as possible. Hardly had I curled myself up in the bottom of the boat, with my rubber blanket wrapped about me, than the gadwalls began returning, the first bunch, consisting of eight or ten birds, being fairly in between my stand and the decoys before I was conscious of their presence. With the crack, crack of the sixteen two gray bodies instantly responded. These lay among the decoys, in calm water, and in less than half an hour sixteen birds were thus killed, affording one of the pleasantest experiences, barring the inclement weather, that fell to my lot during the trip. Another hour passed without affording a single shot; then the clouds broke up into little detachments and were borne away before the wind, which drew around into the north and blew colder. The flight now appearing to pass not far from the point, I gathered up the decoys and pushed southward in that direction. Arriving at the point, I sought the shelter of the rushes and spent the ensuing half hour expending considerable ammunition at long chances, as the flocks were inclined to avoid the point and swung into the channel when approaching it. From here I was enabled to obtain a view of the slough its entire length and was very favorably impressed with the character of the place. The crooked channel extended for probably two miles or more south and perhaps half a mile northward, making a goodly sized shooting ground, and this being, as we afterward learned, centrally located, drew its supply of birds from all directions. My explorations consuming the ensuing two hours, I was then ready to return to camp. A better landing place on the main land was discovered, and, drawing the boat into the cover and secreting the paddle and decoys, I started for the fort, laden with the legal bag for a single day's shooting. The fort was reached after a weary tramp, and there I found a late dinner being eaten by the boys, all of whom had met with excellent success during the morning. The rest of the day was devoted to the thorough cleaning of guns, drying of clothes, etc., for the morning had been a most disagreeable one and all were soaked to the skin. Nearly every day for the space of a week the lumberman and I visited the same slough, usually shooting until noon and then spending the remainder of the day in camp or making short excursions with team to different ponds within driving distance of the fort. Our larder was never without prairie chickens, grouse, snipes, duck and all varieties of game, as we were in a district which abounded with it, and after the first day or two we regulated our shooting so that no birds might spoil on our hands. The team made two trips back to Sisseton and at those times carried our game into town, where is was distributed freely from the hardware store.

On one occasion the attorney, Nels and the writer took an afternoon drive and covered a considerable expanse of country. Many ponds and sloughs were visited and one in particular appealed to the writer's tastes in a marked degree. The only signs of any hunters having visited its shores that season were found where a sharp point jutted out into the lake some little distance and there the remains of an old campfire were scattered and the bent poles where the wigwam had stood told that the site had been occupied by the red man. The slough probably covered a hundred and fifty acres of land and was almost divided by a dense mass of rushes which ran through shallow water from east to west and afforded most excellent cover from which to shoot. Out on both sides the water was covered with a heavy growth of canes, with here and there large spaces of open water. A shot fired from the shores started hundreds of birds in motion and for half an hour the guns were kept busy. We had brought no boat with us on the drive, therefore were unable to reach the most desirable stands, otherwise we could have spent the entire afternoon on the two sloughs and brought away a large number of ducks. However, we were well content to sit later in the shade of a grove of trees on the shores and watch the flocks of ducks return and settle into the canes, feeling that we would make the place a visit at some subsequent date and spend an entire day there, but this we were unable to do as our party became gradually reduced, one by one, and we ourselves finally found it necessary to turn our faces homeward without having the pleasure of again testing the possibilities of the two sloughs.

The ride back to Sisseton over the rolling hills country was keenly enjoyed, and upon our arrival there was much to be done before the departure of our train, which was to leave between 7 and 8 o'clock. After the necessary packing had been accomplished we were invited by the doctor to participate in a game dinner served at a French restaurant, at which game of several varieties and nicely prepared was spread temptingly before us. Then good-byes were said, hands heartily shaken, and, with our paraphernalia safely aboard the train, we were at last actually leaving the shooting grounds. The sleeper was taken a few hours later and the sun was shining and our train running into the Twin Cities when we awoke. The daylight run through to Milwaukee was made on schedule time and our annual outing became a thing of the past but for the recollections which remain ever with us.

I can certainly recommend the country visited on the above-described trip to anyone desiring reasonably good shooting and shall be pleased to give further information regarding locations, etc., to parties who may wish to correspond with me. Within the past few months Mr. Nelson has secured a lease of the territory adjacent to the fort and will very likely be in position to care royally for shooters who visit him. Circumstances rendered a trip to the Dakotas out of the question last season but if nothing occurs to prevent, I expect to spend this year's vacation with Nels at the fort. Accommodations for ladies also can easily be arranged for, and there certainly never can be found a more admirably located headquarters for a congenial party than at the fort, for innumerable sloughs extend in all directions, several of which can be reached in a few minutes' walk. The water from the big spring is excellent, the dry prairie air is invigorating, and enough shooting to satisfy any humane sportsman will be found close at hand. Take your wives with you for a change, fellow shooters. They will enjoy it just as much as you will, and it will make future excursions of this character all the easier for you and many be the means of beating the family physician out of his fees during the long Winter ahead of us. Mrs. Greenhead says she is going this Fall, and periodically trots out her togs for my inspection. I have had the sixteen's stock shortened a bit so as to fit her shoulder, and I expect when her corduroy cap shows on one side of the channel of that long slough west of the fort, where I shot every day for a week two years ago, and mine is visible on the opposite side of the channel, that there'll be "something doing."

Away back toward the commencement of this article, which has become considerably longer than I anticipated at the start, reference was made to the death of one of the members of our little company, and I have purposely postponed narrating the particulars until the present time, as the subject is a very painful one to me. Perhaps an extract from a letter written me by Maurice Schindler, under date of October 14, 1903, from Sisseton, will accomplish what I find difficult to attempt myself. It is as follows:

"I am sorry to tell you that Dr. Carleton was drowned in Buffalo

Lake last Sunday, October 11. We went out to the lake the evening before. There were seven in the party and we all went out hunting in the morning, came back to camp at noon and cooked dinner, but no doctor came. We went out after dinner and in about half an hour I got seven ducks. I dropped a teal and went to get her, and when I got into the grass I saw the doctor's little dog sitting in the doctor's boat and found the doctor, with his left arm hanging over the side of the boat and his body in the water. It was about 3 o'clock when I found him and his watch stopped about 10, so he had been in the water several hours. I got the boys together and we finally succeeded in getting the body to camp, and later to town. That was the saddest hunt we ever had. We went out Tuesday and dragged up his gun. Everyone feels as though he had lost his best friend."

For days after the receipt of this letter recollections of the dear old doctor were constantly before me. Ever thoughtful and considerate in his treatment of others, his kindly face will be missed upon the streets of the little town of Sisseton, and when the remaining members of the company with whom he was wont to participate in frequent shooting excursions assemble around their fire after a successful day spent out on the ducking grounds, they will sadly mourn the loss of a true comrade and a trusty friend. Though the day were inclement, though the birds refused to move, though his long waders accidentally became filled with ice-cold water, no word of complaint escaped him during three weeks of close companionship. Dear old man! May his spirit in that mystic realm find rest and contentment. I was utterly unable to reconcile myself to the thought of the doctor having met his death by drowning. Judge, therefore, of my relief to learn upon receipt of a second letter from Maurice Schindler that the examination disclosed the fact that death was due to heart disease.

(This portion of Part 2 contains articles from Forest and Stream)

A TRIP ON A HUNTING CAR
by Jersey
1883

On Saturday morning, Sept. 29, at 4 o'clock, a party of fifteen of us, including your correspondent, who is proud to be known as a Jerseyman, left Harrisburg, Pa., on the Pullman hunting car Davy Crockett for the wilds of Minnesota and Dakota Territory on a two weeks' hunt for chickens, geese, ducks, etc. Our car was a model of its kind being furnished with electric bells, sleeping apartments, dining and observation rooms, kitchen, refrigerators, and in fact everything necessary to make our stay on it a pleasant one. A half dozen kennels for our dogs were also a part of the fixtures. The car was in charge of Robert Winfield, who with two assistants (including cook), all furnished by the Pullman Co., "were of the finest." The larder was sumptuously furnished with lots of good things to tickle the inner man.

We left Harrisburg amid the cheers and best wishes of a host of friends, arriving in Chicago on Sunday morning; leaving that city in the evening and arriving at St. Paul the following day. A hasty look of a few hours over that busy city and away we go again, bound for Ashby, Minn., which we reach at 7 o'clock the next morning. Here was to be our first stop for hunting. Upon our arrival teams are quickly secured, our guns put on board, and the dogs released from their kennels. Over the almost boundless prairies, covered with grain fields further than the eye can reach, away we go a happy party of four. After a drive of ten miles along the shores of Pelican Lake our dogs are started and the hunting begins. For hours we hunt, but not a chicken. Our party were beginning to think that chickens were a myth, when about thirty yards from us up jumps a buster. (When I say "buster" I mean a great big overgrown chicken.) Never shall I forget my feelings, never the astonishment I felt at sight of him. To me he looked the size of a goose as he sailed away from us. Bang, bang, went our guns but he never stopped. We had the fever badly. Following him for nearly a mile we again flush him when the object of our hopes again alights, and as we once more see him rise I, with an unerring aim, pull trigger and down comes his majesty. Cheer after cheer and yell upon yell do I indulge in. The proudest man in America is hugging that bird to his cheek, is caressing his first chicken, and that man a Jerseyman. Talk about fun! Talk about happiness!

No man knows what real, true, unalloyed fun and happiness are until he kills his first chicken. The boys gather around me. I am the lion of the party. Proudly do I hand them the bird for their inspection.

In a short time we find a bunch of seven birds, and then the fun begins again. Bang, bang, go our guns, but we have got our hands in this time, and we bag six of the seven. Off we go again and succeed in adding three more to our score. Arriving at our car, we find we are low boat, as far as the count is concerned—one team bringing in twenty-nine and the other twenty-four birds. The next day is almost a repetition of the first, excepting that our team leads the score with forty-one chickens, twenty-eight ducks, and several geese.

On Friday morning we bid Ashby good-bye, and we are off for Valley City, Dakota Territory. Just before reaching Moorhead City, Minn., we were visited by a party of cowboys who, after helping themselves to our cigars, lemonade, etc. left us to the silence of our feelings. Poppy R. (Crockers) was highly indignant at their want of courtesy, while the well-known voice of Pat as he roared, "Mark

Elcho, I'll lick you." was the only sound that broke the silence until we reached Fargo.

Saturday morning we reached Valley City, Dakota, and found there two warm-hearted, genial sportsmen in Mr. Davidson, of the *Daily Record*, and Mr. Scott, a lawyer of that place. With them we passed the time, shooting chickens, ducks and geese to our hearts' content. Loads of game were captured each day, and when the time came to say farewell, we did so feeling that truer friends or better sportsmen we had never met. May their cartridges never stick in their guns, nor their aim be untrue.

On Tuesday morning we started for Fargo, on our return home, stopping over a day, where we were kindly attended to by Col. Fred Cobham, Dep. U. S. Marshal for Dakota. The thanks of our party are due Col. C. for his untiring efforts in our behalf.

Away again on Wednesday, stopping at Minneapolis, Milwaukee and Chicago each a day, we arrive in Harrisburg on Sunday morning well pleased with our trip and with the friends we made. Surely Horace Greeley's head was very level when he gave the advice, "Go West, young man, go West."

A GOOSE HUNT IN NORTH DAKOTA
By George F. Goodwin
1891

About the 20th of October the writer, in company with W. S. Parker, a druggist of Lisbon, N.D., and Dr. O. G. Winters, of La Crosse, Wis., left Lisbon via Fargo, for Devil's Lake for a few days' sport among the wily wild geese. Taking the morning train from Fargo, a six hours' ride upon the finely equipped Great Northern Railway through a portion of the Red River Valley brought us to the lake with the satanic name, where, by previous arrangement, a team and driver were in waiting to convey us to the hunting grounds. We made our headquarters at the house of a substantial German farmer.

We were up betimes the next morning, eating breakfast by lamplight, and having carefully loaded our ammunition, decoys, etc., into the commodious two-seated buggy, were soon off into the thick darkness of the early morning, headed for the lake where the geese had spent the night. A lively ride of three miles in the crisp morning air behind a span of cranky bronchos managed by a reckless driver brought us to the lake just as the first faint streaks of daylight began to show in the eastern horizon.

Stringing out along the shore at intervals of 20 or 50 rods, and securing such cover as best we could behind the high grass and small bushes that fringed the high banks, we anxiously awaited the morning flight. We had not long to wait; small flocks soon commenced to rise from the center of the lake and start for the feeding grounds, but they seemed to fly in all directions except ours, and the few that came our way kept safely out of reach;

finally, just as we were beginning to get chilled and discouraged, a nice flock of "honkers." or Canada gray geese, came within our reach; and, waiting until they were fairly past, we gave them the contents of our trusty Parker ten-bore (charged with 5 drs. of powder and 1 1/8 oz. of No. 2 chilled shot), and had the satisfaction of seeing two fine birds come down with a "swish" upon the prairie. In the meantime the other boys were banging away with good success, and the firing became general all along the line. By sunrise the geese were nearly all out of the lake, and, gathering up the results of our morning shoot (a dozen fine birds), we loaded into the buggy again and followed in the direction of the northward flight. About three miles out we found a stubble field thickly covered with geese and brant feeding, and driving them away without shooting, we proceeded to dig our pits and put out our decoys and dead geese. By the time this was fairly accomplished, our empty stomachs warned us that it was "high twelve," and we adjourned to a neighboring house and partook of our noonday lunch.

Getting back into the pits about two o'clock , we awaited the afternoon flight from the lake. It was nearly three o'clock before the first triangle appeared on the distant horizon; soon the honk, honk, squawk, squawk, of the coming flocks was heard, and the order is given, "Down there," and we prepare for action. Soon they are over us and taking the decoys beautifully; all ready—one, two, three; bang, bang, bang; whizz, swish, thump; five fine birds as the result of the first volley. From this time on until dark they kept coming at irregular intervals, the short waits adding zest to the sport.

Space will not admit of a detailed account of our three days' hunt; of the crack "double shots," nor of the many misses; of how one old "honker" when he was struck took a bee line at an angle of about forty-five degrees for the pit where the writer was ensconced, and only missed his head by a scratch; nor of the sharpened appetites with which we devoured the baked goose and other goodies of the good German *frau*, nor of the yarns spun around the evening fireside amid wreaths of smoke from our cob pipes.

Suffice it to say that we returned with a bountiful supply of geese and brant, and with minds and bodies refreshed for our respective duties. I purposely omit specifying numbers, fearing that it may overtax the credulity of your readers, and fearing also that the story might not be as large as some one else has told.

We all thought that we had seen large numbers of geese and brant together before, but when we saw the ground literally covered at times for half a mile wide and two miles long, and when we stood on the banks of the lake at evening and saw them coming in, drove after drove, and heard the honking and squawking of from five thousand to six thousand geese and brant in unison until it mingled into the indistinct roar that was simply deafening, we concluded that this was indeed "The Goose Hunter's Paradise."

DAKOTA GAME BIRDS
By Elmer T. Judd
1891

Editor's Note: The author of this note, Elmer T. Judd, was an ornithologist and it is included for the scientific value. He published a booklet: "List of North Dakota Birds Found in the Big Coulee, Turtle Mountains and Devils Lake Region; As noted during the years 1890 to 1896." (1917)

I send you a few notes on the game birds of Towner county, North Dakota, as I saw them during the spring, summer and fall of 1890. I arrived in Towner county May 10, and from that time until late in the fall I saw game birds of some kind nearly every day. The main flight of geese and ducks had gone north, presumably to their breeding grounds, leaving only those which for reasons of their own had determined to try their luck where they were at that time.

May 1 I saw first willets and bartramian sandpipers—called plover—the 13th I saw a good many mallards, some widgeon and bluewing teal, four ruddy ducks (the only ones seen during the year), hooded mergansers, two sandhill cranes, and flocks of geese that looked very large to me and they were when compared with what I had seen in old Connecticut. The 16th I had my first goose hunt. With two friends I went to the Big Slough, some 2½ miles northeast of town. We arrived late; the flight was over. The geese and ducks frequented the place for the purpose of rest and to drink. Charlie, thinking to give the two novices a chance, went back and around a hill, coming on to the shore of the pond opposite our stand. Every bird immediately took flight, several hundred coming over our heads. Billy picked out his bird, killing one with first barrel and missing with the second. As for myself, I scored a complete miss. As the flock went over my head, I thought the geese were so thick that a shot could not get through without striking a bird, so I drew up and shot both barrels into the flock, and, so far as I could see, never stirred a feather. Small wasn't the word for the way I felt. This proved to be the last flock of geese we saw until the fall flight.

On the 19th I added the gray duck to my list; the 20th an American coot; the 23rd the pintail duck; the 25th prairie chickens were seen, also a large flock of black-bellied plover. May 21 I found a mallard's nest with eight eggs; the 31st another with eleven eggs. June 4 I added the marbled godwit to the list. June 18 saw female gray duck with six or eight young two or three days old. June 14 a friend brought me a young prairie chicken less than a week old. His dog had killed it. There were a number of good broods of prairie chickens raised within a short drive of the town. A few were shot before the law was off by local hunters. The farmers at this season are very busy, or in all probability more would be shot. In 1888 chickens were rarely seen in this vicinity, while the sharp-tailed grouse were quite numerous; but now it is changed. The prairie chicken is increasing and the sharptail disappearing, although said to be the only grouse in and around Turtle Mountains.

Sept. 8 I found a flock of twenty chickens, apparently two broods, as they were of different sizes, nearly full-grown and very strong flyers. Previous to finding the chickens I had put up an old male sharp-tailed grouse, who proved to be too sharp for me, as, after following him over three miles and shooting at him several times, I gave it up, thinking it would be too bad to annihilate the only specimen of its kind I had seen.

Two days later, with my friend Charlie Canfield, I had some fine shooting for a short time at the same flock of chickens, getting seven. They were about the last killed in this place. Sept. 20 I saw a small flock of brant which were the advance of the fall flight here. The 25th I saw the first flock of snow geese, which were common from then on. Oct. 5 Hutchins's brant and white crane made their appearance. Some flocks of sandhill crane had been seen flying over, but they did not stop to feed. Oct. 7 it commenced storming and it rained or snowed every day until the 17th. It was an unusual thing for so much water to fall at this season of the year, but the hunters thought it a great blessing, as it filled up the sloughs and coulees. Before the storm general complaint was heard from shooters that there would be no geese or duck shooting as there was no water. From then on geese and mallard ducks were without numbers. Figures can give no idea of the size of the immense flocks that were seen. The largest flock I saw was in one continuous line over a half mile in length and they were flying from 20 to 50 abreast. Nearly every resident agreed in saying that there had never been so many mallard ducks seen in one fall as there were during the last weeks in October, 1890. They were considered small game. Every one could eat goose. One man, who had killed a good many ducks, took a buggy load into town. He could not give them away and they were fed to hogs. I heard of an old half-breed who sneaked on to a flock of geese and killed twelve with one charge from an old muzzleloading shotgun of not over 16-bore. The geese I saw, and could identify, were snow geese, which were abundant and led in numbers. Hutchins's brant were quite common and often seen in large flocks of snow geese, besides many flocks that kept by themselves. The Canada geese were common but not seen in any great numbers at one time; the American white-fronted or speckle-bellied goose was quite frequently killed out of flocks of snow geese. I also saw several that I could assign to no place, apparently hybrids, or they might be classed as sports from the varieties of the genus *Bernicla* or brant geese.

There was a severe cold snap the first week in November, after which the geese were seen flying in the triangular-shaped flocks in which they migrate, and from then on the numbers seen grew rapidly less and all were gone by Nov. 15, with the exception of now and then a small flock which would be seen flying rapidly toward the south, until about Dec. 1. After geese and ducks go south it is seldom a game bird of any description is seen on the prairies of North Dakota. I append the weights of a few of the geese and ducks I killed during spring and fall.

Snow geese in adult plumage: 7 weighed respectively 5 lbs. 6oz., 5 lbs. 5½oz., 5 1/4 lbs., 5 5/8 lbs.,, 6 3/8 lbs. In young or gray plumage 8 weighed 4 lbs. 6 oz., 4 lbs. 10 oz., 6 lb. 12 oz., 4 lbs. 10 oz., 5 lbs., 5 lbs. 2 oz., 4 lbs. 8 oz., 4 lbs. 4 oz.

Mallards: 6 drakes weighed 3 lbs., 2½ lbs., 2 lbs. 10 oz., 2½ lbs., 1 lb. 10 oz., 3 lbs., 2 3/4 lbs; 3 ducks, 2 lbs. 2 oz., 2 lbs. 8 oz., 2 lbs. 10 oz. One gadwall drake weighed 2 lbs., one pintail weighed 2 lbs., one widgeon drake 1½ lbs., 2 ducks, 1½ lbs., 1 1/8 lbs. Blue-wing teal, 5 drakes, 4 ducks, weighed without any variation 3/4 lb. each.

THE SAGINAW CROWD
By William B. Mershon
1891

Editor's Note: William B. Mershon was one of the more noteworthy sportsmen who came to North Dakota to hunt in the 1880s. He was a resident of Saginaw, Michigan and with other hunters used a converted Pullman railroad car as a mobile hunting camp. It was named the "City of Saginaw" and in an August 2, 1883 note in <u>Forest and Stream</u> Mershon stated: "The Saginaw Hunting Club have had fitted up a car that is a model of beauty and comfort, and we are planning a trip to Yellowstone Park on September 1." And from the book, "Recollections of My Fifty Years Hunting and Fishing" (1923) he wrote: "In September '83, on my return from the Yellowstone Park, I, with a few friends, stopped in eastern Dakota to shoot ducks,...." Also in that book: "We commenced going to Dawson with the car, Saginaw, a year after this (1884) and continued to so every year until 1899. More will be found concerning Mershon's hunting trips in other places in this book.

We have been somewhere every year; while not always the same old crowd, still a good many of the old hands have been along. Last year we left for our old stamping ground in Dakota, Oct. 13, taking the good car City of Saginaw, over the C. S. & N., Wisconsin Central and Northern Pacific. The party was small. Bob Schultz and I were the only ones of the old crowd, and two tenderfeet in the shape of A. H. Morley, of this city, and A. P. Bigelow, of New York, with George, the porter, and old John to look after the kitchen, constituted the party.

We arrived on Thursday, the 16th, and were met by our guide and the livery stable man with the cheering news that the birds had not come down yet, that the shooting was poor and the sloughs all dry. However, we were comforted by the remark that on a barley field about ten miles north a number of birds had been seen the last few days and possibly we could get a shot there. It proved to be a very good day. We started at once and arrived on the ground about 10 o'clock.

As soon as we came in sight of the stubble we saw that we were going to have some fun. It was situated on the side of a hill, about half a mile distant was a little lake and there was a continual stream of geese and mallards coming from the water to the barley field and back into the lake. The day was dark, and by the time we had our decoys out and pits dug it began to snow, and seemed as if the air suddenly became filled with geese and mallards. We did not wait for lunch. The shooting was good for about two hours; 37 ducks, mostly greenheads, 35 geese and two great white whooping cranes that Bob had the good fortune to get, was the tally as we put them in the wagon. The cannonading at last drove the birds away and although we waited for their return flight in the evening, they did not come and we drove back to town, exceedingly well satisfied with the day's sport.

We did not get as many birds any day after that, though the bag was fair, getting a few plover and quite a number of sharp-tailed grouse. I also killed a prairie wolf with my rifle at, I should judge, fully 300 yds., most likely a lucky shot. We were driving over the prairie and went through a very rough patch all grown up to weeds, and right in front of the horses out sprung this wolf and a badger. The badger went into a hole, but the wolf, after running about 300 yds. , stopped to look back. In the meantime I had shoved a cartridge into my .38 Marlin, and taking careful aim, fired, and as good fortune would have it, struck him right back of the ear. When we counted up that night we did have a pretty good bag; 68 geese, one white crane, the wolf and two sharp-tailed grouse.

Hunting Car "City of Saginaw"

We were preparing to take a trip about 35 miles northwest after deer. In a strip of rough country cut up by hills and gullies, a good many blacktails had been seen the week before. We were making all preparations and were to start on Thursday the 23rd. Wednesday, Bigelow, the guide and myself went to the north of the car about twelve miles and located a big flight of geese, and were expecting grand sport for that night. About two o'clock in the afternoon I was taken with a severe chill and burning fever, and a congestion or knotting sensation in the left lung finally drew me all out shape, and it resulted in a severe attack of pneumonia. Temperature was up to $105\frac{1}{2}$ when the doctor came in to see me the next day. To say that the long ride home that night was miserable but feebly describes it. Had to be lifted into bed and at the advice of the doctor we started for home the next day. The Chicago and Grand Trunk people put us on their fastest east bound train out of Chicago and we reached home late Saturday night. This ended my shooting for last year. It was a great disappointment to the rest of the crowd.

The birds came home in nice condition and were given to our friends. One beauty of shooting out there is that the nights are so cold that the game gets thoroughly chilled, and with even ordinary care you can save it two weeks.

    We are now planning for another trip. Our party will consist of ten or twelve, the old crowd, and we are getting together now every evening and talking over loads, how many shells to take, getting decoys painted up, making out our list of supplies, and getting the old car in order, and, in fact, beginning to have as much fun out of it as we will have after we get there. Lots of wheat this year and plenty of water ought to make the shooting good, but whether it is or not we will have a grand time and possibly may write you about it later.

"THE SAGINAW CROWD"
William B. Mershon
1891

<u>Editor's Note</u>: *This brief note was important to me when I found it because it has information about two hunters, William A. Bond and Albert R. Barnes, of Chicago, who hunted in Kidder county from 1889 to 1902. The article verified that Bond and Barnes stayed with early day homesteaders, Mr. and Mrs. J. D. Williams, whose ranch was on the south side of Lake Williams which was named for him as well as the town of Lake Williams. That location is four miles from my hunting camp and so Bond and Barnes hunted in some of the same lakes and marshes that I have over the past 30 years or more. A more complete account of Bond and Barnes with details of game shot and habitat conditions at that time is in Part 3 of this book.*

SAGINAW, Mich., Nov. 12.— "The Saginaw Crowd" returned Oct. 24. Of course we had the best time yet. Every one was well pleased with the trip, and found as much game as usual, though more hunters there after it. We could count thirty-five foreign sportsmen staying with the farmers at this one little prairie town. I inclose a clipping taken from the local paper:

> The hunting party of which Messrs. Bond, Barnes and Paddock were members returned to their homes in Chicago on Sunday evening, after a stay of nearly four weeks at the pleasant home of Mr. and Mrs. J. D.

Williams, in New Yorktown. These gentlemen have been in the habit of making this place their headquarters for several years for a season of waterfowl shooting, and have almost come to be considered as members of Mr. Williams' family. They are thorough gentlemen—of great prowess and superior marksmanship, as is evidenced by their score this season, showing a mortality of 3,600 birds, 3 deer, and 1 antelope.

Reads almost like slaughter. Over 3,600 birds; and after all these people were there a month and had a party of about half a dozen.

Under date of Nov. 8 I have a letter from Harry, our teamster, saying that the weather has been nice ever since we left, and lots of game. He said that about a week before he wrote two of the farmers there went out and shot sixty geese in one afternoon. It was blowing hard and made the shooting good. The next day one of the party went on another field and killed fifty single-handed in two hours. Again two men on a barley field stubble in one afternoon killed sixty greenhead mallards. In fact we found the mallard shooting over decoys on the stubble to be about the nicest sport yet; great big greenheads and what a fine bag they made. Sharp-tailed grouse were also plentiful. A party of three would get from twenty-five to thirty-five in a day's shooting, which we considered excellent as we had no dogs with us. We found more snipe than usual. The writer bagged thirty-nine in one day's shooting, besides ducks and other game.

If I can find time to get at it, will write up the incidents of the trip, making another chapter for *Forest and Stream* relating the seventh pilgrimage of "The Saginaw Crowd."

WITH GOKEY, OF DAWSON
By Emerson Hough
1897

Editor's Note: The author of this article, Emerson Hough, was a prominent and well-known writer of Western novels. It is rather lengthy but I thought interesting and of historical importance. One of the principal subjects of the article was Joseph J. Gokey. The book on the Dawson Centennial 1880-1980 has an interesting article about Gokey written by a Dawson resident who knew him, John A. Gilk. George Bird Grinnell included portions of the <u>Forest and Stream</u> article in his book, "American Duck Shooting" (1901).

Last week I spoke of a little hunt which my friend, the Chief, from New York, and myself, intended taking out in North Dakota with State Game Warden Bowers and his friend, Deputy Warden Gokey, of Dawson. We took the hunt and had one of the pleasantest little experiences either of us has known for a long time. We left St. Paul on the evening of Monday, via Northern Pacific, and taking up Mr. Bowers at Fargo, N.D., where he lives, we spent the rest of the night on board the train conversing about all those things which come up to the minds of children out of school. It was daybreak when we reached Dawson, and soon thereafter we were introduced to one of the most celebrated and justly famous citizens of the great State of North Dakota, Gokey, of Dawson.

In appearance we found Gokey to be strictly weird, about medium height, but with long black hair hanging on his shoulders. His garb was of corduroy, his hat no derby, but the soft covering of the plains. His manner was that of the genuine West. In two minutes we were all acquainted, and in four we had our plans for the hunt completed.

Gokey, of Dawson, has done more to make his State famous than any politician within its borders. He is known all over his own State, and, moreover, in every other State of the Union. He has friends by the score among the best and wealthiest sportsmen of America. Not to know Gokey is to argue oneself unknown, and that is why the Chief and I went out to see him.

Gokey, of Dawson, was once upon a time a New Englander, and his parents wanted to make a business man out of him, but he was always sneaking off to go hunting, so they gave it up. Some score or more of years ago he resolved to come West, where he could breathe deeper and oftener and under less restraint. He reached Dakota in the buffalo days. He knew the antelope before they were gone. He will tell you that even to-day he believes that he can take you, inside of four days, to a place in the unknown Dakota lands, where you may see a buffalo, a real live wild buffalo. But he does not state for publication where this place may be found.

Gokey, Of Dawson.
Photo By Dr. P.H. Mason.

When Gokey located, years ago, in the little prairie town of Dawson, he faced the problem of making a living just as the rest of us have to face it under one condition or another. In the little towns of the West the channels of trade run in miniature, and perhaps a single one does not offer a living of itself. In the cities each man does one thing, or part of it, but on the prairies he is obliged to do many things.

Gokey, of Dawson, is above all things a hunter, yet not a market hunter, and not a butcher. He takes out parties into the best duck and goose country of Dakota. This season is short, of course, and for the rest of the year Gokey does many things. He is deputy game warden, and a rattling good one. He is justice of the peace, of course, for the most prominent citizen is always elected to be justice of the peace in a Western town. He says that not since the first year of his arrival in Dakota has he been without holding an office of some kind. Also, he is a harness maker, and a very good one. He repairs guns and all sorts of firearms. He loads shells, and sells supplies for guns. More than that, he is a professional photographer, and makes some very sweet pictures of Dakota babies. Not content with this, he is also a dentist. He pulls teeth after a painless method which he advertises. When the patient tells him that he has been hurt, Gokey, of Dawson, apologies and tells him that he forgot to rub on that painless stuff, and offers to put the tooth back and do it over again. I asked him where he was graduated as a dentist, and he said he just picked it up. Not yet done is the catalogue of Gokey, of Dawson. He is leader of the town band, and plays the clarinet with exactness and confidence. I have an obscure notion that his painless method of dentistry is in some way connected with the clarinet, though of this I am not sure. Gokey, of Dawson, is a musician, a scientist, a philosopher, a business man, a jurist, a corking fine duck shot, and the very best fellow in the world. No one ever saw him out of humor. Day or night, he is always with a laugh upon his lips. He will not wear rubber boots, but goes into the water, no matter what the weather, in old shoes and trousers direct. Yet he has never known to shiver; he never had rheumatism, and he is never sick. He can break a dog, handle a gun, or pole a boat with the best of them. I nearly forgot to add that he is the town barber, and he shaves and cuts hair as well as he shoots ducks. No man ever knew him who did not love and admire him. There is only one of him in the entire State of North

Dakota, and if you see him once you are bound to go back and see him again.

Picture to yourself Gokey, of Dawson, engaged at his work, or more properly speaking, at his works. I do not say that he can try a case at law and shave a man at one and the same time, but suppose this doubtful situation is not offered him. Suppose that he has merely to make a set of harness while he is trying a case, or to load some shells after he has given the band the regular lesson in Sousa's marches (which they really play). Suppose that he merely has to shave a man, after he has fixed up a broken gun, or something of that sort, and is then about to make a picture of a Norske infant. You approach Gokey so employed, and mention to him the possibility of a little hunt. Presto! You find the real business, the real preferences of the man. He continues the law case. He postpones the parents of the Norske infant. He lets the harness wait, and tarries not at all to evoke sweet notes upon the clarinet. In four minutes Gokey, of Dawson, has his two rough-looking but speedy horses hitched up to his light covered wagon. His dogs, rough-coated but old-headed, trail out behind. On a little two-wheeled cart of his own invention a duck boat travels on behind the light wagon. His useful gun, his well-worn coat and suit are in evidence. Gokey, of Dawson, is no longer jurist, barber, artist, merchant. He is in every shining, happy lineament Gokey the hunter, unapproachable in his chosen craft.

It is thus that I would lovingly picture him, nor can I suggest greater happiness for any person, whatsoever be his condition, than at some day thus to see Gokey, of Dawson, and to think that he is to be head of an expedition out over the big gray plains, where the air is sweet and keen, and where the blue sky has long, dark traceries drawn across it by the wavering flights of the fowl.

We had two days at Dawson, Warden Bowers, the Chief and myself, and though we had had no sleep the previous night on the train, but had visited and talked like schoolgirls till the gray of dawn, we lost no moment getting off for our hunt. On this first day Gokey determined to take us only about six or seven miles out of town, to the Dead Buffalo Lake, near the old Sibley battle ground. On the way out he and Warden Bowers told us all sorts of cock-and-bull stories about the numbers of ducks we should see (all local ducks, of course), and to this I listened politely, as one used to many such stories which had never found fulfillment. Here let me apologize. The stories in this case more than came true.

At the head of the Dead Buffalo Lake there is a narrow strip of water separating it from a smaller lake above, and between this little sheltered basin and the wide, deep water where the wild celery grows, there is a more or less constant flight of ducks. We put out our team and hastened quietly as we could down to this fly-way, seeking not to alarm the birds till we had taken our stand on the ridge between the lakes, where the rushes grow much higher than a man's head and run out almost entirely across the narrow channel. One of the dogs ran on ahead of us, and even before we could run over to the pass, there arose an enormous black cloud of ducks, which began to stream over the pass and to spread out over the big lake below.

Hot Times on the Pass.

Each of us had his pockets full of shells, and before we had deployed as skirmishers across the pass the pockets began to empty. The ducks came in a constant stream, without intermission for many minutes, nearly all of them low and almost in our faces, and with that velocity of flight seen nowhere except on a duck pass. The four of us with shouts and calls and eager vociferations of "Mark! Mark! Mark!" poured in such fire as we could. Mr. Bowers cut down his first two birds after his regular style, and Gokey, wading out into the middle of the channel, began to fold up birds with the smoothness of the old-time shot. I came near stopping my own gun to watch the sport of duck shooting on the pass, which I consider to be one of the most difficult and exciting forms of shooting. High up in the air the passing bird would suddenly close up, its head falling back, and come down like a stone with an excellent great splash. For the Chief, I can say he was diligent, and often I saw him cut down his duck, sometimes dropping it at his feet as he stood on the dry ground. Both the Chief and myself were raw at first on the pass, but after the flurry we got down to it and shot with our average of badness I suppose. All of us killed ducks, many ducks, so many and in such mingled fashion that for a time no one could tell whose duck it was that fell out of the flight under the pattering fusillade. The retrievers were busy wading and swimming, and we, too, at times paused to pick up a bird or so. In half an hour the flight slackened, and we stopped to take account. Many of our birds fell back of us in the water, and unless killed dead some such birds were as good as lost; for they would dive and disappear as soon as they got to the water. We could see that many of our ducks were canvasbacks and redheads. I shall make it short by saying that the first hurried flight did not last long, and that during the day, which came off very hot, the birds did not move much, Gokey very wisely declining to go out and stir them up, as he said that would drive them off their feeding beds and cause them to leave the lake. The evening was still, and the birds did not move as we had expected. Moreover, we were most of us tired and sleepy, and not disposed to kill everything in sight. After we had picked up our dead and found such of the cripples as we could, we had somewhere between thirty and forty ducks, I believe, nearly a dozen and a half of which were fine fat canvasbacks and redheads. This we voted plenty good enough for us.

Not so Gokey. Both he and Bowers declared we had seen no shooting at all. They held conference, and soon announced that on the following day we must be prepared for a long ride. We were to go to the famous Chase Pass, about twenty-four miles northeast of

Dawson, and to see what both these gentlemen declared to be the best flight of ducks in the whole country.

Dreams Realized.

Here again I am obliged to say that the representations held out did not begin to equal the reality. The Chief and myself have traveled a little in this big country of America, and have seen ducks all the way from British America to Mexico, yet never, even on the Gulf coast of Texas, did we ever see so many ducks, such comfortable, obliging ducks, and ducks so accessible and incessant. It was a wonderful sight of wildfowl, one of those sights which make the unthinking say that there are "just as many ducks now as there ever were." Gokey said this was always a great place for ducks, but that this year the birds were more numerous than for many years previous, thanks to high water and to the license law, which cut off the non-resident market shooting and reduced that of game hogs who knew no moderation. Gokey said that up to the past two years it was a daily sight at Dawson station to see the entire platform lined with ducks waiting for the train to bear them out of the State. He said that in warm weather it was no unusual thing to see two or three wagon loads of spoiled ducks hauled out into the country and dumped into a coulee. He seemed to take comfort in the hope of better things. Both he and Warden Bowers are assured of the wisdom of the non-resident act, whatever the non-resident himself may think about it. I think both the Chief and myself would be disposed now to say that if a shooter can in anyway afford it, it would pay him better to pay his $25 in North Dakota, where he can get some shooting and where the birds are not being destroyed in such quantities for the markets than to go to some more liberal but more illy-stocked State for a sporting trip. I know this license law has stopped much shooting and cut off much non-resident travel to North Dakota, for the gun stores of St. Paul and Minneapolis complain that it has hurt their trade with sportsmen who outfit for shooting trips to the Northwest. Even the railroads don't like the law, for it lessens their traffic. The ducks, however, are to be congratulated upon it, and so are those whose fate enables them to get a look in at one of the greatest remaining sporting grounds of America.

Home of the Wildfowl.

It was 11:45 in the morning when our long ride over the easy prairies came to a pause at the famous Chase Pass. From the high ridge which rims in this valley we looked down and saw two great lakes, each reaching away four or five miles from the point of view, each perhaps half a mile or more across. Between these two bodies of clear water there stretched a high ridge of hard, dry ground, apparently a quarter of a mile across from water to water, and about 40 ft. above the surface of the water at the summit of the ridge. There was a light wind moving, and the water was rippled and moving, so that we could see no ducks at first. As we drove down nearer to the bank we caught sight of thousands of black, bobbing figures, all over the whole face of the waters. In shore, and now not over a few hundreds of yards from us, there rested upon the bars literally a black mass of ducks, thousands upon thousands. This is not the enthusiasm of a man who has never seen many birds before, but is the literal and calm truth. I never in my life have seen so great a body of wildfowl at one time. Soon the birds began to soar up and circle blackly about, and in time the air was dark with a countless multitude of circling, twisting and turning fowl, each bunch with a different direction from the others. It was enough to drive one crazy.

Neither Bowers nor Gokey showed any signs of losing his mind, though I feared for the Chief. For my own part, I have a vague recollection that I stood upon one foot while the team was being turned out and the deliberate preparations made for the hunt.

"Take plenty of shells." was about all the advice Warden Bowers had to offer. "You'll need them all, for you won't kill every shot."

So we took each a back load and hurried off to the pass over which the birds were streaming. We had been told that on this pass, no matter what the weather, the ducks fly all day long. This we did not believe, but set down as "agi'n natur'." Yet we found it true this day at least, though the morning started in very fair and warm.

We found that a series of pits had been dug along the ridge, a few feet below the summit, deep enough so that the shooter would be concealed when he crouched down. In these pits we saw many old shells, but these were weather-beaten, and showed to be those of last year. We were the first to shoot on this wonderful pass in the wonderful duck year of 1897.

The Battle.

Gokey took the furthest pit, Bowers next to him, then myself, then the Chief, who thus was furthest to the left as he faced to the west, from which direction the first flight came. We hurried under many passing flocks as we trotted into the firing line, and as soon as we got located each began to shoot. The ducks were most accommodating, and came to us at first in a vast mass, out of which it was next to impossible to pick out any individual birds. The speed of the flight was terrific, and the hiss of the wings cutting low and close or whispering high overhead was never absent from the ear. Nor was there absent the steady cracking of the guns. Gokey's regular double report, mingled with the cornsheller activity of Bowers's repeating Winchester smote my ear on the right, while nearby on the left the sharp crack of the Chief's little 12-gauge sounded incessantly. Not one shot out of four landed its game, but, none the less, there was a series of heavy thumps all about us, more especially to the right of the firing line, where the two Dakota men were in action.

After a while we had a little let up and I looked over to see how the Chief was getting along. I then had about a dozen ducks piled up in my pit, most of them belonging to Bowers, I presume, but when I approached the Chief he was sitting with his head in his hand, gloomily looking down at a hen spoonbill which he had chased into the grass and killed with a stick.

Couldn't Land.

"What's the matter, Chief?" I asked him, kindly and like a perfect gentleman.

"The truth is," said he, sadly, as he looked up from the hen spoonbill, "I can't land on 'em. Now, I've been holding for the solar plexus of about 4,000 individual ducks that have sashayed across here, but I can't seem to land on 'em. When I lead they—don't misunderstand me—they duck, as it were. They ain't there. How about that? Are these things too good for everybody? How did you fellows happen to get any? Did you shoot into the flock, and hit another flock?"

Duck Delirium.

I explained to the Chief that I got ducks by watching closely where Mr. Bowers was shooting, and then shooting into the same flock with him. He regretted that he was so far out of the way of this sort of assistance that he could not avail himself of anybody's skill but his own, and he hadn't any. (The Chief is good over decoys, but this was his first day on a redhot fast pass, and he met the customarily difficulty in shooting before the birds were over on the next lake.)

The Chief and I then concluded to visit a while, and we shot together out of his pit for a few rounds. By this time the birds had begun to come back from the east, and now the fun grew yet more fast and furious. The flocks would start from the eastern lake high up in the air. "Mark east!" would come the warning down the line, and each man would get below the level of the ridge. As the birds approached the high ground they would drop rapidly, and come over the pass parallel with the ground and very low. They would roll over the top of the little ridge beyond us, dip down into the coulee across our front, disappear for a moment, and then come surging and boiling and whistling up in a long, swift, feathery wave over the crest of our breastworks hissing almost into our faces as they swept on out toward the water. Never was such an exciting situation in the world!

Never in all my life did I see such shooting. It was a glimpse, a glance, and then a swift wheel to get a fair shot at a disappearing bunch almost over the edge of the reeds which lined the water's edge behind us. Sometimes the ducks flew almost into our faces. Often we dodged down to escape what seemed an imminent danger of losing a hat or a head. Twice I shot ducks ahead of me which fell 30 ft. Behind me. Once I had a fat duck come crushing into the pit beside me, and once I dropped a teal against the bank of my pit. A more perfect embodiment of a hot corner on ducks never existed. It was almost bewildering in its tension. It was a delirium of ducks.

The Chief and I shot from his pit together, and after a time we both began to improve, coaching each other on the lead as the different flocks came by. I could see that he was stopping his gun when he fired and holding about six feet ahead on birds where he should have led twenty. I could see the line of his smoke cut in apparently a dozen feet behind the bird which he thought he was leading almost too much. He did an equal service by me, and soon we began to acquire the lead, a distance which seemed utterly absurd at first. The pile of birds at our pit began to grow. At lunch time the Chief had become a finished performer on the pass. A very nice looking farmer lady came out with a very nice looking lunch, and as she drove up, the Chief and I rose and cut out four ducks from a passing flock, just to show the lady how it was done. Alas for me! I fell down on my next chance, but the Chief killed a pair out the next flight over. Then, as we gathered at the reed bed for luncheon, he cut down a high single, and a moment later yet another. I saw a glance of triumph come into his eye. He had caught the knack of it.

At lunch we paused now and then to kill or try to kill the ducks which continued to pour over. Mr. Bowers told me that he and some friends once killed fourteen ducks at that same spot, while they were eating lunch one day. I think we dropped half a dozen or so before we had cleaned up the lunch. A bountiful and well-cooked one it was, and to have it thus brought down warm from the farmhouse was the last touch of comfort on this dry, comfortable, and absolutely ideal fly-way. A good part of our lunch was made up of four grouse, which we had picked up along the road; almost the only grouse we saw in this part of the country, where they are very scarce this year.

Amenities on the Duck Pass.

After our lunch we resumed position in the skirmish line, minus Gokey, who had a headache and did not shoot for a while. It was an old story with Gokey, and it did not take him long to kill the twenty-five birds which make the limit *per diem* for a shooter in the State of North Dakota. With the Chief and myself it was different. We got a good deal bigger run for our money than anybody else, because we shot worse. It now began to be a struggle of courtesy between us all. "I never touched that bird; it's yours, my friend," I would say to the Chief. "Your bird, sir," he would reply, with equal courtesy; and so we would argue over it. Bowers and I nearly scared the Chief to death by covertly piling up a lot of our birds in front of his pit, and then proceeding to count them before him. We made it out to be twenty-nine birds, and the warden told him it would cost him $400!

It would seem that one should soon kill his limit on a flight like this, and so he can, even though he be new at the sport of pass shooting—the hardest shooting in the world, and not to be compared with the easy work of shooting over decoys. Yet I have noticed that even the best shots will spoil 100 shells to pick up twenty-five ducks on a pass like this, and it takes a little while to shoot 100 shells, especially after the first flurry is over and one steadies down and behaves like a shooter, picking his shots and taking care. We had shot a little over a couple of hours before we thought it best to rectify our rough counts of individual bags and to go after the birds which had fallen dead back of us in the reeds. Bowers and I went over the crest of the ridge to look for some birds we had killed on the hard ground, and while we were there we saw the prettiest bit of shooting done on the trip.

The Chief was then alone in the pit over which the main flight was passing, and he had his eye on the birds. He took toll out of everything that crossed. Five times we saw him rise and fire at flocks and small bodies of birds, and each time he got meat. Once he killed all three of three ducks that went over down wind, high and fast—a handsome bit of work. Twice he dropped his double out, and out of five accepted chances he did not miss a shot. It was good enough fun to sit and watch this, and Bowers and I both concluded we had no more advice to offer him. When we got to his pit we found him radiant and hugging to his bosom the light 12-gauge with which he was now thoroughly infatuated. He expressed himself as for once absolutely satisfied with the world. "Did you see me deflate that last un?" he asked, cheerfully.

When we picked up our birds we found that, counting a half-dozen birds we had given the farmer's wife, we had our limit, or so near it that we did not care to go closer—ninety-eight birds in all.

Thereupon came up human nature, as the Chief and I both realized. It was the first day we had had outdoors with a gun for a long time, and the best chance to kill a lot of ducks either of us had ever had in all his life. I confess that my personal wish was to kill some more. I wanted to try just one or two shots more. I wanted to see if I could kill a double out of the flock just heading for us. I wanted—well, I admit I wanted to go ahead and shoot a lot. But this we did not do, and after we saw the awful pile of game we had when we got it together, every one of us was mighty glad we had killed no more, even the question of the law aside. All of these birds, except those eaten by ourselves, were taken to Fargo and there disposed of, Mr. Bowers and myself laboring faithfully till we had them all given away. It is sure we killed enough. How many we could have killed had we all shot all day long as steadily as possible, I should not like to say. I believe we could easily have fired from 500 to 600 shells apiece, and have killed perhaps one-fourth or more of that number of birds apiece. But what a butchery that would have been, for even our one party. What a butchery it would be for many parties, taken for not one day, but for many days. I never had the lesson of moderation more forcibly impressed upon me. It was not at first pleasant, I admit, and I vaguely found the customary excuses for doing what I wanted to do, just as human nature always finds such excuses; but once the temptation was overcome we each of us felt happy. We are each ready to say that the killing of twenty-five ducks on a red-hot pass is fun enough for one day for any man, and that the law is a good one and should stand and be respected. This limit is one which should be set in every gentlemen's shooting club all over the land. It is enough. It is at the moment hard to realize it, but it is enough. Stop at twenty-five, and you feel bad at the time, but good after a while.

So we went away long before evening, while a cold storm was blowing up, and while over the greatest duck pass of the Northwest the long black streamers of the flight were growing thick and thicker. Into the night, over roads made softer by a drizzling rain, we drove, reaching town late, but very well contented. And so ended our day with Gokey, of Dawson, whom we voted a man in whom alike truth and skill abode. We left him with genuine regret, for we had sat at his board and eaten there of duck cooked as one finds it not from Dan to Beersheba, for Mrs. Gokey can cook as well as her versatile husband can shoot. When the Chief and I go out after our winter's meat next year, it is more than likely that we shall endeavor to have that occur in the company of Gokey, of Dawson. And betimes a load is shifted from my mind. Many men in the course of a year write and ask me where they can find shooting. In human nature, this means not a little shooting but a lot of shooting. I can answer truthfully: go to Gokey, of Dawson. There are no chickens there this year, and there may be very few next year, as indeed there may not then be so many ducks; but if the duck shooting then is one-half what we know it was this fall, it is absolutely certain that the visiting shooter will be more than satisfied.

It Protects.

The main body of non-resident shooters will not be at Dawson until about Oct. 1, when the goose season begins. Then the special cars and the special parties will begin to flock in, and Gokey will be busy all the time, as well as all the other guides. If you go hither, Gokey will take you out shooting. He will shave you, play to you or take your picture. He will try you if you break the law. He will put one-third of your $25 in his pocket, and don't you forget it; and if you kick will arrest you and try you before himself, and levy on your stuff if you don't pay.

Protection is beginning to protect out in the far Northwest, but it does not by any means follow that the end of the world has come, or that all the fun and all the shooting must come to an end. If you think that, look at the Dawson *Registrar* a week from now, or ask the opinion of Gokey first citizen of North Dakota.

I call Gokey thus deliberately. Warden Bowers is an old friend of mine, and a square man. He can throw Gokey in a fair wrestling match, as he proved many times on this trip. But can he shave Gokey, play to him, picture him or try him, all at once? I know not. There is but one Gokey, and he lives at Dawson.

E. Hough. 1206 Boyce Building, Chicago.

THE SAGINAW CROWD
By William B. Mershon
1902

Editor's Note: With this article William B. Mershon summarized the twentieth annual hunting trip to the Dawson area. More details of his experiences are found at other places in this book.

The twentieth annual hunting trip of the Saginaw Crowd was described by Mr. W. B. Mershon in the Saginaw Courier-Herald, from which we copy as below, for the Saginaw chronicles belong in *Forest and Stream:*

You have asked me to tell the readers of The Courier-Herald something about Dakota shooting, and the recent trip of the Saginaw party. I have not time to comply with your request fittingly, but briefly would state that this year was the twentieth annual trip of the Saginaw Crowd to North Dakota. The first trip was made in our old hunting car, "City of Saginaw," in 1883, which was the year the Northern Pacific was completed, and we followed the excursion party that went to drive the golden spike binding the East to the West. At that time our old car, which had not nearly as large accommodations as our present one, contained twenty-two passengers. We slept double, even in the upper berths, and to-day I wonder how it was done.

In those days the game was far more plentiful than now. We stopped at New Buffalo and had duck shooting that was grand, but the next year, when we stopped at New Buffalo, the water had dried up a good deal and the shooting was far poorer, so we moved on to Dawson, Kidder County, which has been, with one or two exceptions, our annual place of rendezvous.

Fifteen or twenty years ago, around Dawson, was one immense

wheat field. It was a boom town and locality, but as the settlers found that it was only about one year in seven they could raise a crop of grain, they have gradually petered out, until today there are very few grain fields in that vicinity, and the few people there are subsisting by raising cattle and sheep.

On account of the abundance of grain, the geese on their southern flight congregated there in vast numbers. Kidder County is filled with lakes and sloughs, as the prairie marshes are called. We used to pay more attention to goose hunting than anything else. The prairie chicken was unknown in that country then, but there were quite a good many sharp-tailed grouse. Of late the prairie chickens have increased, and the sharp-tailed grouse have decreased, so on our recent tip, out of ninety birds killed, probably three-fourths of them were prairie chicken, or more properly speaking, pinnated grouse. But as I said before, our main joy was in goose shooting.

The modus operandi was to drive out during the forenoon early, and find some big grain stubble on which the geese were feeding, for until disturbed or the feed has been used up, they will continue to come to the same locality. They like the barley stubbles best, but failing in them, they go to the wheat stubbles, where the left-over and lost grain is most plentiful. Finding one of these feeding grounds, we would remain in the locality until the birds had eaten their fill and left for the lakes or watering places, which is usually about 10:30 or 11 o'clock in the morning. We would then go into the stubble and begin digging pits, one for each shooter. If there were four in the party, we would make four pits 10 or 12 feet apart, and about 40 inches deep and 30 inches in diameter, just large enough to sit in comfortably and have your eyes on a level with the ground. The earth was not piled up around the excavation, but scattered, and when the pit was finished, the stubble was pulled, going a distance from the pit for this purpose, and then this pulled stubble was transplanted, all around the freshly dug pits so as to make it appear like an undisturbed stubble field. The hunter in a grass-colored suit, sitting well down in his pit, was almost completely hidden.

Now came the placing of the decoys. These were 30 or 40 in number, and were always placed to the leeward of the pits, and 20 to 40 yards distant, for the geese coming in with the wind would always turn and swing to the decoys, to alight against the wind. Thus, with their eyes fixed on the decoys, the geese coming into them, would necessarily have to pass over the pits in which the hunters were hidden, to alight among their sheet-iron counterfeits, for the decoys were made of sheet iron, heavy enough so they will not wobble in the wind, painted to resemble geese and stuck in the ground. They are merely profile, but by putting them at various angles, generally headed toward the wind, the incoming birds could see them until they really got over them. It was laughable at times to see geese coming up sidewise to these decoys, suddenly loose sight of them altogether, and you could see them crane their necks around in every direction to see what had become of their supposed brethren.

Now, after preparing the pits and setting out the decoys, and getting our shell boxes, which generally contained a good stiff charge of smokeless powder, and about one ounce of No. 2 chilled shot, we would adjourn to some sunny hillside for our luncheon and smoke, but if it was cloudy and windy, we would have the right to expect the early return of the birds from the lakes to the feeding grounds. On pleasant days, from 4:30 to 5 o'clock, was about the time to look for the birds, but on cloudy days or windy days they would come an hour or two earlier.

A novice would always misjudge the distance and shoot before the bird would be within gunshot. I have known some of my Saginaw friends to stand up and deliberately blaze away at an incoming bird, coming directly toward him, when I am certain it had not approached nearer than 200 yards. But remember it is a prairie country without a single bush to gauge distance by and absolutely clear sky and a bird weighing from twelve to fifteen pounds, and so it is not to be wondered at that they look big and right on to you, when they really were a rifle shot away.

The captain of the party is generally put in the center pit and is supposed to give the word of command when to fire, so that each man can get in his right and left if possible. It is generally arranged so that the center man takes the center of the flock, the man on the right the birds on his side and the one on the left the same. Big birds as they are, and apparently slow flying, it is extremely difficult for a novice to keep cool and shoot right. Many a good man at the trap has learned to his confusion that he could break a clay pigeon easier than he could kill a goose at first. After a while, they catch on.

Wing-broken birds should be gathered immediately, otherwise they will slink away and run off into the stubble, and in an incredibly short time they get beyond finding distance.

In the old days, these goose shoots netted good sport and good bags. It was not unusual for three or four of us shooting together to get 25 or 30 birds in an afternoon or morning flight, and I have known instances where four of us shooting together have gotten as high as 65 birds in one shoot. They are fine eating, fat as they are on the wheat, and being generally young birds and not having toughened themselves by long flights to the south. With the Saginaw party, no game ever was wasted, for what we did not use or give away out there, we brought home for division among our friends.

With the disappearance of grain fields around Dawson and the widening out of grain culture in North Dakota, the flight has changed, or in other words, spread out, so it is not so concentrated.

I am speaking of black geese, of which there are three or four kinds; the geese that are most prized and the ones that decoy. The white, or Arctic goose, will not decoy and does not have specific places for feeding, for whatever field the first flock drops down upon, the others will follow, too, and some whim will strike them in the midst of their feeding, and they will all move off to another field, a mile or two distant. The white geese are far thicker than they used to be, and there are dozens of places in North Dakota, where you can go late in the fall and find these birds in thousands and tens of thousands. This year at Dawson we did not get a single goose; first, for the reasons given above, and next, because the weather was like mid-summer, and the northern birds had not come down. At Devil's Lake, the greatest of the northern feeding and resting places for waterfowl, where geese are usually in thousands, it was said at the time we were in North Dakota that no birds had reached there from the north yet. But we did have nice shooting upon sharp-tailed grouse and prairie chicken, though the law ran out on the 15th, and we were not equipped with dogs; but at this time of the year prairie chicken do not lie well to dogs and are in bunches or 'packed' for the winter. They are generally found in the wheat stubbles or along the weed patches adjoining them.

The northern ducks had not come down to any extent and were mostly local birds that were on the lakes and sloughs; they were there in large quantities, but had been shot at so much they did not fly during the day; and while sometimes an evening flight would be good for a few minutes, generally they availed themselves of the bright moonlight nights for their flying from one place to another. Some of the lakes were well filled with canvasbacks, and out of 254 ducks that our party of eight got in the two weeks we were there, 37 of them were canvasbacks.

But the Saginaw Crowd does not go so much for shooting birds and the game that they can get as for the rest and recreation, getting away from business, politics, coal strikes and everything else of that kind, that one has to contend with eleven months of the year, and is in great luck if he can skip the twelfth month; filling one's lungs with that grand, pure air of the treeless plain, outdoor exercise and freedom from all care, pay far better than a wagon boxful of ducks and geese. We had birds enough to eat, birds enough to give to our railroad friends passing through Dawson, and that was enough, and I hope that the Saginaw Crowd can take these annual trips for twenty years to come. Three members of our party have joined the silent majority, and will go with us no more, and those that are left notice that they cannot stand so much tramping nor so much fatigue as in days of yore.

The enthusiasm of youth is lessened but we hope that the last spark of it will not vanish for many years to come.

PART 3

Editor's Note: This article contains an account of duck and goose shooting in Kidder County, North Dakota by two men from Chicago, William A. Bond and Albert R. Barnes from 1889 to 1902. It is noteworthy because it contains the only record that I know of for the kinds and numbers of birds shot for a lengthy period of time. Not only were the two men excellent wildfowlers but they left notes about the water conditions that existed in several well-known lakes and marshes in the Lake Williams area.

DUCK AND GOOSE HUNTING IN KIDDER COUNTY 1889 - 1902

(Based on Robert C. McClanahan's 1939 unpublished memorandum)

By Harold F. Duebbert
2001

This article is based on an unpublished report concerning long ago duck and goose shooting in Kidder County, North Dakota. It contained the records of waterfowl and other game shot by two men, William A. Bond and Albert R. Barnes, of Chicago, Illinois between 1889 and 1902. The records were summarized in a report by Robert C. McClanahan who was a biologist with the Bureau of Biological Survey, U. S. Department of Agriculture. McClanahan interviewed Mr. Bond during December 15-19, 1939 and recorded portions of his hunting records.

At that time, Mr. Bond was 90 years old and had begun to hunt when he was 14. In 1887, he began keeping a journal, which he called a score book, and continued to do so until 1932 when he quit hunting at the age of 82. The hunting records were in four large volumes totaling more than 1500 pages written in longhand for a 43-year record. Mr. McClanahan recognized the impracticality of copying the entire journals. Therefore, he took from the original records the number and kinds of birds shot each day, a weekly summary, and a yearly summary of the same information. The location or existence of the original journals is unknown at this time. Thus, the report compiled by Mr. McClanahan represents a valuable contribution to knowledge about long ago duck and goose hunting in North Dakota.

I have had a lifelong interest in reading accounts of duck and goose shooting in the olden days. Many hunters have a similar interest and in recent years several books have been published with copies of long ago duck and goose hunting. For these reasons, I thought it advisable to place the information from this unpublished report in a more permanent form. Reading the Bond-Barnes hunting records was very exciting to me. For over 30 years I have hunted in the same area, and indeed in some of the same lakes and marshes written about by Mr. Bond over 100 years ago.

In Table 1 the records of ducks, geese, and other birds shot during the 14 years 1889 to 1902 are presented. Of the total of 11,624 birds shot were 9,878 ducks, 972 geese, 16 swans, 170 sandhill cranes, 11 whooping cranes, and 577 snipe. Other game shot included grouse, deer, jackrabbits, badger, and avocet. In 1891, 59 grouse were shot and 57 in 1892. Without access to the original records it is unknown how the large numbers of birds were utilized. Proximity to the Northern Pacific Railroad would have made it relatively easy to ship birds to eastern markets or friends back home. Canvasback duck was rated as epicurean fare in the finest eastern restaurants including Chicago where the hunters lived. Local farmers and ranchers would have appreciated getting some of the ducks, geese, and cranes to provide food for the table. When interpreting the numbers of birds shot it is important to realize that from one to six other hunters were sometimes added to the Bond-Barnes party. And the hunt covered five or six weeks in most years.

The records also contain interesting notes about water conditions in the various lakes and marshes in the Lake Williams area. It is noteworthy that nearly all of the main lakes and marshes (sloughs) were named before 1900. Those mentioned in the Bond-Barnes report include South Lake, Bond Lake, Deer Lake, Iowa Lake, Des Moines Lake, Round Lake, Lake Louise, Ranch Lake, and Chase Lake. Reference to Bond Lake was interesting to me. I have often wondered how it got its name. I have made inquiry of Mr. Galen Bowerman, a life-long resident near Bond Lake, whether a family named Bond ever lived near the lake. He answered "no" and that the lake had been named Bond ever since he could remember. So, I propose that the lake was named by or for Albert A. Bond who is the subject of this article. Some distance away, north of Woodworth, is a lake named Barnes. It could possibly have been named for Albert R. Barnes who was Bond's hunting partner.

As an ecologist and career waterfowl biologist (retired), I was interested in the notes on water conditions in the Lake Williams area between 1889 and 1902. The records from the Bond-Barnes journals provide some of the best information I know of for that period. There was no mention of water conditions between 1889 to 1893. Large numbers of ducks and geese were taken in those years so water conditions must have been suitable for good hunting. For 1894, it was mentioned that water levels were low in several sloughs with names that are unknown to me. In 1895 Bond and Barnes arrived on the Northern Pacific at Crystal Springs on September 27. They stopped at Fischer's Ranch on the way north and arrived at Marston Moor in the afternoon. The next day they travelled to the Williams Ranch and found the prairie all burned over. Many of the large lakes were dry. Water in South Lake had receded 250 yards from shore. During October they found very few ducks in the area and those mostly marsh ducks. Not many cans or redheads. As shown in Table 1, 280 ducks were shot in 1895 (poor water) compared to 1180 in 1892 (good water).

In 1896 it was reported that hard rains had fallen in the Dawson area. But the small sloughs had no water, which was attributed to the very dry conditions the year before. South Lake had about eight inches of water and many ducks but no cans or redheads. More cranes were reported than for many years. Bond Lake was mentioned for the first time and it had considerable water. It was noted that each member of the party had to buy a $25.00 license. This must have been the first year that non-residents were required to do so.

South Lake had plenty of water in 1897. Deer Lake had plenty of water and a great many ducks. It is noteworthy that 1400 ducks were shot in 1897 by three hunters and that was the largest total for the 14 year record. I suggest that the lakes and marshes in the area were in a highly productive biological condition after being dry or in drawdown for the previous two or three years. The only record for 1898 was that Bond Lake had low water. In 1899 Chase Lake was very low with few ducks. The channel of Lake Louise was dry. Bond Lake was dry. South Lake was nearly dry. Deer Lake was dry. Ranch Lake was very low. All water areas around Lake Williams were dry except Iowa Lake and Des Moines Lake. The poor water conditions were reflected in the record showing only 152 ducks shot that year. No water records for 1900 but only 242 ducks were shot that year. In 1901 Deer Lake had low water and was overgrown with grass but had large numbers of ducks. South Lake had plenty of water. Some other sloughs had good water levels but the names are unknown to me. No water records were given for 1902 which was the last year that Bond and Barnes hunted in Kidder County. They then began hunting in the Bear River Marshes, Utah and continued to do so until 1932.

Following completion of the Northern Pacific Railroad across

Kidder County in 1872, many hunters from the eastern United States used that form of transportation to come to hunt. Letters and publications in popular magazines such as *Forest and Stream* and *The American Field* wrote glowingly about the abundance of game to be found in the newly settled state. Perhaps Bond and Barnes learned about it that way or may have had acquaintances in North Dakota. Hunters including Barnes and Bond often had as their destination Crystal Springs, Tappen, or Dawson. From there on travel had to be by horse and buggy and often lodging was arranged with local farmers or ranchers. Knowledge about how Bond and Barnes lived while hunting in Kidder County can be obtained from the following account. In *Forest and Stream* for December 3, 1891 I found a short article by William B. Mershon. Mershon was a well-known hunter from Saginaw, Michigan who hunted in the Dawson area from 1883 to 1903. It is very likely that Mershon, Bond, and Barnes were acquainted as they hunted in some of the same areas and the years overlapped.

A pertinent reference from the article mentioned above is quoted here in its entirety: "The hunting party of which Messrs. Bond, Barnes, and Paddock were members returned to their homes in Chicago on Sunday evening, after a stay of nearly four weeks at the pleasant home of Mr. and Mrs. J. D. Williams, in New Yorktown. These gentlemen have been in the habit of making this place their headquarters for several years for a season of waterfowl shooting, and have almost come to be considered as members of Mr. Williams' family. They are thorough gentlemen—of great prowess and superior marksmanship, as is evidenced by their score this season, showing a mortality of 3,600 birds, 3 deer, and one antelope." According to the 1960 History of Pettibone the J. D. Williams ranch was two and one-half miles west of Pettibone. It would have been well located as a base for Bond-Barnes as most of their hunting places were within a few miles of it.

It would indeed be interesting to know something of their

hunting methods and day-to-day experiences. In some places reference is made to using a boat so perhaps decoys were used. Pass shooting was common in the early days. Geese and cranes were probably hunted in harvested grain fields and decoys could have been used there also. No mention was made of the kinds of guns used. It is likely that the original journals contained a wealth of information that would be interesting if they could somehow be located. A friend and I are investigating some possibilities of where they might be. If any readers know anything about the Bond or Barnes families I would appreciate hearing from you. Possibly descendants of Mr. J. D. Williams might have recollections or family diaries with references to Bond and Barnes the hunters.

Records from the McClanahan report provide some suggestions that variations in water conditions, waterfowl abundance, and shooting success are similar to those in modern times. As shown above most of the lakes in the Lake Williams area were dry or nearly so in 1899. One hundred years later, in 1999, those same lakes were at record high levels and held 15-20 feet of water. This serves as a graphic example of the wide range of variability that may be expected in wetland basins within the glaciated prairie pothole region. In the 35 years that I have hunted in the same area as Bond and Barnes I have maintained a diary of each hunt. Also, I have noted and recorded variations in water levels and general habitat conditions. I have seen some lakes and marshes vary from being bone dry, often for several years, to holding 15-20 feet of water as in 2000. One of the most remarkable examples is Horsehead Lake near Robinson. For most of the 1970s and 1980s it was a barren alkali flat or held less than three feet of water. Beginning in 1993 water levels began to rise as a result of much above average rainfall and snow for several years. By 1999, the lake held around 20 feet of water and a population of northern pike. The pike and probably other fish species moved into Horsehead Lake from nearby Cherry Lake through a small stream and other sources.

In the future when I am hunting in areas hunted by Mr. Bond and Mr. Barnes I will sense a kind of spiritual connection with them. It is apparent that both men were wildfowlers in the deepest sense of the word and enjoyed hunting together.

Evidently they had jobs or a life situation that permitted them to be in North Dakota to hunt for four or five weeks each fall. One can imagine the thrill they felt to be in a newly settled land with an abundance of waterfowl and cranes to mark their gunner's eye. Through the original journals of Mr. Bond and the summary of them by Mr. McClanahan we are able to have a glimpse of hunting in Kidder county as it was 100 years ago.

Special Acknowledgement

I wish to thank Arthur W. Hawkins and Henry M. Reeves for providing a copy of the McClanahan report to me. Reeves also helped in preparation of this article.

Table 1. Waterfowl and other birds shot by William A. Bond, Albert R. Barnes, and others 1889-1902.

Year	Ducks	Geese	Swans	Sandhill Crane	Whooping Crane	Snipe
1889	277	187	0	38	0	0
1890	735	275	2	57	0	43
1891	1340	265	2	28	4	136
1892	1180	38	0	2	0	6
1893	584	11	4	0	0	3
1894	758	28	3	8	4	30
1895	280	104	5	9	0	20
1896	677	5	0	0	1	28
1897	1400	35	0	1	0	120
1898	682	14	0	13	2	68
1899	152	0	0	0	0	0
1900	242	0	0	0	0	19
1901	769	3	0	2	0	57
1902	802	7	0	12	0	47
Total	9878	972	16	170	11	577

TOTAL OF ALL BIRDS: 11,624

AMONG THE GEESE AND
SAND HILL CRANES IN NORTH DAKOTA

By Fred Kimble, In: Supreme Duck Shooting Stories, by William Hazelton (1930), reprinted by *The Gunnerman Press* (1989).

Editor's Note: The fact that Fred Kimble was an expert and well-known trap shooter of his time and records of hunting in the early days makes this an outstanding article. The Stinchcomb mentioned was Elmer E. Stinchcomb whose life was detailed in the History of Pettibone 1920-1960. In it is stated: "Elmer E. Stinchcomb was born in Sandusky, Ohio in 1861. He came to North Dakota Territory as a young man and homesteaded about 12 miles north of Dawson in Kidder County." This was near the present Schumacher Lake and Horsehead Lake and one can imagine what great shooting was possible during the time that Kimble hunted there. Once again history comes alive for me as I have killed many ducks, geese, and sandhill cranes in that same area.

My Parker No. 10 double gun handled large shot well, putting its charge of No. 1 or No. 2 shot into a 30-inch circle at 40 yards.

I had heard much about the goose shooting in North Dakota, so I took a trip up there [*Editor's Note: Probably in 1890s*]. I stopped with a farmer 12 miles north of Dawson, North Dakota. A colony of New York farmers had taken up a tract of land just south of the Manitoba [rail] line, and planted it all in wheat. It was called the New York settlement and my stopping place was the nearest house to the railroad. All the other farmers had to pass the house in going to or from town.

This large tract of wheat was the first in the line of flight of the geese and cranes on their way south and it was a great feeding ground. I stopped with a farmer named Stinchcomb and W. B. Mershon knew him.

Here was a good opportunity to try out my Parker on long-range shooting and I took advantage of it. I used No. 1 shot. One afternoon, shooting from a pit in a stubble field, between 3 o'clock and sundown, I killed 46 Canada geese and 37 sandhill cranes. Five of the largest geese weighed 16½ pounds each, while the lot would average around 11 pounds. The total weight of the game shot inside of three hours was over 700 pounds. It filled our wagon box.

I could kill both geese and cranes up to 65 yards and had no trouble in killing pairs up to 60 yards when straight overhead.

Both the old Parker gun and myself decided it was time to go home after putting in a solid month with the geese and cranes. When we arrived at Dawson on the railroad I found that reports had been brought in from day to day by the farmers and to hear them tell it, a goose couldn't fly high enough to get out of the reach of that old gun. What it had done to the geese and cranes was the talk of the town. The farmers were supplied first and the game not used by them was shipped to Minneapolis and Chicago. The trip had been successful in every way. In fact, as fine a trip as I ever had in all my career and one never to be forgotten.

HUNTING RECORDS OF WILLIAM B. MERSHON IN DAWSON AREA

Editor's Note: William B. Mershon of Saginaw, Michigan figured prominently in the history of wildfowling in the Dawson, North Dakota area. Many of his experiences are immortalized in his 1923 book "Recollections of My Fifty Years Hunting and Fishing." One chapter, "Hunting at Dawson, N.D.," is presented herein in its entirety and other references are excerpted to save space.

HUNTING AT DAWSON, N.D.

The following, entitled "A Ten Days Trip to Dakota," was written by me at the time; at any rate, I have found it among my old hunting records. It ended abruptly, as you will see, and it was not completed until 1907. I am not reproducing it because of literary merit by any means, but it teems with the enthusiasm of youth. Later on when we were going to Dakota regularly we became familiar with many of the things that were so delightful because of their being new and the first time.

We used to get tremendous bags of geese. The plan was to drive through the stubble fields early in the morning and find where the geese were feeding, make an examination of the ground after the geese had left and see if there was much food left, or if they had been feeding there long, which could be told by the droppings or feathers, and if we had good reason to believe it was a regular feeding, we put in pits. These were holes in the ground between four and five feet in depth and about thirty inches in diameter. The earth was spread out so as to not make much of a mound around the pit and then we plucked or pulled stubble in bunches that we replanted in rows so that the ground would look to have been undisturbed and the stubble would look as if it had originally grown there. If there were two or more of us shooting, we arranged our pits in a row six or eight feet apart. The man in the center acted as Captain and gave the word; the rest were supposed to keep down and not move. The geese fed twice a day. They came into the stubble at daylight and fed until ten or eleven o'clock and then returned to the lake. They came in again between three and four o'clock and fed until dark. On bright still days they flew high and came in later in the afternoon; on stormy days they came in low and began flying earlier, in fact, I have known them to fly all day. Metal profile decoys were used, and it was no uncommon thing for us to kill fifty or sixty geese in one afternoon's or morning's shoot.

    The biggest shoot we ever had was sometime in the early 80's on the Troy farm near Tappen, the station just east of Dawson on the Northern Pacific. It was a stormy day; snow squalls all day long. The field we located in was a mile square of wheat stubble. Our party of five divided, three in one part of the field and two in the other. The geese were flying all day, thousands upon thousands of them. We killed 163 that day. We had a farm wagon with extra side boards for carrying eighty bushels of wheat. Our kill nearly filled that wagon box. I know that night when we drove back to Dawson, which I think was eight miles distant, we were cold and wet and we all stuck our legs down in the geese and the warmth of their bodies kept us comfortable. We frequently brought home three hundred or more geese with us, and the arrival of the car in Saginaw was known in advance and our friends by the score flocked to the car to share in our bag. Not a bird was ever wasted, and these wheat fed young geese were very highly considered for the table.

    With the goose shooting we had good duck shooting. Lakes Isabelle, Etta and Sibley literally swarmed with all kinds of wild fowl. Every tree claim and sand hill were full of sharptailed grouse. Bag limits and non-shipping out of the state in those days were unknown.

A Ten Days' Trip to Dakota

In September '83, on my return from the Yellowstone Park, I, with a few friends, stopped for two days in eastern Dakota to shoot ducks, and having such fine sport we then and there determined to come again the next year. The best of resolves are more often broken than kept, and when the time came this fall for carrying out the idea, I could not get a party large enough to enable us to take our good hunting car "City of Saginaw." This to me was a great disappointment as there is so much comfort to be had in going in your own car, having your own cook, and as our car is fitted with large ice boxes, we are enabled to save our game to bring home for our friends.

However, on October tenth we left here, three besides myself, and in Chicago were joined by Bob L. of New York and Fred Lord of the Northern Pacific R.R., the latter having business north and spent a day or two with us.

Monday morning found us at Moorhead, Minn. Standing on the rear platform we could count dozens of flocks of geese, hundreds of ducks, snipe and curlew, and every little way a flock of "chickens' would go booming over the prairie. We breakfasted at Fargo just over the line in Dakota, and at ten o'clock stopped with our friend Goodsell at Buffalo. He was expecting us but did not give very encouraging accounts of game; the weather had been so fine that the ducks and geese were still north. Mr. Goodsell has five Canada geese that he caught when young, and by keeping their wings clipped, keeps them tame. Great wild looking fellows they are and whenever a flock of their relatives comes in sight, they set up such a honking that renders the wild ones very uncertain and they often circle around and around the barnyard, almost alighting.

After dinner we loaded ourselves, traps and dogs into wagons and set out for the ranch twelve miles distant. As we drove over the wheat stubbles great flocks of sandhill cranes would take wing just before we would get near enough to shoot. Once this did not prove the case and Charlie blazed away, killing a great big fellow just as he had gotten well under motion; his head and legs dropped and with wings outstretched slowly circled down in a most ludicrous way, but the best he could do, poor fellow. We were all delighted, of course, and as the crane was very fat, visions of a roast floated before our eyes, only dispelled by Mr. Charles saying he was going to express it home to the taxidermist. We found out afterwards he was given to these freaks. For two days did he lug his specimen around and finally he forget it; left it one night at the depot on the platform, and I saw it going off under a chap's arm early next morning. I said nothing, as it would do someone some good probably.

But to resume: We arrived at the ranch about three o'clock and after making an engagement for supper we spread out along the sloughs. I saw at once our shooting would be poor, for where the year before I had found ponds black with ducks, now only a flock or two were to be seen. The banging of the guns soon started the birds and we had fun enough for the first night. Early next morning we tried it again and by noon were ready for a change, only having bagged eighty-four ducks and four geese, beside a very few snipe. We held a council of war and determined to pull up stakes and make for a place farther west that we had heard great reports from. We got into Buffalo just in time to take the train and arrived Thursday morning on our hunting ground, some 250 miles farther west. Here we had all the shooting we wanted, as you shall see.

Our first concern was to secure means of transportation to and from our shooting grounds, so Bob and I were appointed a committee on transportation and proceeded to interview the livery man. Like a great many of his class, he sized us up for our pile; wanted $8.00 per day for a rig that would carry but three, and said we must pay extra for bringing in our geese. Now the latter part sounded well because it looked like game, but we did not propose to pay some $16.00 or $20.00 per day for riding six or eight miles; that is as we hoped to stay several days, but Mr. Livery Man thought he had us and would not come down a cent. Inwardly wishing him a reserved seat in the place Bob Ingersoll says does not exist, we set about another scheme, and soon we had arranged with a fellow by the name of Long who had a good outfit that would carry our entire party at a reasonable figure. And I will say that Long proved to be a treasure. Little at a time we learned his history, though a very small portion of it I am sure. Educated at one of our eastern colleges, for some reason or other he had gone west soon after graduating. All alone he had trapped the winter before on some Indian Reservation where he had no business to, and had lost all his traps, pelts and outfit; he had been to Jimtown to refit and was now on his way back to some point on the northern Missouri River, way above Bismarck. A mule team, three year old colt and puppy were his only companions. At night he would spread his blankets under the wagon and sleep the sleep of the just; he called it putting up at the "Globe Hotel."

As Bob was bent on duck shooting and the rest of us hankered for geese, we divided; that is, Bob divided; took a buggy and set out for the sloughs four miles south of the track. We piled into Long's wagon and went in the opposite direction. We soon came to a large stubble and it was covered with geese, some feeding but most of them with necks stretched up a yard or two looking at us. Some were for getting out at once and trying to get a shot, but the old head of the party having been there before, said "No." Not one was disturbed but turning to the right we drove on to the large Alkali Lake a few miles further on, here unhitching the team; some loafing, others strolled around the shores of the lake. Ducks and geese covered the surface. I had never seen such clouds of water fowl. When taking wing the roar was like thunder; they would circle around and gradually settle down in another part of the lake. Occasionally we shot a goose or a duck and I got two birds that I set down as avocets. They stood about twelve or thirteen inches high; were white below and gray and black above, and the bills curved upward, being over two inches long, I should judge; I took no measurements, or if I did, I have forgotten them now. I tried to save the skins, but with my usual luck, spoiled them.

About noon the geese began to come in from the stubble and after the first flock they came in a steady stream, alighting far out in the lake. The din was deafening as each flock was welcomed by those already there. Hastily eating our lunch, traps are loaded into the wagon and back we go to the stubble where they were seen feeding in the morning, for if not disturbed they were sure to return toward the latter part of the day. And now for the hard work of goose shooting—digging the pits. Charlie, Eben and myself took the lower end of the field whilst the others went to the upper end, a mile or so from us. After an hour's digging three very respectable pits were finished, about twelve feet apart and covered with short stubble, and so disguised that we were confident the most wary old gander would not harbor a suspicion of danger. We had placed our Danz profile decoys around us in most bewitching positions, taken frequent pulls at our water bottles and discussed all points as to how we would do it, when the birds came. Charlie has a new 10-gauge Westly Richards hammerless, Eben a 10-gauge Scott, both heavy guns, and were shooting five drams of powder and 1 1/4 ounces No. 2 shot. I was the odd one. I was then, and am now, a 16-gauge crank. The year previous I had taken two guns with me, 10 and 16 gauge, W. & C. Scott & Sons, and after one trial of the small gun, had never fired the other again. So there I sat in the middle pit with my "pop-gun" as they called it, and no end of chaff did I have to take. All I could say was, "Wait and see." To tell the truth I thought they might clean me out as they were both crack shots, and by shooting 1 1/4 ounces shot as against my little 7/8 ounces, they certainly had the advantage in a flock at least.

While all this talking was going on I had my eyes peeled in the direction of the lake. At half past three we had said "Time they began to come," and then I caught sight of a long undulating line low down, way over towards the Alkali waters. "Down, boys!

Digging Goose Holes Near Dawson, N.D. - October 1893

Quick! Here they come!" And then all was excitement in an instant. On they came, saw the decoys and made straight for us, honking, necks outstretched, with lazy wing. I can't say who fired first, but we do know that we all had arisen and fired when the birds were twenty yards too far. In the clear air the great fellows looked to be right on to us when, in fact, our first shots were at sixty to seventy yards; if we had only waited they would have come right over us, but what is the use of kicking? We would know better next time, and besides, four Canada geese lay dead on the hard ground before us, the result of six barrels; not so bad.

I was to take the middle birds, Eben those to the left and Charlie the right. Two had fallen from the center but both avowed they had fired at the old gander that was slightly ahead and leading the gang. So it was ever after; I could not keep one or the other from shooting at my center birds. At any rate, I claimed them, as they had no business to shoot at them.

Now that the ice was broken, in came flock after flock, and by the booming guns at the far end of the field, we knew our friends were having sport too. Oh, for another hour of such excitement! The sport lasted but an hour and then not a goose was to be seen. It was grand. But somehow or other I heard no more from my friends to the right and left as to the shooting qualities of the "pop-gun." Once in a while Charlie had remarked in excellent French,"...you got that fellow, Billy." I found that if I got on to them I killed my goose slick and clean, but if I was not very careful and trusted any to scatter, I got left and no goose. But the flight had ceased and we gathered up our dead and what a pile they made. We had four or five different kinds—pure white fellows with black on the ends of the wings; and one yellow legged fellow that the natives called a California goose, with a breast all blotched with black, looking as though he had been wounded the year before and black had grown instead of the original yellowish gray; great big Canada geese and smaller ones that seemed nearly the same.

The American Field - Nov. 30, 1889

Soon the two from the other ground came in with the wagon

and our pile was counted and found to contain fifty-eight geese. Whoop la! Talk about fun, well that was a sample of it. Back to the little village in the soft twilight such as comes over the great Dakota prairies after a bright October day, with song and laughter and tale of how this one missed and that one hit, we came among the twinkling lights of the station. Soon Bob comes in from the slough and reports ducks without end but says he did not shoot well or would have had more game. We all say that same thing. However, his geese and great greenhead mallards added to our already shamefully large pile. All hands turned in and the birds were soon drawn, tied in bunches and expressed to friends in St. Paul and elsewhere. Then supper, smoke the pipe of peace while arranging for the next day's fray, and then sleep. In the morning two of our genial friends and companions took the train for Fargo there to join us Monday morning on our way home. How they hated to go and we equally regretted their departure, but business was to be attended to, so we bade them goodbye and promised a good report of our doings for the two days we were to stay.

After breakfast was eaten Mr. Long's express was brought to the door and in we piled, bound for the slough and mallards. Arriving at our destination we took possession of a small shanty used by some hardy pioneer as a roosting place when tilling the large fields around us. No other buildings were in sight. To the southward for two or three miles stretched the slough and such a place as it proved to be for water fowl.

To complete this story at this late date, February 16th, 1907, I can not help but comment upon the terrific change that has taken place since the events related took place.

The big slough just mentioned, in later years we came to know as Lake Etta Slough and the Big Slough back of Sam Devore's house. For years the latter slough has been dry. In 1884, it was almost a sea, although the bottom was hard and with rubber boots one could wade a good ways into it. Such clouds of water fowl as we saw here and at Sibley Lake and Buffalo Lake (all places that became familiar to us later on at Dawson). I have never seen before and never have seen since. I remember standing on the edge of the Sam Devore Slough when something alarmed the water fowl and they fairly darkened the sky when they got up, and the roar reminded one of a heavy train moving at a rapid rate of speed over a long, resonant trestle.

The first afternoon, E. waded in the smart-weed and the duck grass that hardly came to his knees and put up and killed 17 mallards. The team followed along opposite on the bank and as fast as he got two or three birds he put them in the wagon. He had been bragging a good deal about his shooting, a habit of conceit that has stuck to him all these years. So I made up my mind the next evening that I would take it out of him a bit. Bob and I had lugged our soap boxes out to an advantageous point for the evening flight, we were satiated with shooting and had been loafing around all day. The soap boxes were an invention of Bob's as a seat, so we could squat down without breaking our legs or getting wet. I was shooting my 16-gauge gun and about the first bird that came along was a snow goose up quite high, but I covered it and let go a load of 6's and the bird folded up and fell within a few feet of where I was sitting, absolutely stone dead. Though dictating this more than twenty years after the event, the picture is as plain in my memory now as it was the day it happened.

At dusk, just as the great red glow of the gorgeous Dakota sunset was at its best in the west, the ducks began to come fast and furious. I do not think I shot more than twenty minutes. My gun was hot. Frequently I had to dodge to avoid being hit by the teal coming into the hole like bullets. Sometimes they came so fast and so low and close they startled me and I put up my arm to shield them off. It seemed as if they must knock me over. I only shot those that passed between me and the clear, red bit of sky and would fall free in the open water, for I never then nor do I now permit myself to shoot ducks that would fall in the rushes and can not be found. So with this brief shooting spell, fast and furious as it was, nearly all the birds fell in the open. I did not attempt to pick them up that night. The trail was long back to the hard ground, although the water was only knee deep.

E. had a pretty fair bag. He was rubbing it into the rest of us as usual. I said nothing but asked him to go out with me and help me pick up my birds in the morning. I remember I picked up and brought in 46 ducks besides the goose and they were largely teal and mallards. This was going some. It took the wind out of E.'s sails. It does not sound very well today; it is sort of game-hoggish. We had not at that time begun to appreciate that game was disappearing. The year before I had partaken of a buffalo hump in Montana and it was the last piece of wild buffalo meat I ever ate.

This ended our shooting. Two days with the ducks and one with the geese was sufficient. There were no laws in those days regarding shipment of game out of the state and we were able to bring home a fine lot of birds to our friends.

We commenced going to Dawson with the car, Saginaw, a year after this and continued to do so every year until 1899.

THE OLD HUNTING CAR
AND
THE DANCE OF THE SANDHILL CRANE

From: *Recollections of My Fifty Years Hunting and Fishing.* William B. Mershon (1923)

<u>Editor's Note</u>: *Yes, I know, sandhill cranes are not waterfowl but the hunting of them is so much like going for ducks or geese that I thought this note in the article was worthwhile. Also, Mershon's description of his morning among the cranes is exactly as it is often seen today. Incidentally, I share his opinion about the eating qualities of crane.*

In 1883 Coups Circus got into difficulties and its advertising car was sold at sheriff's sale at Saginaw. ...The car was remodeled and made into a hunting car. There were six lower berths, six upper berths, and a kitchen at one end and an observation room or dining room in the other, a large ice box, storage room and all that sort of thing.

In 1883 the car was filled jam full to go to Yellowstone Park. It was attached to the train that followed the Villard-Hatch party when they went to drive the golden spike that connected the eastern and western ends of the Northern Pacific. This was in September of 1883. ...We did a little duck shooting on the way out. We stopped at New Buffalo, N.D. Mr. Goodsell from Grand Rapids had a ranch a few miles north and there were sloughs around that ranch that were filled with ducks. Up to that time I never had seen as many ducks as I saw on those sloughs. In going through Dawson we were told what a wonderful place it was for all kinds of waterfowl, especially geese.

...by the late 80's we were going to Dawson regularly with this car, never less than eight, sometimes ten.

In 1894 we built a new car and formed the Forest and Stream Co., Ltd., consisting of ten members. ...It was perfectly plain, but it was a larger, stronger car; six wheel trucks; more convenient and roomy. We had the luxury of a bath room and tub. Could carry 500 gallons of water and there was room for about 750 pounds of ice, so that we were quite independent....

We used this car to go to Dawson every October until the goose shooting failed there, and after that when in 1900 we changed to Pleasant Lake, N.D.....

When we hunted around Dawson, N.D., between 1884 and 1890 we saw these birds (whooping cranes) almost daily. [*Editor's Note: This is one of the only references I know of that relates to the abundance of whooping cranes in the early days.*]

It was about 1899 that I was goose shooting in Kidder County, North Dakota. It was about the 10th of October. I had driven north from Dawson the day before—about fifteen miles—for I had learned that the geese were feeding on the stubble fields in that locality in quantity. My companion and I got to the feeding ground in time the night before to dig our goose pits and get them stubbled, so that they were well disguised.

(The next morning) We were side by side, our pits not more than a dozen feet apart, the decoys out, and comfortably settled as the sky was reddening in the east, toward which we were facing. We were on the lower side of a slight hill whose crest was outlined against the reddening sky. Before the sun had shown its rim above the horizon, we saw coming from various directions, sandhill cranes in twos and threes and in flocks of fifteen or twenty. They came from every direction, silent and without a call, centering on the hill crest some three or four hundred yards in front of us and directly toward the sunrise.

They kept their weird and strange performance (dancing) up for about eight or ten minutes. By that time the sun had shown itself above the sky line and at a signal, that we did not hear, the dancing ceased as quickly as it had begun, and one by one or in groups of a dozen or more, these cranes left as silently as they had come, flying in all directions. Some came over us so we took toll out of them. They were goodly birds, with a body like a young turkey and when roasted were just as good, in fact, we preferred them to any of the other game unless it was the sharptailed grouse, but the roasted crane we always thought was the choice morsel compared to young wild goose, duck or even the canvasback.

CONCLUDING THOUGHTS

I hope you have enjoyed browsing through and reading these accounts of hunts by wildfowlers on the Dakota prairies in days of long ago. Perhaps many of you will recognize places you have hunted or experiences similar to those hardy people who ventured into Dakota Territory. I found it interesting that those early-day hunters had a strong passion for the hunt and a feeling of camaraderie that many of us have today.

We all know that conditions in the Dakotas have changed greatly since those early days. We will probably never again see the numbers of ducks and geese that occurred back then or the opportunity to shoot the numbers of birds they did. One exception may be snow geese whose population may now be higher than it has ever been. Times change and we as hunters have to change with them. I recently heard a prominent psychologist compare the past with the wake of a motor boat; it tells you where you have been but it doesn't record much about where you are going. Other writers and speakers emphasize the importance of living in the now for good emotional well-being. A friend of mine often reminds me, "You can't go back." We can only cherish the memories of hunts in years gone by but the challenge is to adapt to conditions we face now and in the future.

The birds are still the same as they have always been. And we should be grateful that it is possible in the present to find places to practice our skills of the hunt. Just as the ducks and geese have to be resilient in adapting to changing conditions, we must do the same. At times in my life I have said I would have liked to have lived 150 years ago when the stories reported in this book were lived. I suspect other wildfowlers have thought the same thing. I once heard a talk by Chris Madson, editor of *Wyoming Wildlife* magazine, in which he said: "Contemplating the past is not a pleasant experience—especially for waterfowlers." I have often felt that way when I read about conditions in the original prairie pothole region before it was modified forever by the activities of we humans. On the other hand, I am encouraged at the present time because of the apparent increases in environmental awareness among people across the land. Several organizations seek to implement worthwhile programs to benefit waterfowl by the preservation and management of vital habitat. If you care about the future of wildfowling I encourage you to join and support one or more of them.

In a sense all of us are living a page in history each time we participate in the great experience of wildfowling. In the future hunters will look back on these times just as we look back into the past. The excitement of a fall sunrise over a prairie marsh and the whistle of wings will always take a wildfowler's breath away.

REFERENCES CITED

Anonymous. 1966. *Tappen: Eighty-Eight Years of Progress*. Steele Ozone Press, Steele, ND. 397 p.

Anonymous. 1980. *Dawson Centennial 1880 - 1980 - The First 100 Years*. Steele Ozone Press, Steele, ND. 386 p.

Bovey, M. 1947. *Whistling Wings*. Doubleday and Co., Inc., Garden City, New York. 162 p.

Connett, Eugene V. 1949. *Wildfowling in the Mississippi Flyway*. D. Van Nostrand Company, Inc., New York. 387 p.

Grinnell, G. B. 1901. *American Duck Shooting*. Willis McDonald & Company, New York. 627 p.

Heilner, V. C. 1939. *Duck Shooting*. Alfred A. Knopf, New York. 540 p.

Leffingwell, W. B. 1888. *Wild Fowl Shooting*. Rand, McNally & Co., Chicago. 373 p.

Leffingwell, W. B. (Ed.) 1890. *Shooting on Upland, Marsh, and Stream*. Rand, McNally & Co., Chicago. 473 p.

Leffingwell, W. B. 1894. *The Art of Wing Shooting*. Rand, McNally & Co., Chicago. 192 p.

Luehr, E. and H. Stuart. 1960. *Pettibone, N. Dak. 1910-1960*. Steele Ozone Press, Steele, ND. 332 p.

Mershon, W. B. 1923. *Recollections of My Fifty Years Hunting and Fishing*. The Stratford Company, Boston. 259 p.

BOOKS ABOUT OLDEN TIMES WILDFOWLING

Bruette, W. 1930. *American Duck, Goose, and Brant Shooting.* Charles Scribner's Sons, New York. 415 p.

Forester, F. 1860. *Field Sports of the United States.* W. A. Townsend and Co., New York. Two vols. 749 p.

Hazelton, W. 1930. *Supreme Duck Shooting Stories.* (Reprint Edition by Lawrence G. Barnes (1989), The Gunnerman Press, Auburn Hills, Michigan. 160 p.)

Lewis, E. 1855. *The American Sportsman.* Lippincott, Grambo and Co., Philadelphia. 494 p.

Long., J. W. 1874. *American Wild-Fowl Shooting.* J. B. Ford and Co., New York. 285 p.

Muderlak, E. 2000. *When Ducks Were Plenty.* Safari Press, Inc., Long Beach, CA. 384 p.

Mathewson, W. 1989. *Wildfowling Tales 1888 - 1913.* Sand Lake Press, Salem, OR. 186 p.

Mathewson, W. 1989. *Western Bird Hunting.* Sand Lake Press, Salem, OR. 289 p.

Mathewson, W. 1995. *Old Wildfowling Tales - Volume II.* Sand Lake Press, Amity, OR. 240 p.

Miller, S. M. 1986. *Early American Waterfowling 1730s - 1930.* Winchester press (New Century Publishers, Inc.), Piscataway, NY. 279 p.

Williamson, F. P. 1979. *The Waterfowl Gunner's Book.* The Amwell Press, Clinton, NJ. 282 p.

NOTES

NOTES